# THE MILFORD MALE

## The Autobiography of a Small Town Iowan

Air Force Officer and Combat Pilot
Special Operator
Attorney
Lobbyist
Regulator
Political Consultant

## KEITH EDWARD LUCHTEL

Happy Jack Publishing

# DEDICATION

This work is dedicated to my family, especially my wife, children, and their spouses and my grandchildren.

"My family" also includes my grandparents, parents, sister, brother, and their spouses and extended families.

It is also dedicated to the men, and their families, of Carolina Moon, Eagle Claw, and the many other friends who lost their lives in the service of our country in Vietnam and elsewhere.

# CONTENTS

# ACKNOWLEDGMENTS

My thanks to my first Editor, Beth Burgmeyer of Happy Jack Publishing. Beth is a nationally recognized author and editor who risked taking me under her wing. She also directed me to Cover Editor Tina Lampe to whom I also owe thanks! They make a great team. I am most appreciative of their valuable efforts on my behalf.

I want to thank author and friend, David Furneaux, for recommending them to me, and me to them.

I also thank my wife, Patti Moss Luchtel, for her work in proofreading and suggesting content. She has endured more than 50 years correcting my errors!

I want to thank the men who made up the 19th Cadet Squadron of the United States Air Force Academy from August of 1960 to June of 1964. We shaped each other's lives. I am grateful for the effort and attention to our training (not always appreciated at the time, I admit) by those members of the Classes of 1961, 1962, and 1963, Their combined efforts turned my Class of 1964 into the best class ever graduated. Thanks guys!! And my thanks to the classes of 1965, 1966, and 1967 upon whom we practiced and developed our leadership skills. We fell just short of making yours the best classes ever! We tried our hardest, but as they still say at USAFA, NO ONE HAS DONE MORE THAN '64! Last I knew we still lead in medals and General Officers. Oh, and in humility too!

I want to specially recognize that group of men who made up the Class of 1964, 19th Squadron, designated "The Playboy Squadron." My Band of Brothers (see next page for a list of the Playboys).

# The Playboys
## The Class of '64, 19<sup>th</sup> Squadron
## My Band of Brothers

| | | |
|---|---|---|
| Ammerman, Dave* | Baer, Les | Bartlett, Frank |
| Bedarf, Rich | Bliss, Ron* | Bushnell, Marty |
| Dula, Brett | Ganong, Gary | Gordon, Jeff |
| Graham, Jim* | Growden, Ron | Holder, Chuck * |
| Kearns, Dan* | Manekofsky, Harvey | Manning, Jim |
| Pauer, Kurt | Pierce, Jim | Prenez, Jon* |
| Robbins, Mike | Sears, Jim | Young, TR* |

*Deceased

# PREFACE

I WAS BORN in September 1941, and raised in Milford, Iowa, located just south of Lake Okoboji, a main tourist attraction. It was and is a pleasant small town in Iowa. I had a great family. My family and the community and the values they instilled were a lifelong influence on me. Milford was well served by its local newspaper, The Milford Mail. The other group that greatly influenced my life was my other family: the members of the Class of 1964 at the United States Air Force Academy, especially those who were in the 19<sup>th</sup> Squadron, known as the Playboy Squadron. I owe the title of this book to one of my roommates, James L. Graham, who, when he first saw my home-town newspaper, immediately named me "The Milford Male." Jim got an advance look at this: he died from cancer after a long battle on July 19, 2017. We talked often during this fight, shared a lot of memories, and enjoyed a good laugh over this title.

With the passage of time my military colleagues took to calling me "Lucky"—derived from my last name and the fact that I was, indeed, very lucky. The nickname has carried over into my civilian life where I have also been blessed with good luck.

What follows is a recounting of my life, the people in it, and some of the lessons learned along the way. In the process of writing this, I discovered how much World War II influenced my life and that of my family. That discovery gave me an additional perspective on how much my wars in Vietnam and other places influenced my life and cast shadows I am only now coming to understand.

# PART I
# BEGINNINGS

# 1

# Grandparents

IN SMALL TOWN Iowa, grandparents were people of influence. However, I was denied the opportunity to ever know my maternal grandmother who died because of a ruptured appendix when my mother, Gertrude, was 15.

My widowed maternal grandfather, Ed, was a farmer and had six children, the youngest of whom was Rosalie. She was two when her mother, Alice Bertha Houlihan, died at age 40. The oldest was my mother. She gave up her high school education and stayed on the farm to help raise her siblings.

Grandpa Ed loved politics. He was a Democrat in very Republican northwest Iowa. I can recall the sadness expressed by the family when President Franklin Roosevelt died in April 1945 even though I was only three and a half years old. And I recall the disdain for Tom Dewey who was expected to defeat President Truman in 1948. Four years later, I became involved in my first political campaign. Grandpa Ed died in May of 1950, spared knowledge of his oldest grandchild supporting a Republican for president!

My paternal grandparents were Herman (Frank Herman) and Theresa. They too had six children. Two others died in infancy. Theresa was a homemaker, which in the days of her youth called for quite a bit of the pioneer spirit. They lived in the then very southwestern part of Milford. It was truly on the outskirts of town. I recall a chicken coop in the backyard. One of my earliest memories is of grandma going out to find a chicken for dinner. The nominee was not willing to be served. Grandma was only willing to commit to a brief chase before the hatchet was flung at the chicken, nearly severing its head. As far as the chicken was concerned, it had. I was impressed!

Grandpa Herman was a lot of things: a talented painter of outdoor hunting and fishing scenes, a musician who had his own small orchestra, and a church decorator (he could make ordinary wood look like marble), and house painter. He also was an avid fisherman. He too was interested in public affairs, but I don't remember him being a member of a political party. I do recall that we discussed political issues. He was also interested in international affairs. I remember sitting with him listening to radio commentator Gabriel Heater. It was Mr. Heater who informed us of Stalin's death the evening of March 5, 1953. We celebrated loudly when we heard the news on Grandpa's console radio.

My grandmother was a quiet, kind woman who seemed a bit withdrawn. I now think it was the result of their son Gilbert's death in World War II. Both grandparents were of German descent. We had family members who spoke German and had limited English speaking abilities. My grandmother was reputed to have served as an interpreter for friends and relatives who struggled with English. I have had an interest in languages for as long as I can remember. My grandmother began teaching me German before I started school. My father had a hatred for the Nazis which was reflected in his disdain for all things German, especially the German language when spoken by his son. He was very irritated with Grandma for teaching me and asked her to stop. Mostly she honored his wish.

# 2

# Aunts and Uncles

MY MOTHER AND father had interesting siblings who were also an influence on me. I was born exactly three months before Pearl Harbor was attacked by the Japanese. The first five years of my life, the attention and energy of the nation and Milford, Iowa, were dominated by "The War."

Dad had three sisters: Alma, Mildred, and Florence. Alma became a nurse and lived in Minneapolis when I was growing up. She was married to Art Warneke. I didn't see her often, but I enjoyed her and her family when I did. Florence lived in Sioux City and was married to Marvin Leritz. I saw her and her family more often as they had a summer cottage at Lake Okoboji. Mildred lived her life in Milford. She was a musician whose career began when she was very young. She provided piano accompaniment to silent movies. She was known professionally as "Jim Luchtel." As I recall, the name "Jim" related to a cartoon character. She married a musician, Matt Richter, and they primarily entertained at square dances in the upper Midwest. I grew up listening to them on the radio from stations in the local area and adjoining states. They also provided entertainment in the lake resorts, primarily Vacation Village Resort on Lake Okoboji.

Dad had two brothers: Gilbert and Harold (Dutch). Gilbert was a very talented artist and musician. He could have been a member of the Glen Miller Army Band but chose the infantry instead. His plan was to serve his country and return to Milford where he would resume working with his father and his older brother in the church decorating and house painting business. Dutch was the youngest and was a Naval Aviator who finished training as the war was ending. He had a successful career in banking in Nebraska. He was married to Jean Bradley whose father owned several small banks. Dutch flew for several years in the Navy Reserve out of Lincoln, Nebraska and owned and flew a light airplane. He was an inspiration to me, and I treasured the times he flew his F9F jet fighter over Milford. I was told that even as an infant I would react to a passing airplane. It was a big deal when Uncle Dutch would occasionally provide a Milford flyover.

Staff Sergeant Gilbert R. Luchtel, 382nd Infantry, was killed in action in the Philippines on November 12, 1944 at age 22. I was three years old at the time, but I remember his last visit to Milford that fall. It left a big impression because the men of the family went out in the backyard and took turns with their shotguns shooting tin cans thrown in the air. There was also a sadness I didn't fully understand that overtook the Christmas of 1944. I am not sure when the family was notified of Gilbert's death, but I think it was close to Christmas.

My Dad later told me that he and his sister Mildred (Jim) both had premonitions of his death prior to receiving notice. Dad said he was awakened in the middle of the night by Gilbert's calling out to him.

Following my combat experiences and the loss of many friends, I have come to realize the profound impact Gilbert's death had on my grandparents, parents, and me and my siblings, and the extended family. The personal experiences dealing with the impact of my friends' wartime deaths on their families, and on me and my wife, have caused me to reflect upon and better understand the impact of Uncle Gilbert's death on my family.

My mother had two sisters: Lois and Rosalie, who were both homemakers. Rosalie was the youngest and I remember her wedding to Grant McDonald. Grant also served in World War II. She and her husband farmed west of Milford. They moved to town when Grant retired from farming.

Lois and her family moved to the Los Angeles area where her husband, Bruce Littlejohn, worked for Northrup Aviation. Northrup designed and built the first supersonic jet fighter trainer, the T-38 Talon, which I flew in training. It still is a great airplane! I enjoyed my tour of the Northrup plant in California with Uncle Bruce as a T-38 pilot and nephew.

Lois was an interesting person. She had a friend I knew as "Aunt Ruby" who years later I realized was Ruby Keeler, the famous dancer and wife of singer Al Jolson.

My mother's three brothers were Earl, Leland (Lee), and Marion (Pat). All three served with distinction in World War II in the infantry. Pat was a medic. They were decorated. Uncle Pat was awarded the Silver Star twice. Uncle Earl was a remarkable marksman. He was known to shoot flying pheasants with a .22 caliber rifle. These three farm boys all eventually left farming after their return from Europe following the end of The War.

Earl and Lee farmed in the Milford area, but Earl eventually moved to Phoenix, and Lee to Los Angeles. Earl was married to Dorothy Toohey (they eventually divorced). Lee was married to Helen Severtson. Pat was the first to move to the Los Angeles area, having done so soon after returning from Europe at the end of the war. Pat became friends with several artists and actors as he began to build his men's clothing businesses. He also invested in real estate.

I really liked all my aunts and uncles. I especially liked Dutch, the flyer, and Pat. Pat was a prize fighter and bought boxing gloves for me on one of his visits. He tried to make a boxer out of me, but I wasn't much interested in the sport. I didn't know anyone my age who was interested either. Pat was very handsome and attracted lots of female attention. Later, I came to understand that he was gay. But that was not obvious, meant nothing to me growing up, and he was very masculine in appearance and had a very charismatic personality. He was twenty years older than me. He was a great storyteller who led an interesting life. He eventually settled into what was to become a long-term relationship with Dr. Charles Brubaker, M.D.

These aunts and uncles and the cousins they provided all played a role in my childhood. Uncle Pat's relationship with Dr. Brubaker came about in my late teens. Dr. Brubaker survived Uncle Pat and I still regard him as a family member whose company my family and I continue to enjoy.

# 3

# Parents and Siblings

DAD WAS REPUTED to have been a great baseball player in his youth. Rural Iowa had what were called "town teams" made up of good players from local areas. They were highly competitive and formed "all-star" teams to play semi-professional teams that traveled the Midwest. He was fond of telling about the time he played on a local all-star team against a team from the Negro League. He got a hit off Satchel Paige. Satchel Paige later achieved great success, pitched in the 1948 World Series, and is in the Baseball Hall of Fame. Satchel was four years older than Dad. Some would say that Satchel was the best-ever major league pitcher. One of his Negro League touring stunts was to have his infielders sit down while he pitched strikeouts.

Dad suffered the loss of opportunity brought about by the onset of the great depression prior to World War II. He hated painting and went to college to pursue a business education. The depression forced an end to that endeavor after one year. I recall finding his grades report for that year—all A's.

Dad spent the rest of his life in the painting business. He eventually dropped the contracting part of it and opened a paint and wallpaper decorating store. Carpeting and drapes were added. A gift section was also added but was unsuccessful. The business struggled on for several years. I still feel bad thinking about his struggles which I didn't fully appreciate at the time.

The War impacted the lives of my family and changed the course of my life. My father was disappointed that he failed his physical on two different occasions when he volunteered for military service after Pearl Harbor. My earliest memory is of my dad boarding a train for his second attempt to report for duty. I have in mind it was wintery and Mom was very upset. These two failures affected him the rest of his life. He felt denied of the opportunity to serve, which adversely impacted his feeling of self-worth.

I remember Dad telling us about starting a church job in Northeast Iowa in 1939. They were just getting started when the Nazis invaded Poland. Dad immediately put the crew into high gear so that the job was far enough along to make it impractical for the church to back out of the contract. He always had a great interest in the news of the day and no faith in there ever being "Peace in Our Time."

Another war memory is the panicked reaction my mother had when she found me playing with our food ration stamps or coupons! I had no idea what they were or their importance.

My grandfather and father continued the painting and church decorating business after Gilbert's death. My father, like me, did not have the musical or artistic talent of his father, brother, and sister. My grandfather spent a lot of time painting pictures which he easily sold. He also was an avid fisherman. I now believe that my grandfather's interest in fishing and painting wildlife scenes were refuges. His interest in the business faded and my Dad struggled to keep things together as best he could. Eventually the business evolved into house and commercial contract painting in the Okoboji area.

Dad was well liked and a very faithful Roman Catholic. It broke his heart when the church started buying cheaper paint from the local hardware store and gave a carpeting contract to an out-of-town retailer who wasn't even a member of the congregation. When he finally decided to retire, he had a big sale which he advertised on the radio and in the newspaper, The Milford Mail. Not one sale was made that day. He was devastated. The local people were good folks and I like to think they didn't want to take advantage of him.

He hauled his inventory home, and years later, my brother (he did the lion's share) and I hauled the paint out of the basement and solidified it so it could be disposed of in the landfill. It was frustrating work made more difficult by the memories it evoked.

My mother was a homemaker, as were most of her friends. She was active in the church and loved the lake. We spent many a summer afternoon at the local beach, about a mile from our home. Dad would try to join us after work as he too loved the lake. My mother never could swim, but Dad had us kids swimming at young ages.

We had a boat which was an old cabin cruiser. We spent most of the weekends on the boat. We didn't stay out overnight, but usually spent half a day Saturdays and all-day Sundays (after Mass) on the boat. Mom would fry chicken and we would picnic on the boat or beach the boat and eat on shore. We would sometimes get together with Dad's sister from Sioux City and her family. Those were good times and back when Dad was contracting. Though he hated painting and managing painters, he apparently was successful. I think his sense of obligation kept the business going. But I also feel he was weighed down by the loss of his brother. He had a great customer list, and for the most part, they became life-long friends. But I do remember his frustration with some of his slow-paying customers who had plenty of money but delayed paying him for as long as possible. To this day I remember that and pay for work done around our house as soon as a bill is presented.

My mother was an avid bridge player and established a bridge marathon program at the church. All interested women were welcomed regardless of religious affiliation. That was a most unusual outreach for those days. I understand that program continues today. She also loved gardening and had artistic talent. Only my sister inherited those talents!

Dad and Mom played lots of bridge together. Bridge and movies were their social life. They were in bridge groups that met frequently and included a lawyer, school superintendent, and physician. They enjoyed a nice group of friends.

They also had friends who were pastors of various catholic and protestant churches for whom Dad had done church decorating work.

My parent's best friends were Dr. and Mrs. Buchanan (bridge players too). Doc was quite the character and, as was usually the case with a small-town physician, very influential. They had lots of fun together, and sometimes vacationed together. On one such occasion they made international news.

On the return drive home from a trip to Florida, the men were driving through the night and the women were asleep in the back seat. They stopped somewhere in the south for gas in the middle of the night and made a restroom stop while the attendant pumped the gas. It was a long time ago—when gas station attendants put the gas in your car for you and even washed your windshield!

They paid for the gas (no credit card readers or cards to be read back then) and hustled back to the car. They drove off not realizing the women had awakened and availed themselves of the restroom facilities too. The women came out of the restroom and no car! And no purses! They were indeed stranded. They knew the men were listening to WHO radio in Des Moines, a clear channel-station that reached all over the country and into Mexico and Canada. They called the radio station and asked them to alert Dad and Doc, which they did. As you might imagine, the announcer had fun with that! A listener in Mexico sent them a little miniature toilet (a doll-house piece, I guess) for their car.

Dad was totally unafraid of heights. While doing our Ground Observer Corp duties (more about that later), he was very comfortable sitting on the edge of the business building roof with his feet dangling while enjoying his birds-eye view of downtown Milford. It made me a nervous wreck as I was (and am) afraid of heights! But I am fine in an airplane or even a parachute. When the County Courthouse flagpole needed to be painted, Dad was pleased to go up to the top of the courthouse and paint it. I don't think he charged for anything other than the paint. He may not have charged for that since he got so much enjoyment out of doing it. In his eighties he liked climbing to the top of the local grain elevator to enjoy the view while sitting on the edge. He caused a lot of consternation when it was finally noticed there was someone sitting up there dangling his feet!

My sister, Michele, is five years younger, and my brother, Dean, is twelve years younger. We have always been best friends. That friendship has extended to include our outstanding spouses! It makes for fun times when everyone is supportive and proud of the others.

Michele put herself through college and graduated in four years with her degree in special education from the University of South Dakota. She had always wanted to be a teacher. She took a job with the Oxnard, California, school district as an elementary school teacher. She stayed with that district until her retirement. She married David Emery, a bank holding company officer in charge of audit and security. Dave supervised audit and security operations in bank offices in the Oxnard area. He is a great Southern California tour guide having grown up in Santa Barbara. He really impressed our daughter Kristina when she was a young teen by taking her to see Michael Jackson's secluded in-the-middle-of-nowhere residence.

Michele and Dave sold their beautiful home on a golf course in Oxnard in the spring of 2018. They now live on a golf course in West Des Moines. This time their beautiful home includes a pool table. Lots of good times ahead for all!

Dean attended Wayne State in Nebraska on a baseball scholarship. He is the family jock. He was a star pitcher and later took up tennis where he had success in tournament play, primarily in the Midwest. At one point he held a ranking in the US. He also attended Lakes Community College and was recognized as an outstanding alum in later years. He married Arlene Berry from Estherville, Iowa.

He worked for a year or so in Dad's store in Milford. He then took a job working in our cousins' retail clothing store in Milford, "The Three Sons." He was in that job for about 20 years. He left and started his own company, Okoboji Home Watch, providing concierge and security services to lakes area property owners.

Arlene graduated with a teaching degree but spent most of her working years at Stylecraft Furniture Company, a Milford manufacturing company. She handled purchasing for the company. She also worked part-time as a photographer and reporter for The Milford Mail for about a year. She was elected to the Milford City Council. They have three children: Barry (Kelly), Landon (Megan), and Molly (Bryson). They currently have eight grandchildren, three from Barry and Kelly, three from Molly and Bryson, and two with one on the way from Landon and Megan. Dean will have his baseball team! Dean and Arlene moved to West Des Moines in 2016 where all their children and grandchildren also live.

# 4

# Saint Joseph's School

THE WAR ENDED in 1945. Although not quite four years old, I still remember the town's fire and emergency sirens blaring and someone running through our backyard yelling that the war in Europe had ended. I don't recall anything about the end of the war in the Pacific later in the summer. I do recall talk about the Atomic Bomb, but I didn't understand its significance or that it brought about the end of the war in the Pacific. I have a vague recollection of my mother's brothers returning from Army service. The next memorable event in my life was when I started school at St. Joseph's Catholic School in Milford in 1947.

We lived across the street from the VanderWilt family. The father was superintendent of the public-school system. They had a son who was a month younger than me. I was born in September and Bob in October. We could have started school the year before, but Bob's parents suggested we wait a year. It worked out well for both of us. I got into the Air Force Academy and Bob VanderWilt was captain of the Iowa State University basketball team. Bob's accomplishment was especially noteworthy. We played together almost daily. One day we were playing in our yard when he went home not feeling very well. The polio scourge was in full bloom. I eventually went inside after convincing myself that I didn't feel well either. I suffered from allergies and my mother assumed that was my issue.

Bob's parents became concerned and took Bob to a doctor who suspected polio. He was placed in the hospital and the diagnosis was confirmed. My parents were contacted because I had likely been exposed too. Now we had two sets of parents on the street in a high state of alarm. It was soon confirmed that my issue was due to allergies.

I don't recall how long Bob was out of circulation, but he obviously made a great recovery.

While the rest of the world was settling into post-war normalcy, my world was turning upside down. St. Joseph's had nuns! Nuns wore habits in those days and somewhat resembled penguins. Sternness was apparently a virtue if one were to be a nun in 1947 through '56! A sense of humor was not required. Smiles were sparingly given. The nuns in those days were not noted for their cheerfulness. It was the beginning of a long slog!

A memory of the early grade school days: my Uncle Gilbert's remains were brought back from the Philippians and reburied in St. Joseph's Cemetery in Milford. A funeral Mass was conducted followed by graveside services with an American Legion M-1 Rifle salute. Presentation of the flag was made to my grandparents after it had been removed from the casket and ceremoniously folded into a triangular bundle.

Prior to the service, one of the nuns came up and asked me why the casket was closed. Even as a grade school kid I thought she must be crazy! I told my Dad about it and he was not pleased!

At school I made a new friend, Robert Killian. His parents owned the town's only hotel, a couple of blocks from our house. He and I became friends. Unfortunately, Robert was the first of my contemporaries to suffer an early death. I believe he was only about six years old. He was playing around the hotel trash fire and caught his clothing on fire. He was severely burned. Despite help from his siblings and Dr. Buchanan, whose office was across the street from the hotel, Robert died in the local hospital.

In grade school I did well and was very good at math and anything to do with science. I was terrible at music. Terrible! Couldn't sing a note—still can't. But my family included professional musicians. A highlight of Christmas Midnight Mass was my grandfather's violin rendition of Christmas carols during communion time and after Mass. I still think of him whenever I hear "Silent Night." The nuns attributed my lack of musical development to recalcitrance and rebelliousness subject to cure only by application of a ruler to knuckles, followed by recovery while standing in the corner. Fun days! They could never quite grasp the concept that I just didn't have any talent.

We had a vacant lot next to our home that became the neighborhood sports center. We had a basketball hoop on our garage and a ping pong and a pool table in the basement. I grew up playing baseball, basketball, and football. St. Joseph's didn't have formal sports teams, but it had a nice baseball diamond and an adequate gym for basketball. Being involved in sports was a big part of growing up in Milford.

I was also active in Cub Scouts and Boy Scouts. Both provided good experiences and complimented the system of values instilled at home and in school.

My mother was sure that a musician dwelled somewhere within me. I took accordion lessons and was a pretty good mechanical player. My Aunt Mildred (Jim) was a professional musician who played the accordion and the piano. She could hear a song on the radio and play it after having only just listened to it. I remember listening to her and her husband, Matt Richter, on the major Midwest radio stations. Eventually, at my mother's request, she assessed my musical talents as marginally existent. That got me off the hook. I should note that Aunt Jim attempted to teach the famous Lawrence Welk to read music. She claimed to have not been very successful, but that he had tremendous natural ability to play musical instruments and lead other talented musicians. No such talent was present in me!

Speaking of Lawrence Welk, we had relatives that owned a gas station in north central Iowa. Lawrence would come through on his way to a gig and fill up with gas. He would pass back through afterwards and fill up again. He would then pay for both fills by putting money in a can by the door. Many years later, our relatives attended a Lawrence Welk Show at the Hollywood Palladium. They managed to make it to the dance floor and worked their way up to Mr. Welk. The wife tapped him on the shoulder and said, "I bet you don't remember us."

He looked at her and a conversation like this ensued: "Sure I do, Clara! And hello, Ray. By the way, I can pay for my gas going and coming these days! Great seeing you folks again! And thanks again for trusting me on the gas!"

I digress. My early fascination with airplanes continued. I was diagnosed with asthma while in grade school. The local doctor and family friend recommended that I be seen by a specialist in Omaha. My parents and the local airport operator, Stanley Fuller, were very good friends. The Fullers had been their landlords before they built their house. It was decided we would fly to Omaha. My first flight! I got to sit in the right front seat next to the pilot. The airplane was a four-place Navion. I still have a fondness for them although they hardly exist outside museums. I don't know exactly when that would have been, but I was probably no more than five or six. But that first flight confirmed my earliest suspicions—I was going to be a pilot no matter what!

My mother also developed health problems. Later in life she became a breast cancer survivor. These illnesses really set the family back financially. There wasn't much in the way of health insurance available at the time. And the government programs we have now grown accustomed to did not exist.

By necessity I learned a lot about homemaking while Mom was ill (don't tell Patti, I am adding this after she finished proofreading). I am still adept at mending with a needle and thread—well, I can at least still sew a button on. Anyway, my wife Patti long ago discovered I was familiar with the use of vacuum cleaners and laundry equipment.

The nuns at St. Joseph's did a great job of preparing us for high school. By the time I was ready to start high school I had determined that I wanted to go to West Point and become an Air Force jet pilot. But those plans changed when it was announced that the Air Force would soon have its own academy in Colorado Springs. It immediately became my goal to attend the United States Air Force Academy.

During these years, another life-long interest continued to develop—politics and international relations. Some say I was born an old man, and perhaps they are right. I enlisted in my first political campaign at age eleven hanging "I Like Ike!" doorknob signs urging the election of General Eisenhower as president. I really did like Ike! I was eleven and hooked. Sorry, Grandpa Ed!

# 5

# Family Values

MY PARENTS WERE very devoted Roman Catholics and patriots. The guiding principles of my youth essentially flowed from those core sets of values. Woe unto us should we ever lie, cheat, or steal! Mass was mandatory every Sunday and Holy Day. Lent was to be observed, and midweek devotions were added to the church schedule. In those days it was fish every Friday. Many of us grew up with an aversion to seafood. Catechism was a daily course of study during Catholic grade school and junior high. The nuns made sure that we were acutely aware that "impure thoughts" were truly the work of the devil.

I was involved with scouting beginning with Cub Scouts and concluding with Explorer Scouts. Patriotism was a core value as was the Golden Rule. Those values influenced routine activities which focused on appreciation of the outdoors, camping, and individual interests that were channeled into earning merit badges. Problems with asthma prevented me from participating in some of the camping activities.

My parents taught that all people were God's creations and should be treated as such, regardless of their worldly station. People of different religious beliefs, cultures, or races were to be treated with equal dignity and respect. There was not much diversity in

Milford, Iowa, when I was growing up. A very few wealthy people who had summer homes at Lake Okoboji had African American servants. My father did work for many of these people and I recall that he had very friendly relationships with their servants.

When I was in high school, I met Wilburn Hollis, who became one of the first African Americans to earn All-American honors as a quarterback. He was a product of Boys Town in Omaha, Nebraska. Boys Town had a summer camp at Lake Okoboji just down the beach from where I went swimming with my family. I met him there. Willie went to Boys Town at age 10 and became well known as an exceptional multi-sport athlete. He was one year older and two grades ahead of me. We were not close friends, but we did spend some enjoyable time together. He was my first African American friend. He sustained an injury in his senior year in college that terminated what otherwise would have been a great football career.

Following the end of World War II, soldiers from the area began the return to civilian life. Some, however, served as occupiers in Germany and Japan. Some of those soldiers returned home with "war brides." Since there were many citizens of German heritage in the community, the German war brides gained easy acceptance. That was not always the case with Japanese war brides. I don't recall any Japanese who lived in our community before the war. Remember too that my Uncle Gilbert was killed by soldiers of the Japanese army.

As a child I naturally had a very bad impression of the Japanese. They had killed my uncle! One of the returning soldiers brought home a Japanese war bride. I remember my parents discussing this couple and the difficulties they were having fitting into the community. I still remember my mother and father deciding they should invite the couple to our home for dinner. They thought that would send a message to the community that the young woman should not be held responsible for the wrongs committed by her country's leaders.

In those days the local newspaper, The Milford Mail, published a social column listing the entertainment activities of residents. My parents knew the dinner they had for the soldier and his wife would be the basis for an item in that column. I was probably six or seven years old at the time, but this example of my parents' concern for the well-being of others made a lasting impression.

The federal government had created a civilian sky-watch program called the Ground Observer Corps during World War II. It was disbanded after the war. In 1950 it was revived as a Cold War defense organization. By 1952 there were 16,000 observation posts and 75 reporting centers. The observation posts were staffed with volunteers who reported aircraft sightings to the centers. My father and I were a volunteer team.

Dad was also interested in airplanes and later served as the Milford Airport Commissioner. But he never took flying lessons. We both habitually noted every airplane that passed overhead. It made sense to turn that interest into something productive. We did six-hour shifts as I recall. We operated out of a little shed constructed on the roof of a downtown business building that contained communications equipment. The Ground Observer Corp program was terminated in 1958. The volunteer observers were encouraged to participate in civil defense through the Radio Amateur Civil Emergency Service, which we did. I had an amateur radio license and my dad got his license a year or so after I got mine.

# 6

# Milford High School

IN THE FALL of 1956, I transitioned from the Catholic grade
school and junior high to the local public Milford High School.
There was no longer a Catholic High School in Milford. That was
more of a transition than most would think. It was big news in the
early 50s when the public-school system hired its first Catholic
teacher! In my case, religious bigotry was not really an issue.
Through summer baseball and scouting I already had several
protestant friends in the public-school system.

Which reminds me, I recall being told that before my time there
was a Ku Klux Klan unit in the Milford area. Since they didn't have
any African Americans to harass, they had to make do with Catholics.
The Klan didn't do well in Milford. They were ridiculed and mocked
when they tried to intimidate by parading through town in their goofy
robes and hoods. I don't think they did anything destructive. After
some heckling, it dawned on them how foolish they looked. Some
people just seem to have a need to find someone to hate! That is a
phenomenon I have observed throughout the world.

Despite my initial trepidation about going to the public school
for the first time, it was a very good experience. I was elected
president of the freshman class and participated in band, basketball,
and drama. In my junior year I was medically cleared to play

football. I lettered in each of these activities, including track. I hated track, but the football coach required it. However, if you had a job, the football coach would excuse you from track. I got a job! It was a lot more fun than track. I had learned early in my athletic "career" that running laps was a punishment for an error or infraction. That has influenced my feelings about running to this day.

I really loved baseball and played every position on our summer team. The high school did not have a baseball team, but the town through service clubs supported a summer baseball program in which I participated. The catcher on the team was from a rural high school near Milford, Jerry Johnson. I still remember him breaking his little finger during a game. I took over as catcher until he could play again. Jerry became a significant player in my life. I did some pitching but was nowhere near the pitcher that my little brother became. But I was a better hitter—right, Dean?

I had little musical talent, as earlier stated, but somehow (small school, perhaps?) I became a member of the Milford High School concert and marching bands. I took clarinet lessons. That enhanced my career as a mechanical musician of minor achievement, whose musical career terminated upon high school graduation. When I was medically cleared (asthma) to play football, I dropped the marching band gig. They probably quickly learned they sounded better without me!

The school plays were lots of fun, especially the practices and get togethers after practice. Along that line, we had a speech contest based on a patriotic theme. I won and got to give my speech on the local Spencer radio station, KICD.

I was elected to other leadership positions during my high school career and graduated as salutatorian behind our valedictorian, Marilyn Russell. Marilyn and I competed for top grades. It was a friendly competition and we dated from time to time. There was no doubt in my mind that she was the better student. But I was the better athlete!

Speaking of dating: it was a different era. I did date some, but not very much. We were a small class in a small high school. My memories from those days are fond. Many of us still get together and have lots of fun recalling those days. Some friends married people they dated in high school. Some of those marriages have endured to this day, some haven't. This circumstance seems to apply to all marriages regardless of when and where established. The resort nature of the lake offered all kinds of dating opportunities. It was a fantastic place to grow up. Pretty dull in the winter months, but lots of fun during the summer.

The Roof Garden at Lake Okoboji was a dancehall which drew several of the great performers of the day. Many of them were young stars and had nothing to do when not performing. While I never worked at the Roof Garden, I had friends who did. It was easy to become acquainted with the younger performers. I remember taking a young African American singer on a trampoline date after her show. We had a lot of fun as did the other singers in her group who were with us.

I met Conway Twitty one summer. We spent some time together that summer and the next one. He had a big Cadillac convertible that we trolled with. He picked me up at our house one evening and met my mother. She was hesitant about my friendship with this rock star. He charmed her and pointed out that he sang Danny Boy in his act. She decided he had to be an okay guy. Good that she never heard his version!

Phil Harris and Alice Faye were summer visitors. They were nationally famous entertainers who had friends with a big home on the lake. They would come by plane while I was working at the airport. They were nice to me. They would visit for several weeks and brought with them their beautiful daughters, Alice and Phyliss. Alice was a year younger and Phyliss three years younger than me. They resembled their movie star mother. I was smitten, but mostly from afar. There was a long line!

I got interested in amateur radio around age 14 and got licensed as a "ham" (K0LCI—the "0" is a zero with a slash line though it and it is pronounced "zero") while a freshman. It led to a keener interest in world affairs and languages. I had a multi-language phrase book used to help communicate with hams in other countries. I still maintain my license, but I have been inactive since the 90s. While in high school several of my good friends and classmates (Lee Carr, Gary Moeller, and Ron Vandenberg) also got their licenses.

My dad was always interested in ham radio too, but he never had the opportunity to pursue it. After I got licensed and bought some equipment, he worked on getting a license. He passed his Morse Code and radio theory tests and was licensed as K0PEQ.

In the spring of my junior year I was playing catch with some friends in our front yard one nice afternoon after school. We had a radio playing. The music was interrupted for a news bulletin: it was announced that my grandfather had just died of a sudden heart attack while fishing on Lake Okoboji. I was shocked of course. A few minutes later my dad drove up and got out of the car. I ran to him and said I had heard a bulletin on the radio saying Grandpa had died. He said it was true. He wasn't pleased that the radio station rushed it onto the air before there was even time to notify family members. But I realize now that Grandpa was newsworthy as a local celebrity even at age 77.

My high school class graduated 42 people. We were the smallest class at any time during my high school career. I formed many good friendships which have endured to the time of this writing. We had a gay fellow and a mentally handicapped fellow in our class. On balance these two were treated well by their classmates and others in the high school. The mentally handicapped boy, Johnny, was the son of the town doctor and his wife, best friends of my parents.

Johnny was a year older than me. We spent a lot of our younger years together because of our parents' friendship. Johnny was my friend growing up and I was his protector in high school. Consequently, I learned how to fight. He was occasionally subjected to bullying and harassment by a few fellow students, but not by members of our Class of 1960. One fellow in another class was a persistent bully. It finally resulted in a real fight after school. The bully thought he was tough and a good fighter—he learned he wasn't good enough. I was very angry!

My maternal grandfather, the active Democrat politician, died of cancer at age 67 when I was nine years old. He spent the last few months of his life in our home. I loved him dearly and even today mourn his loss. It was the first time I felt God really let me down! I had been praying frantically for his recovery.

In my junior year I began the process of application to the United States Air Force Academy. I was aware of the existence of the evil Republican State Senator Roy Smith. I say "evil" because my grandfather appeared to generally think poorly of Republicans. I knew he and my grandfather held opposing views, disagreed about many things, and were political opponents. But I never knew Grandpa to personally attack any Republican. I knew we lived in a very Republican part of the state. I learned that did not bode well for aspiring Democrat politicians. Grandfather Ed died two years before my hero, General Dwight David Eisenhower, was elected president as a Republican.

My real first political insight came about because of my grandfather's illness. The evil Senator Smith visited him on a regular basis. I later surmised that he was probably supplying my grandfather with some adult beverages. They had great times together! I could hear them raising their voices and arguing their points. But I also heard much good-natured laughter and noted the respect and affection they held for each other. I fondly remember those visits. As I got older, my admiration and appreciation for their respect and regard for each other grew to influence my outlook to my great benefit. I learned early that it was possible to disagree without being disagreeable. That lesson has served me well throughout my personal and professional life.

The Senator was aware of my love for my grandfather and the pain of my loss. He stayed close. I had frequent contact with him, as my parents were also close to him. When it came time to apply to the Academy, he offered his help. Our congressman was a

Republican (Charles B. Hoeven), a friend of the then-retired Senator Smith. The first hurdle in the process those days was to secure one of 11 nominations for one (sometimes two) of the appointments allocated to Members of Congress to each service academy.

Senator Smith advised me and my parents on the application process. He arranged for me to meet people involved in that process, and he gave me his encouragement. During one of the meetings he arranged, a housefly intruded. The men in attendance commented and the fly happened by me. In one of my luckier maneuvers, I struck out at it with my hand and caught it. They were all in awe of my quick reflexes and commented on what a great pilot I would become given the chance!

Fortunately, I obtained one of the 11 nominations. Since my parents had no political influence, being Democrats in a Republican realm, I was also lucky in that Congressman Hoeven based the final appointment on the outcome of the testing of the nominees by the Air Force. I was the runner-up. The winner was an engineering student finishing his sophomore year at Iowa State University. I was the winner of a consolation prize: an offer of enrollment in the Naval Academy Preparatory School. The service academies, other than Air Force at the time, had preparatory schools for promising applicants who were qualified but did not obtain an appointment. Attendees would be enlisted in the service which put them in a different and somewhat less competitive applicant pool. The Air Force used the Naval Academy's prep school. The Air Force Academy later established its own prep school.

I had no idea what I was being offered. I discussed it with my Naval Reserve Aviator Uncle, Dutch, who was not sure either. I eventually decided to simply call the admissions office at the Air Force Academy and ask to speak to someone who could explain this opportunity. I was given the Colonel who was the Director of Admissions. We had a very long and thorough discussion about the prep school, me, my desire to fly in the Air Force, and my other options.

The class I wanted to join, the class of 1964, was to convene in Colorado Springs within a few days of my conversation with the Colonel. I was in the process of deciding whether to accept the preparatory school offer or enroll at Iowa State University. I had been accepted in the college of electrical engineering at ISU. Before deciding, I received telegraphic notification that I had been appointed a member of the class of 1964 at the United States Air Force Academy.

That visit with the Colonel obviously changed my life! I hastily made my final preparations and took my first airline trip which was to Colorado Springs. I arrived the day before we were to sign in and spent the afternoon at a motel with a swimming pool. It was to be my last taste of luxury for many months to come.

Family friend and physician, Dr. J. J. Buchanan, played a significant role too. He had served as a Navy physician in World War II. I always suspected he glossed over my allergy problems and gave me a glowing report. Recently I became acquainted with his granddaughter, Bobbi, also a physician. Dr. Bobbi, in response to my inquiry, laughed when I expressed my suspicions that he played a significant role in my admission. She said he was very proud of having put his thumb on the scale.

After I was appointed to the Academy, my parents decided the least they could do for Congressman Hoeven was to switch parties. We have been a Republican family since. Much later I came to know a Democrat legislative leader from that part of Iowa, Senator Jack Kibbie. I took an instant liking to him, partly because he was from my home area. Then I learned he had known my grandfather. Jack and his wife, Kay, remain good friends.

# PART II
# EYE ON THE SKY

# 1

# Into the Wild Blue Yonder

*Doolie Summer*

EARLY THE DAY after arrival in Colorado Springs, I joined classmates for the first time for a bus ride into the future. The class consisted of 750 subdued young men from a reported applicant pool of 70,000. It wasn't long before we wondered if the other 69,250 weren't the lucky ones! When we were off-loaded from our buses, we were led to an in-processing center where we were issued uniforms, paperwork, and instructions. One of the instructions included our four-digit and one letter serial number which we were told to memorize immediately and to never forget.

We were shown to a door which opened into the cadet area where screaming upperclassmen awaited in ambush. They took us one-by-one and immediately began yelling instructions which were baffling to us. Our lack of comprehension resulted in an order to drop and give pushups. The first time I was so ordered, I managed to scuff the spit-shined shoes of the upperclassman. Talk about a capital offense. That set the tone for the rest of the day. We got our uniforms, we were measured for more uniforms, we had our hair almost completely sheared off, and we were run by the medical clinic.

We were introduced to eating at attention. Although seated, we were required to sit rigidly erect, eyes straight ahead, feet together, arms and elbows locked against our sides. We were not to make any movement related to feeding ourselves until ordered to do so by an upper-class cadet. First, we had to pass the containers of food to the upperclassmen. This was to be done in a specified manner while maintaining our rigid positions to the fullest extent possible. We were then permitted to serve ourselves and await a command to eat. We ate while maintaining our rigid positions. While eating, it was customary for the upperclassmen to propound questions to us individually. The subject could be anything. Name the members of the Joint Chiefs of Staff, for example. What was the score of the Cub's game last night?

When we finally retired to our rooms, we were in a state of utter exhaustion and confusion. Day One of Basic Cade Training (BCT) or "Doolie Summer" had been completed. It didn't get any better the next day, or many days thereafter.

We were embarking on a four-year ordeal that ended on June 3, 1964, when 490 of the original 750 (65%) of us raised our right-hand and swore the oath of a second lieutenant in the United States Air Force. We were also awarded a Bachelor of Science Degree. Many of us would go on to jet pilot training and earn the wings of a United States Air Force pilot. Some would become navigators. Many others would go directly to graduate school to pursue advanced degrees in aeronautical engineering and similar technical fields. One would go to Cambridge University as a Rhodes Scholar. One of my roommates, Mike Robbins, was awarded a Fulbright Scholarship. Several other classmates received similar scholarships.

The beginning of this journey involved a grueling grind, challenging us mentally and physically. One of the first "drills" involved a run of significant distance on the Academy grounds. The upperclassmen ran with us and they hardly broke a sweat! They seemed like supermen. Eventually we figured out that they looked good because they were acclimated to the high-altitude (7,258 feet) environment of the Academy, and we were most definitely not. We soon became acclimated too. But the first few days were made even more brutal because of that disadvantage.

The physical demands were exhausting, and the mental stress was not any better. We were expected to memorize certain information and be able to yell it out whenever asked by an upperclassman who stood in our face while we held an exaggerated position of military attention. For example, we were required to memorize the full name and position of each member of the President's cabinet. Thank God there weren't as many cabinet members as there are today. Of course, we had to know all stanzas of the Star-Spangled Banner and the Air Force song. This was our summer of 1960 at the United States Air Force Academy.

We began to lose classmates beginning early in this summer ordeal. Others fell by the wayside up to the week before graduation. Two classmates washed out just before graduation. Some left voluntarily, others left because of academic failures, disciplinary issues, and honor code violations.

Harry Chapin was one of those who left voluntarily during summer training. He wanted to fly. But he soon realized military discipline didn't fit his free spirit personality. He recognized his real passion was music. He became one of the world's most famous singer-songwriters with millions of records sold. He was also a philanthropist interested in addressing world hunger. He was posthumously awarded the Congressional Gold Medal for his humanitarian work. And he remained an Academy booster who performed gratuitously in the Cadet theater at the Cadet social center, Arnold Hall. Harry died in an automobile accident in 1981 at the age of 38. A surviving daughter, Jennifer (Jen) Chapin, has followed in her dad's footsteps and become a popular recording artist. I had the pleasure of spending some time with her when she performed in Des Moines.

The Air Force Academy was my big break in life. I survived the grueling Basic Cadet Training (BCT) but two of my roommates did not. Both were good cadet candidates. One was the son of a famous author. Both suffered injuries in the training that disqualified them.

Our class (the sixth) was only the second class that would spend all four years at the newly constructed facility in Colorado Springs. The first years of operation were at Lowry Air Force base in Denver. The dormitory rooms were two-man rooms (no female cadets in those days). The loss of two roommates was a real problem. I was left to fend for myself in my room. Our rooms were subject to almost daily inspections which required the work of two. Every nook and cranny were subject to white glove inspections for traces of dust, and the floor had to be buffed to a polish and the sink kept in perfect condition when not in use.

The important lessons of BCT included learning how to work with a roommate to meet all the impossible demands imposed and how to work with your classmates as a member of a group. There never was enough time in the day to do everything.

Developing the judgment and discipline to identify and address priority needs first was an unstated training goal. It was a real challenge to keep up without a roommate. On the other hand, I only had one of us to clean up after! We had limited telephone privileges and cell phones hadn't been invented. Our limited social time mostly occurred in our room with our roommate. I was in solitary confinement when not "on the yard" with my classmates.

After the loss of my second roommate there was an odd number of Basic Cadets left in my class. I had no roommate for the last four or five weeks of BCT. This really put me at a disadvantage. After about a week of this, a First Classman (a senior, a God, relative to our status) knocked on my door one evening. There was nothing worse than having a First Classman visit your room. Nothing good ever came of it.

But this time the First Classman quickly told me to relax, be "at ease" and chat with him. He stated that I wasn't going to get a roommate unless something happened to another classmate. He went on to say it was nearly impossible to make it as a Basic Cadet without a roommate. The upperclassmen in charge of our training understood that and had designated him as someone I could go to for help when I was "down" or needed help with something.

After a good chat, he left my room. But he immediately re-entered, closed the door, and offered this advice: "Luchtel, I will let you in on my secret for surviving this place. Don't take this place too seriously. Every day there is something that happens that is just plain funny. If you can't find something to laugh about when you're getting ready for bed, I want to know. Keep your sense of humor and have a least one good chuckle a day about this system and you will be fine!" I later learned they had picked the right person. He was an outstanding member of the class of 1961. He was sincere in his offer of assistance. It ended up I was able to cope on my own. The advice he gave that night carried me through those four years and all the years that I have racked up since. He led me to a concept that has served me well.

BCT was a demanding couple of months designed to prepare new cadets for life in the Cadet Wing (student body) which required adherence to strict academic and military training standards. Successful completion of the ordeal led to promotion from Basic Cadet to Cadet Fourth Class (Freshman).

◆ ◆ ◆

## The Honor Code

Governing the total environment was the Cadet Honor Code: "We will not lie, cheat or steal nor tolerate amongst us those who do." A very simple statement with a profound impact on all cadets. The toleration clause was the most difficult. Its application made it an honor code violation to not report a fellow cadet's violation of the Code. In the 1960s this was a very rigid code and several classmates suffered the penalty that applied to violations: expulsion. Some very good and honorable men (as the label is normally applied) fell by the wayside as a result. Some even self-reported their own violations. We mourned the loss of some outstanding classmates who sometimes succumbed to errors in judgment, which probably seemed minor to them at the time, but resulted in their expulsion. I think about them occasionally and hope they recovered from their tragic loss and have gone on to lead successful lives.

The Code is administered by the cadets. Its administration and application have been modified over the years. In my time, each squadron had an "honor representative" who served as a delegate to the Wing Honor Committee. There was oversight by the Commandant of Cadets, an Air Force Brigadier General. It was rare for the General to interfere or interject himself into proceedings. He was empowered, however, to reverse or modify a finding of the Committee.

In BCT we enjoyed our training on the Code. It was taught in a relaxed atmosphere and its benefits became obvious to us. We learned to appreciate the difference it made in the social and military environment. We came to value the fact that our fellow cadets would not take advantage of us in the competitions that would follow. The Code was recognized as creating a secure environment conducive to intellectual development and acquisition of lifelong friendships. It created an expectation that was not required by other academic institutions, as many of us learned while subsequently pursuing advanced degrees.

It should be noted that it was prohibited to use the Honor Code to enforce the disciplinary system. From my lawyer's perspective it might best be described as prohibiting "entrapment" through use of the Code. Cadets could be questioned and were honor bound to give correct answers, but "fishing expeditions" to enforce discipline were not allowed. There had to be some "probable cause" to launch an inquiry. If your shoes didn't look shined well enough, you could expect to be asked if you had shined them. But you weren't to be asked if all the shoes back in your closet were properly shined unless the inquiry was made during a room inspection.

The disciplinary system used a demerit system. Bed looks sloppy—demerits, shoes not shined—demerits, late to class—lots of demerits, sleep through breakfast—loss of privileges, meaning restriction to quarters when others were privileged to go to the social center or library, and so on. Garner too many demerits, even in small doses, in a month and you would find yourself suffering specified consequences which could range from a restriction to quarters, marching punishment tours, to expulsion. The infractions were classified into three degrees of severity: first, second and third class. Class three offenses were the worst. Some could result in summary dismissal. Punishment tours required marching back and forth along a set path shouldering an M-1 rifle as if on parade for one hour. I think you were given a five-minute break each hour if serving multiple hours. I served one such punishment tour during BCT as an example of what to expect if I accrued too many demerits or committed a serious breach of discipline. Luckily, it was the only tour I served.

◆◆◆

### A Real Genuine Air Force Cadet

Upon completion of Basic Cadet Training an Acceptance Ceremony was held during which the new class was "accepted" into the Cadet Wing. We were given shoulder boards to wear on our new tailored uniforms.

The "promotion" really did not mean much in terms of lifestyle. We still put in eighteen-hour days. Now those hours included rigorous academic studies. There was almost constant "correction" by ever present upper-class cadets. The difference, for practical purposes, was that while we were still Doolies (Freshmen were called that), we had the full set of cadet uniforms including shoulder boards that designated us as full-fledged Cadets Fourth Class, but still the lowest of the low (Seniors were designated Cadet First Class). Cadet rank was indicated on the shoulder boards. Doolies didn't have any rank to display, we wore blank plain black shoulder boards or epaulets.

The real difference from the perspective of a Doolie was that while we still had 18-hour days of military training, physical training, and a heavy load of academic demands, the upper-class cadets had their focus shifted from training the Doolies full time to engaging in their own military training, physical training, and academic struggles.

Instead of being grouped together, Doolies were integrated into the then 20 Cadet Squadrons made up of approximately 100 cadets, approximately 25 from each of the four classes. Doolies having become members of a squadron gradually became integrated into it as "their squadron." We interacted as Doolies with the upper three classes in the living areas to which we were assigned (Squadron Areas) and ate in the Cadet Dining Hall at assigned tables (long ones that seated 10 Cadets as I recall) containing members of all four classes. The senior cadet sat at the head of the table and was designated the "Table Commandant." Tables were served by white uniformed waiters who delivered the food in serving trays to the Doolies who passed them to the other Cadets. Clever Doolies learned to cater to the preference of the first served, the Table Commandant.

As Doolies we were still subject to "knowledge questions" from any upperclassman who wanted to pursue our "training." For example: Recite the fourth stanza of the Star-Spangled Banner. What foreign visitors met with the president yesterday? Why did they meet? Like we had a lot of time for the newspaper which was delivered to our room every morning and were expected to read!

Meals were not by any means a fun relaxing occasion. I had never eaten grits, which were regularly served as part of breakfast. I soon figured out you could gobble up a lot of grits quickly as little chewing was required. "Grits am good" soon became our mantra.

Individual radios were allowed once we became full-fledged cadets. TV was available in restricted common areas containing one set per squadron. The use of TV by Doolies was restricted to very limited weekend hours. There were no recording devices available to time shift the "good stuff" to the hours when Doolies would have access. Only First Classmen had open access to the common TV room (seniors were "First Classmen," juniors Third Classmen, etc. Doolies or freshmen were Fourth Classmen).

The long grind to graduation on June 3, 1964, continued in earnest with challenging academics, military training, and a rigorous intramural athletic program. Intramural athletics were mandatory unless you were engaged in a competitive intercollegiate athletic program such as football or basketball. Several other sports that qualified included fencing, rifle, and pistol shooting teams. I qualified as a member of the varsity pistol team but dropped out when it became apparent it would curtail what little social life was available. Continued participation would have resulted in increased demands on the time available for study. Collegiate athletes at the Academy did receive some benefits: special "training tables" were set up in the Cadet Dining Hall by team, special academic advisors and tutors were provided, and athletes were released from some military training requirements. The training table was a valuable benefit for a new cadet as the harassment was usually much reduced and the upper-class tablemates/teammates were better natured.

◆ ◆ ◆

### Playboy 19

A big break was my assignment to the 19th Squadron, the so-called Playboy Squadron. Yes, that Playboy. Hugh Hefner apparently did not mind. He even sold a hat with our squadron logo on it. His Playboy Bunny logo appeared on our official squadron emblem. Over time the squadron logo has changed at least twice. None included bunnies! Some squadrons emphasized academics and intramural sports. The 19th emphasized a well-rounded comradery with a work hard/play hard lifestyle.

The members of my class of 1964 in the 19th Squadron formed lifelong friendships that endure to this writing. I hear from at least one of them on an almost daily basis thanks to email and the cell phone. We helped each other survive the USAFA and built bonds that were strengthened by our Vietnam experiences. We were a lucky bunch. We did have a squadron classmate, Ron Bliss, who was shot down over North Vietnam and held as a POW for more than six years. But we did not sustain any combat fatalities in Vietnam.

The Academy had excellent dedicated professors who were specially chosen Air Force Officers with advanced degrees in the subjects they taught. The class sizes were quite small, usually no more than 15. There was never a crowd to hide in! The professors were generous with their time and offered extra instruction for anyone who needed it. I seized that opportunity a few times and managed to survive. I also had a breather: my grandmother died unexpectedly in the fall of 1961. I was granted emergency leave to go to her funeral. That couple of days away from the Academy did me a world of good. My professors were very helpful in getting me up to speed when I returned.

◆ ◆ ◆

## The Daily Grind

The routine was very demanding all four years. Each year was better in that it brought new privileges and status. The curriculum in those days was science and engineering oriented and everyone graduated with a Bachelor of Science Degree without a designated major. What we called privileges were few and far between even in the final year. Privileges were as simple as being permitted a few hours away from the Academy with a sponsor for Fourth Class Cadets, and up to a few weekend passes per semester for First Class Cadets. They were doled out based on a cadet's performance and class. Cadets who excelled in military training were named on a recognition list called the Commandant's List. The Dean's List was the academic recognition. If you made both lists, you were on the Superintendent's List. A rare instance where being on more lists the better!

Our days began with reveille at 5:55 AM and taps was at 10:15 PM (we of course soon learned that was from 0555 to 2215 hours). We marched by squadrons in formation for each of our three daily meals. The weekdays were filled with academics, military training, and athletics. Usually there were no classes on Saturdays, but rigid room inspections were conducted on Saturday mornings. We then were required to participate in a military parade most Saturdays with one general exception: home football game Saturdays. Precious free time began for the underclasses following the Saturday noon meal. Cadets entitled to off-base privileges could use them. Cadets who were on restrictions for disciplinary reasons were usually restricted to their rooms or required to march punishment tours. Cadets were required to attend Chapel Services on Sundays when at the Academy. I don't think that requirement exists anymore.

The typical semester schedule called for 18 credit hours weighted towards engineering subjects. We took courses in aeronautical engineering, astrophysics, chemistry, civil engineering, electrical engineering, mechanical engineering, and physics. We also studied the humanities, including a foreign language (French for me), English literature and composition, economics, history, philosophy, and political science. Economic history and political science courses studied other countries and their economic systems as well as the United States.

The first semester of Doolie Year was based on selected courses of study out of those areas. The course material and academic requirements themselves were very demanding. In combination with the military and athletic training demands the burden was almost overwhelming.

For part of the four years we were required to submit a 100 word essay every Sunday evening. Imposition of that requirement nearly caused a revolt. I hated it like most did but came to realize it was a great idea. I think it enhanced our ability to express ourselves in writing and served us well in our Air Force careers.

I was a big fish in a very small pond in high school. My graduating class had 42 members. Thankfully, I had good teachers and was inclined towards math and science. I finished second in the class. I lettered in the sports I played. The transition from high school star to Doolie was painful!

The first semester at USAFA was a real struggle. The mental

stress was increased by the upperclassmen's "training" sessions at meals and in hallway encounters. The only place free of such training was in the cadet gymnasium and surrounding fields of friendly strife. Intramural sports were a big part of cadet life. The competition between squadrons was intense.

My first assigned intramural sport was soccer. All cadets not engaged in varsity sports were required to participate in a rigorous intramural program. In Milford, we did not play soccer. I think I probably knew what a soccer ball looked like, but I am not sure where I would have seen one. One of the attractions of intramural or varsity sports was that you had "amnesty" when engaged in those activities. It was very bad form for an upper-class cadet to "pull rank" on another cadet, even a Doolie. It was especially bad form if the upperclassman was complaining about being hit during a play. At my first soccer practice I took full advantage. It soon became apparent to all concerned, including me, that I knew nothing whatsoever about soccer. I ran around chasing the ball and enjoyed blocking any upperclassman reasonably close to the ball.

After the second practice, there was a knock on my door that evening. It was the lacrosse coach. He said he had heard that I was a stand-up guy without much soccer talent. He said he needed a lacrosse goalie and asked if I was interested. I had absolutely no idea what lacrosse was! I had never even heard of lacrosse. I didn't know what the ball looked like or even if there was a ball. I didn't know anything at all about how the game was played. I assumed it was probably played on a field like soccer with goals at each end. I noticed that soccer goalies did not do much running around. It might be a tough job, but at least it didn't involve excessive running. So, I volunteered.

I became a very good lacrosse goalie and played four years without significant injury. I learned to love the game. Lacrosse goalies are protected from attack inside a circle near the goal. It is not a large area, but it does afford some maneuvering room where the goalie is protected from direct attack. The ball is about tennis ball size and hard as a rock. The players use long sticks with racquet-like webbing at the end. Passes and shots are launched by catapulting the ball out of the webbing by swinging the stick while releasing the ball with a flick of the wrist. A pass is caught by catching it in the webbing.

The goalie has protection much like a baseball catcher. My team's defense was not very good. I developed the technique of attacking offensive players preparing to take a shot by coming out of my protected area and impacting them before they could get their shot off. The goal itself is much smaller than a soccer goal. It is more like a hockey goal. You could block a shot by pursuing and maintaining an attack angle that denied the shooter a proper shot angle. There were lots of injuries in lacrosse, but I was very lucky in that regard.

My one significant injury occurred at the end of a practice. The coach had me in the goal deflecting practice shots being taken by our offense. He blew his whistle signaling the end of the drill. I took off my helmet with face mask attached. One of the shooters had not heard the whistle ending the drill and launched a shot that caught me in the mouth and knocked me off my feet. I bled profusely and was taken to the Academy Hospital Emergency Room by ambulance. I remained conscious, but I was in a lot of pain. The front tooth closest to the point of impact was problematic for the next fifty plus years before it was finally replaced with an implant.

I merely endured intramural wrestling which I hated. It is really hard work and just wasn't my idea of fun. The only match I won was against an upperclassman. We didn't get along and it was my opportunity to take him on. I think in the process we learned we had a common bond after all: we both hated wrestling. We got along much better afterward. Two of my friends excelled at wrestling, Brett Dula and Terry Isaacson. As I recall, they both were All-American wrestlers. Terry was also our All-American Quarterback.

I liked intramural boxing and was also good at it. I was undefeated except for a draw in the championship match. If there is anything to be avoided in boxing, it is a draw. I was fighting a friend and fellow Playboy Squadron classmate, Ron Bliss. We beat the crap out of each other. He proved himself a true standup guy when he ended up being our six-years-plus POW at the Hanoi Hilton.

The entire Academy program was very demanding and geared to teach some very valuable, but often unstated lessons. There was a constant need to prioritize. There never was enough time to do everything that was to be done. We learned to identify and focus on the high priority issues and put the low priority ones aside. We learned to treat time as a valuable commodity not to be wasted. We learned that not everything could be done to perfection. Perfection is too often the enemy of adequate and timely completion. We learned to be aware of what was going on around us and assess situations quickly and accurately. We had to learn to quickly assess situations and react correctly. I was to learn these were skills essential to surviving aerial combat in a few short years.

# 2

# Settling In

THAT IS NOT to say we didn't have some fun times. Arnold Hall was the Academy's social center. It included a nice theater, a ballroom, and a bowling alley. There was a Cadet Wing Hostess who arranged social functions, which often included a bevy of bused-in local coeds. We could visit Arnold Hall during specified time periods on weekends. We entertained visitors there and on the plaza that surrounded it. We could not take guests into the Cadet Area which included the dormitories, dining hall, library, and academic area. A friend from high school was living and working in Denver. Ruth would come and visit and sometimes bring a friend.

We enjoyed a limited number of off-base "dining privileges" which enabled visits to the homes of approved sponsors. Approved sponsors were close relatives, military officers, and retired officers. I spent my first Thanksgiving as a cadet with a family in Colorado Springs. They hosted several cadets, one of whom, Jim Pierce, was engaged to their daughter Nancy. In 1966 I gave my bride a tour of the Academy while on our honeymoon. We went to dinner at a nice restaurant in the mountains. During dinner a bottle of champagne was delivered to our table courtesy of Nancy's parents. I hadn't seen them, but they saw us come in. Nice surprise, great people! We had a very enjoyable visit with them.

My family visited over the Christmas Holidays. My protestant roommate and one of my other cadet friends, who happened to be Jewish, did not have family visit. My family included them in our holiday activities, including Christmas Mass. Max, the Jewish cadet, seemed to enjoy the holiday activities and found the Mass very interesting.

Max graduated and went to helicopter pilot training. He served his six-year commitment to the USAF, resigned and joined the Israeli Air Force. We kept in contact and Max never forgot his Doolie Christmas. He was killed in action during the Yom Kippur War in October 1973 while flying a special operations mission. I had learned that Max had married and had recently become a father. He was very proud of his daughter. Patti and I were privileged to meet Max's widow and child several years later with the help of the Israeli Ambassador to the United States.

The first year wore on and we survived the doldrums of the Academy in the winter months after Christmas. Our commitment to, and appreciation for, being members of the 19th Squadron and the Class of 1964 was forged. Despite the rigid class system, we also began to become friendlier with our upper-class squadron leaders. It was all starting to come together. And we had gained some opportunities to leave the Academy for a few hours on a Saturday or Sunday. I was going to Denver occasionally. We were on the right path!

The academic grind was grueling. There was never enough time! We lost several classmates the first semester due to low grade point average. We lost a classmate out of the 19th Squadron who self-reported an honor code violation. I don't recall what it was, but I think it was an unduly harsh result for what I considered a minor violation. But that was the absolute nature of the Code that we had pledged to support. I remain a strong supporter of that honor code.

Although the majority of my classmates might disagree, I think the "second chance" approach that was adopted decades later has merit. I wonder sometimes what impact dismissal had on those members of our class who left due to a violation. Hopefully they were able to benefit from their time with us and overcome that setback. Those who self-reported had proven themselves to be especially honorable men in my estimation.

Our first classmate to become a fatality was Bill Hickox, a member of the United States championship figure-skating team. The entire team of 18 members was killed on February 15, 1961, in a plane crash at Brussels, Belgium, while traveling to an international competition.

We yearned for "Recognition Day." This was the day when we would be formally "recognized" and accepted into the Cadet Wing as full-fledged members and soon-to-be upperclassmen. No more Doolie stuff! This was a day in May set aside for a ceremony where we would be presented our collar insignia (propeller over wings or "prop and wings") by an upperclassman followed by a friendly handshake and a pat on the back. We could even eat like normal people in the dining hall, upperclassmen would become friends. A truly great day!

But there remained one obstacle: Hell Week! That week everything reverted to Basic Cadet Training of the prior summer in terms of treatment, in most cases even worse. The recognition ceremony was the culmination of Hell Week that was to occur on Saturday. In those days, we marched in formation to all our meals. Our day started with a wake-up call followed by a gathering in formations by squadrons for the march from the dormitory assembly area to the dining hall for breakfast. At the time there were 20 squadrons in the Cadet Wing and one large dormitory. There were four Groups of five squadrons each. We marched to meals by Group and Squadron. That last day of Hell Week was to be our final ordeal as underclassmen. We could look forward to a real going over during assembly for breakfast and at breakfast that Saturday!

Class spirit is, and always will be, a valued attribute of any class at any service academy. The USAFA Class of 1964 was imbued with unmatched class spirit and we were very proud of it. There was no doubt we were the best class ever assembled and we looked for a spectacular way to display it. Today we have adopted "None has done more than '64" as our rallying cry. We base that on the number of generals produced and combat decorations earned.

We decided to go AWOL (Absent Without Official Leave) in the wee hours of Saturday morning before the normal breakfast formation. All but a handful made their way to a foothill to the west of the Academy where we could look down on the Cadet Area. We put up a sign and prepared to yell cheers down upon the upperclassmen gathered for the breakfast formation. We were sure they would be very impressed with our moxie and cohesiveness.

WRONG! There was much consternation below as it began to dawn on the upperclassmen that basically the whole class was missing. Pity the poor stragglers! The upperclassmen began to look for us. They didn't think to look up at the big hill which was on the other side of the entertainment area. As we broke into a cheer, they were not amused or impressed with our enthusiastic demonstration of class spirit and unity. Most were downright furious with us as they were missing out on one last hazing opportunity! They viewed us as shirkers. Some were so outraged they wanted to withdraw from the plan to "recognize" our class. Potentially we could have been the first class to never get "recognized" by our upperclassmen.

Wiser heads prevailed and a delegate to the hilltop invited us down after breakfast where a Recognition Formation and ceremony was conducted. Not all upperclassmen participated! We were officially recognized, but it was grudgingly. It was at least a couple of weeks before we were accepted by all upperclassmen. There is a hard core of upperclassmen that to this day fail to see the humor of that situation. I think they just wish they had thought of the idea when they were Doolies. And I suspect at least some envy us the courage to carry it off!

We had a change in the Commandant of Cadets not long after Recognition Day. We were all eager to take the measure of the new guy. Commandants of Cadets are Air Force Brigadier Generals. The Cadet Wing was buzzing with speculation about who the new commandant would be and what to expect from him. The appointment was to be announced and the appointee introduced at a special parade after the following weekend. The Playboy Squadron held a scheduled party that Saturday at a remote park-like area in the mountains that belonged to the Academy. It had a nice lodge that was a perfect place for a party. As "recognized" cadets we got to participate with the other three classes. The upperclassmen in our squadron quickly got over the AWOL episode—I think several enjoyed it. The upperclassmen arranged to give us and our dates rides to the party.

We weren't supposed to have alcohol there, but it wasn't a rule strictly enforced. We had invited several of our favorite officers and their wives. They appreciated a good drink! Most of them, anyway. My girlfriend at the time, and I, had some bourbon in the car of the upperclassman who gave us a ride to the party. We "enhanced" our drinks and those of our driver and his date. We offered the same for the officers and wives we knew were "good heads."

My date and I were seated in a booth. An older couple came in and asked to join us. I didn't recognize him and wasn't even sure he was in the Air Force. He and his wife were very friendly though, and we promptly offered to refresh their drinks. They expressed their appreciation and accepted the offer. We visited about the Academy and my impression of it. They mentioned they had recently been transferred there. He had been a pilot in World War II and we enjoyed his stories about his experiences. We had a most enjoyable evening with them. They seemed not to know the other officers in attendance.

The following Monday the announcement was made and guess who the new Commandant of Cadets was! I recognized the picture of General William Seawell immediately and figured I might be his first victim as he worked to build a reputation for discipline and control. My ole drinking buddy, Bill, was surely about to hang me out to dry! I was more than extremely concerned about my prospects. I could see marching punishment tours for the entire three years until graduation—maybe after an extra year added on for good measure. I would be turned into an Air Force Academy Monk! The Order of the Severely Admonished!

The formal change-of-command ceremony and parade were held soon after the announcement. The 19th Squadron was the second-to-last squadron to pass in review. As the first eighteen squadrons passed in review, the cadets saluted the new commandant as he stood at rigid attention and smartly snapped a salute back. When the Playboys passed in review, his face relaxed into a big grin and he doffed his hat to us as his return of our salute. General Bill Seawell, West Point, 1941, had arrived!

He was an instant hero with the cadets as the story of the party and his reaction at the parade circulated. He was indeed a great leader and Commandant of Cadets. He was a veteran combat pilot of World War II, as were many of our officers. He was promoted to full colonel (the rank before a one-star general) at the ripe old age of 26, as I recall him telling it. After getting to know him better, I asked what it was like to be a Colonel at that age. He laughed and said the war had ended and it was a long-damned time before he got his next promotion which was to Brigadier General.

Unfortunately, General Seawall's term as Commandant ended in the spring of our Second Class year. His successor was West Point, 1940. He seemed humorless and out to establish a reputation as a "hard-ass" (don't be offended, it is a time-honored military term for a jerk). He really turned the screws! He even tossed out two classmates a couple of weeks before our class was to graduate.

◆ ◆ ◆

*Third Class Year*

The Third Class (sophomore) year was a lot more relaxed than the Fourth Class year. We didn't have the Doolie Year pressures and were assimilated into the upper-class culture of the Academy. There was a new class of Doolies for us to torment. There were still lots of academic challenges to be met, but those challenges brought benefits too.

We generally had thirty days of paid leave during the summer months. Yes, we were given a great free education and paid half the base pay of a Second Lieutenant. HECKUVADEAL! But we were also charged for our uniforms, laundry services, and several other items which I forget. When we graduated, most of us had a few hundred dollars in our accounts as I recall.

The rest of the summer was spent on military training and development. The first summer was Operation Third Lieutenant (there is no such rank in the Air Force, the lowest officer rank being a Second Lieutenant). The idea was to assign us to Air Force units for some field experience to give us a picture of the "Real" Air Force. I was assigned to a unit of the Strategic Air Command located at Plattsburg, New York. The unit flew B-47 bombers carrying nuclear weapons. I got to fly in one and observe a mid-air refueling. It was a fun time and we were treated very well; much better than Second Lieutenants as I was to find out!

On one of my Plattsburg weekends, my roommate, Frank Bartlett, picked me up and we went to his home in New Hampshire for a fun weekend. The highlight was my first lobster fest or cookout or whatever. I had never seen or eaten lobster which Frank's family and friends thought was unbelievable. It was a great time which I still remember fondly. I had lobster recently, and as always, I thought of Frank and his family.

Summer leave followed my Third Lieutenant duty. I returned to Milford and enjoyed the resort scene. Tragically my Milford friend in Denver, Ruth, was a passenger in a car involved in an accident in Denver which left her unresponsive and on life support with a severe head injury. It was my first consideration of the "pull-the-plug" decision which her parents had to make. They recognized the inevitable and made the right decision. She died soon after. She was a very vivacious and attractive lady. I will always remember looking at her stilled body lying in her casket with a conical black hat on her head.

Ruth had two roommates who were also devasted by her loss. They moved from the east side of Denver to an apartment on the west side. We got together after my return that fall and I met one of their new neighbors, George MacDonald. He was raised in Scotland. He was a few years older, single, and loved a good time. And he had a great accent! He and Ruth's roommates' apartments became the focal point for many of the Playboys. That circle of friends expanded over time and resulted in a couple of weddings. Mac willingly made his apartment available to cadets in need of a place to crash on weekends. He became a great friend of the Playboys and an active correspondent. He lives in Bury St. Edmonds, England, and was visited in 2018 by Playboy J. D. Manning and his wife, Beverly.

Mac was a special friend of mine. I spent a lot of time with him. I remember going to a play in Denver with him. There was a beautiful actress in the play. I was smitten and left thinking it would be great to meet her somehow. We got back to the apartment. As Mac was parking the car, I noticed a lady with some bags by the elevator. I had Mac let me out and I went over and offered to help her. I had not seen her before. She gratefully accepted. We got everything in her apartment and she invited me to have a drink. I told her a little about who I was. She had noticed me and the other cadets around the building. She said she would like me to meet her daughter who was showering and changing clothes after work. It was my turn to gratefully accept a favor. The mother was an attractive lady and I hoped for a "daughter-like-mother." Who should appear after a few minutes but my actress! We had some good times together and she became part of the group when she was around.

There was a Polish couple who lived next door to Mac. Wally and Maria Rej (pronounced "Ray"). Wally had served in the Polish Army and the Soviet Army before making it to the states. They were a few years older, but we became good friends. I was starting to date a lady named Judy who worked in a bank in Denver. Wally and Maria really liked her.

We began to be included in some of their parties. I recall my introduction to Krupnicks, a special Polish drink that involves about three days of making. The main ingredient is grain alcohol. It is mixed with a brew of ingredients that simmer over a couple of days. It is almost lethal. I was nearly wiped out the first time I had just one.

Judy was a trooper and we passed muster with the Denver Polish folks. We were even invited to a real Polish wedding. WOW! Those people know how to have a good time and hold great volumes of alcohol. Judy and I were the only non-Polish speaking people in attendance. I remember going into the men's room and looking in the mirror and telling myself I was not going to get sick and disgrace the Air Force and my beloved country! I managed to water my drinks and Judy did the same.

After the reception finally ended, we were invited with everyone else to a physician's house. He had, no kidding, brewed up a potent Polish drink that we scooped out of his bathtub. When the sun came up, we trapesed off as a group to attend Mass together (the church was only a couple of blocks away and remained standing as of 2018. The apartment house is long gone). We sat in the back! I talked to the priest a few weeks later. He recalled the group, laughed, and said at the time he wondered if everyone was going to survive!

◆ ◆ ◆

*Be an Astronaut?—Maybe Not!*

I was very interested in the space program and was among a select group of cadets who met individually with Astronaut Gus Grissom when he was at the Academy to address the Cadet Wing. He was very easy to talk to. I remember him telling me that he thought he had found the best time to be an astronaut. The trips were short and very exciting. He said that by the time my generation of astronauts got there they would be making long duration trips. He was glad he wasn't going to be around for those. He didn't think he wanted to be cooped up in a zero-gravity space vehicle for weeks or even months at a time. That got me thinking, and eventually I decided that was not for me either. Only one of our classmates, Fred Gregory, flew as an astronaut. He became a space shuttle commander. He also served for a time as Acting Director of NASA. Fred is a real credit to our class and a good friend. I have heard him say that his greatest achievement was to have graduated from the Air Force Academy as a member of the great Class of '64.

A few years later I was a pilot waking up in Okinawa, Japan, for a mission to Vietnam when I heard the news that Gus Grissom and two other astronauts (Roger Chaffee, 31, and Ed While, 36) had been killed in a flash fire in a static test of the Apollo 1 command module on the launch pad at Cape Kenney on January 27, 1967. Gus was 40.

Ed White's brother, James Blair White, was a member of the Class of '64 at the Air Force Academy. He was reported missing in action over Laos in 1969. His remains were not recovered and identified until 2018. He finally is at rest at West Point alongside his West Point graduate brother and father, an Army Major General. The General and his wife suffered two terrible losses.

◆◆◆

*Second Class Year*

The fall of 1962 marked the start of our Second Class Academic Year. That meant more responsibility for operation of the 19$^{th}$ Squadron and training the new class. The academic grind continued unabated. But we had more opportunities to leave the Academy on weekends. We also had the opportunity to explore new areas.

During the summer of 1962 the Academy provided a trip abroad to visit military installations overseas. There were choices of destination: Asia, Central Europe, Northern Europe and South America. There was an emphasis on choosing a trip to a location where our foreign language requirement could be put to good use. I chose the Central European trip, a choice which had unimaginable consequences for me.

On these trips we would meet with embassy staff, military officers, and representatives of host governments. We would visit embassies and tour interesting sites. For example, we visited the Berlin Wall. In London I had an arranged date with the daughter of the Queen's Lady in Waiting (yes, there is such a person). In

Brussels it was the daughter of a government minister. In those cities there were formal military balls held for us by our host committees.

I had a French Air Force officer, a pilot, as my French professor at the Academy. It was not unusual to have officers of allied countries serving as visiting professors. He was a good teacher and influenced my choice of foreign field trip. He was a very fine officer willing to work with this Iowa boy to educate him about France, its culture and language.

The most important life changing event occurred during that field trip to Europe in 1962. I met the girl who was to become my wife, Patti Moss, at the University of Paris. We were introduced by a friend, Jerry Johnson, with whom I had played summer baseball in Iowa. He and Patti were participants in a work abroad program and were spending the summer in Europe with that group. Both had jobs in Paris. Patti worked as a translator/interpreter for a French shipping company. Jerry worked for a bank. While in Paris, our field trip stayed at a hotel not far from where Jerry worked.

I located Jerry and we set out for a night on the town. I asked if he knew where there might be some American girls to check out. (I wasn't that confident of my French.) There were several in his work abroad program. He took me to a common room at the place where the group lodged, the Pavilion Neerlandais at the University of Paris. I was immediately attracted to a girl I spotted across the room. I asked my friend about her. He introduced me to several of his friends, including her.

I was invited to participate in the group's plans for the following day. A member of the group worked at Air France. Air France had an office building with a large balcony facing the Champs Elysees, the route for the July 14th Bastille Day (France's Independence Day equivalent) Parade. Air France had invited the group to their balcony to watch the parade. I asked Jerry to line me up with Patti Moss for that day and evening. I showed up at the Air France office the next day assuming the date had been arranged and immediately moved in on her! My friend had not made the date, but Patti went along as though he had. She thought I was a bit presumptuous, but we were having a good time.

After the festivities, I took Patti to dinner at an American Army Officer's Club in Paris. It had slot machines. I encouraged Patti to play. I have never seen anyone so lucky with the slots! I had so many coins from her winnings that my pockets were bulging. I was giving coins to other players. She was the star of the slot machine lounge. We had a very enjoyable time and arranged to go out again.

The next evening Patti met me in the lobby of my hotel. One of my classmates overheard her talking to the hotel staff in French. When I appeared, he was surprised when she turned and spoke to me in what sounded to his Yankee ear as accented English. He approached and complemented her on her English. He asked, "Did you learn English from American or English men?"

Patti looked puzzled and replied, "American."

He asked, "Do you prefer American men?"

She replied that she did. It dawned on her that he thought she was French. She looked at him and declared, "I am an American from Louisville, Kentucky!" My friend was very embarrassed and quickly made his escape. Patti wondered aloud, "What was up with him?"

I told her, "I think he assumed you are a beautiful Parisian lady of the evening that prefers American men." I confirmed that with him later. He apologized to me for making a fool of himself. We had a good laugh about it at breakfast. I guess he was not familiar with southern accents!

While I don't know that Patti would agree, for me the attraction was instant. I was compelled to get acquainted with her. My time in Paris was brief, so there wasn't time for a long-term romance in Paris. But mutual interest had been established. We occasionally communicated over the next four years.

Patti and I both had plans at the time to marry others. She had Joe in Kentucky and I had Sandi in Iowa. Joe would become an attorney and Sandi a teacher.

Sandi was from a small town in Iowa near Milford and spent the summers at Lake Okoboji where her parents had a summer home. We dated off and on for a couple of years and things got serious before the trip to Europe. She came to my graduation. We thought we would marry. She attended the University of Iowa and became a high school teacher in Cedar Rapids, Iowa.

Sandi and Joe eventually married others. I met Joe once, at the funeral of Patti's father which was in August of 1985. We were both practicing law. I enjoyed meeting him and found him very likeable. Although Sandi and her husband lived in Cedar Rapids, they kept in contact with my best high school friend, Gary Moeller, and his wife in Milford. Sandi and I used to double-date with them. Patti got to know my high school friends and eventually met Sandi and her husband Ken at a party in Milford. It was also the first time I met Ken. It was a great first meeting and the six of us had an enjoyable evening together.

Patti maintained a friendship with Joe as did I with Sandi. We would see Sandi at the lake, and I would sometimes see her when I had business in Cedar Rapids. I played golf with Ken in Cedar Rapids.

Joe died suddenly. Sandi and Ken divorced. Ken died suddenly a few years after they divorced. Sandi contracted cancer several years after Ken died. I was able to spend time with her before she died. I got to know the youngest of her four sons, Tom and his wife, as they were often present when I visited Sandi. Tom is also a lawyer.

◆ ◆ ◆

*Cuban Missile Crisis—End Days*

The Cuban Missile Crisis in October 1962 was a very tense time at the Academy. I remember the Chiefs of Staff of the Air Force and the Army attended the Army-Air Force football game at the Academy and quietly left at half-time. That was a clue!

The Cadet Wing was absorbed in following the reports of the crisis. There was a Sunday night when my roommate and I looked out our dorm room window and wondered whether we would live to see another day. Supposedly Colorado Springs, home of NORAD

(North American Air Defense Command) Headquarters would be a prime target area in the event of a nuclear war.

A U-2 pilot lost his life attempting to gather intelligence to assist the president with information for use in formulating reactions to the crisis. Years later I met a CIA Case Officer who first realized that something was afoot. He saw the Cubans preparing athletic fields. They seemed to be of odd proportions to him. He stepped them off one evening and determined they were preparing soccer fields. Cubans didn't play soccer! They played baseball. Who did? Russians, of course.

Another significant event, to me, was my first exposure to the Central Intelligence Agency. I did very well in international affairs courses. I was selected to participate in an honors class taught by a CIA officer who happened to have been a faculty member at the University of Iowa when he was recruited by the Agency. I had already concluded that good intelligence was a critical requirement for military effectiveness. This officer and the missile crisis reinforced my conclusion and piqued my interest in the Agency and the special operations/covert action business.

I became more interested in special operations and the role Air Force pilots played in them. I recognized the potential to impact world affairs. I also appreciated the vital role intelligence gathering played in military planning. It became obvious to me that intelligence gathering also played a critical role in ensuring global peace by avoiding "accidental wars" resulting from a misunderstanding of a potential foe's capabilities and intentions. This insight played a significant role in later actions and advice I provided in some critical situations.

Attrition, voluntary and involuntary, continued as we moved through the system. Academic pressures were unrelenting. Individual goals changed as we matured. One of our standouts, Klien Gilhousen, left in the middle of our Second Class year to pursue his intense interest in engineering. He became a co-founder of Qualcomm, the holder of 55 patents, a philanthropist, and an internationally known competition acrobatic pilot.

# 3

# Finish Line in Sight

*Becoming Top Dogs: Class of '63 Graduates*

THE SPEAKER FOR the graduation of the Class of 1963 was President John F. Kennedy. He was a hero to many of us. Not just because of his World War II exploits, but because he seemed to genuinely like cadets. He had achieved great status with the cadets when some of our colleagues were invited to the White House. President Kennedy was running late they were told. They were invited up to the living quarters where he was showering after a hard day. Refreshments were provided of course. They were surprised when the president appeared in a robe with a towel around his neck. He shook hands all around and told the steward to take away the Cokes and "Get these men and me a cold beer!"

Our last summer at the Academy, 1963, involved conducting the Basic Cadet Training program. That was no easy task! It took a lot of work and we had little time to ourselves during that tour of duty. We realized how much we had changed in three years. We set out to make the incoming class the best prepared to be successful as cadets.

Summer leave was spent at the lake where I spent a lot of time with Sandi. But I confess, I never really forgot Miss Patti Moss from Louisville.

◆◆◆

*The Home Stretch – President Kennedy Assassinated*

The fall of 1963 marked the start of our last academic year as cadets. We had more off-duty privileges and responsibilities for the training of the classes behind us. We only had to grind it out for about ten more months. We were finally First Classmen, Gods of the Universe—well at least our little part of it!

We did have a good football season that fall and defeated Nebraska at Lincoln. But everything paled in significance to the assassination of President Kennedy. That sucked a lot of joy out of the season, to say the least.

National tragedy is the memory that we all carried from that fall. I vividly remember filing into the Cadet Dining Hall for lunch on Friday, November 22, 1963. After we arrived at our respective seats, the Commandant approached the elevated Wing Staff Area microphone. We were called to Attention. We were put "at ease" by the Commandant (we didn't have to stand at the rigid military position of attention). It was about 12:15 MST. He announced that the President had been shot in Dallas, Texas, and taken to a nearby hospital. We were shocked as was everyone when first informed. It cast a pall over everything.

As I recall, we weren't notified the President had died until we were back in our rooms after a somber lunch. The Academy had a speaker system for announcements that covered the whole complex. We heard the president had died shortly after we were back in our rooms. My roommate, Frank Bartlett, was devastated and collapsed on his bed sobbing. He was an ardent Kennedy fan. We all liked JFK. I remember being stunned and wondering what was next. Classes were cancelled, and First Class Cadets were given leave until Monday. Other classes may have been given leave as well, I don't recall.

In those days, only First Classmen could own cars. I had a 1956 Chevrolet I had purchased that summer. I called my Polish friends, Wally and Maria, in Denver and asked if I could stay with them over the weekend. I wanted to get away from the Academy. They were also devastated and glad to have me. We basically watched TV all weekend.

On Sunday morning, Wally went out for groceries and I was in the shower. I was getting out of the shower when I heard Maria screaming. I quickly wrapped in a towel and ran out to see what was wrong. It was a horrible scream and I was afraid she was being attacked. But it was the accused assassin, Lee Harvey Oswald, who had been attacked by Jack Ruby on live TV! Ruby put a fatal bullet into Oswald as they were moving him to a different location.

We intently followed the coverage of President Kennedy's funeral. It was a horrible time for the United States of America.

I don't remember much of Christmas leave in Milford. I drove to Iowa City to pick up Sandi at the University of Iowa. I remember it was snowing hard part of the way. I spent time with Sandi whose home was about 60 miles away from Milford. I'm sure I enjoyed a big Christmas Dinner with my family. I spent time with family, high school friends, and Sandi. The assassination still cast a shadow over everything.

I returned to the Academy for the last semester. Jim Graham became my roommate. The academic pressures were still there, but I had classes I was really interested in. That made things seem easier.

I had avoided the disciplinary system for the most part of my cadet career. I kept my room clean with the help of good roommates. You can't imagine how great it was to have a roommate after my experience of going it alone the first summer! I had four great ones over the four years. Ron Growden, from Maryland, and I survived Doolie Year together and later roomed together at our pilot training base. The next year my roommate was Mike Robbins, from Southern California, with whom I shared an interest in ham radio and pistol shooting. Kurt Pauer, another 19th Squadron classmate was also a ham radio operator. Mike was a four-year member of the USAFA pistol team. I was on the team for a brief period. Next it was Frank Bartlett, from New Hampshire. My last roommate was Jim Graham, from Virginia.

As members of the 19th Squadron Class of '64 we were closely bonded. Roommates even more so. They remain like family members to this day. All my roommates made the Air Force a career. All aspired to be pilots, but Frank was injured in a serious automobile accident not long after graduation and was medically disqualified for pilot training as a result. Jim had a colorblindness issue that also denied that opportunity to him. Mike and Ron served as Air Force pilots.

I managed to keep my nose clean for the most part and didn't make any of the "bad guy" lists. I made it to classes on time and adhered to the system enough to avoid harsh consequences. Oh, there were demerits issued, but with one exception they didn't accumulate enough to amount to anything of significant consequence. That is not to say I was a perfect cadet, far from it. I loved to engage the system and participate in pranks. I didn't participate in all of them. Some of them were too dangerous for me.

I also managed to avoid the "good guy" recognition lists too for the most part. I had no interest in obtaining cadet rank. I was happy to avoid attention and slog my way to pilot training.

However, the disciplinary system and the performance recognition system intersected during my last semester at the Academy. My roommate, Jim Graham, and I both slept through a breakfast formation early in the semester and suffered the consequences. Our offense was a class two violation punishable by a loss of privileges and restriction to quarters for at least a month or, more likely, two. I don't remember which. With not much else to do, I studied! I was really interested in Astrophysics and got one of the top grades for the semester. I also did well in Mechanical Engineering that semester. At the end of the semester I found myself on the Dean's List for my academic accomplishments. I should have applied myself earlier!

◆ ◆ ◆

*Some Fun and Games Along the Way*

The Academy was a wonderful opportunity for me. I recognized it then and appreciate it even more now. Yes, we chaffed at all the rules. In a foretelling of my ultimate future, I became somewhat of a "Guardhouse Lawyer." Several regulations were written or amended to close loopholes I had found. My favorite was when an unpopular Commandant initiated a crackdown on our appearance when we left base. We were to be dressed in coats and ties. His order didn't say anything about trousers, so several of us left in coats, ties, and shorts. I defended the charges filed against us and won dismissal on the basis the General's order failed to address anything other than coats and ties. There were no Cadet Regulations in place addressing the issue. That was soon remedied, but we had our fun with it.

We were an adventurous lot with a fair share of daredevils amongst us. Classmates climbed the structural members of the chapel steeples and hung banners from them in the middle of the night. The chapel wasn't completed until 1962. It afforded some real interesting scaffolding for fearless cadets to climb in the middle of the night. Some also rappelled down the side of the eight-story academic building during the middle of the night to post complaints about the commandant on the outside of his window. It is a wonder someone wasn't killed doing stunts like these. I did not engage in these pranks—I am afraid of heights! I am okay in a plane or parachute, but not on ledges.

We had a great rivalry with the University of Colorado, which resulted in a memorable stunt. We drove up to Boulder in the middle of the night late one fall to enter the football stadium and sow "USAFA" in winter wheat along the fifty-yard line of their field. The next fall we all had a good laugh at seeing USAFA on the field. You had to know what to look for but try as they might they were unable to eliminate all traces!

The pranks went both ways. A fraternity group from the University came down and kidnapped one of our falcon mascots. They got it back to a fraternity house where it escaped whatever they used to contain it. They called the Academy, confessed to having our missing bird, and pleaded with us to please send someone to come and get it. It was wrecking the frat house, and everyone was afraid of it.

Alcohol was strictly prohibited in the cadet dorm. Occasionally there would be special social events in dorm assembly rooms to which supervising officers and faculty and their wives would be invited. It was not permitted at those occasions to serve wine to guests. But my roommate, Mike Robbins, and I did manage to have some wine available and served it to some of the visiting officers on one of these occasions. We had wine left over and took it up to our room. What to do with wine when surprise inspections of quarters were more routine than surprise? We decided the wisest move was to clean our room sink and pour the leftover wine into it. We could serve our fellow cadets from the sink. Should an inspecting officer or cadet appear on the scene, we could simply pull the plug on the sink and the evidence would soon disappear. Great idea! We got the wine in the sink and were getting ready to issue invitations when who should appear at our door but our Air Officer Commanding!

AOCs, as they were called, were commissioned officers who were assigned to squadrons to supervise the cadets, keep an eye on things, and provide training and discipline as needed. Mike popped to attention standing with his back to the sink. No time to pull the plug. I carried on a conversation with the AOC. It distracted him. He never noticed the wine. Apparently, he had spent too much time on flight lines to have a keen since of smell! Or he had enough of our wine that evening that he didn't notice. We accepted his compliments about the event and saluted as he departed. Then we proceeded to serve our neighboring cadets. It wasn't long before the evidence was consumed. So, no wine went down our drain—even though it was past its time!

Five Squadrons formed a Group; four Groups formed the Cadet Wing. Each Group had its Group AOC. One of our more burdensome duties was to keep the tile floors spotless. We used buffer machines as needed. We had a new Group AOC who had a fetish for polished floors. Saturdays were inspections days and he was driving everyone crazy in our Group with his intense concern for the state of our floors. Usually buffing occurred monthly, if then. For this guy it was a weekly ordeal. The Academy has miles of tunnels under its structures. They interconnect the various buildings and enable delivery of electricity, heat, water, etc. While off limits, some of us used them in the middle of the night to pull off our pranks.

I decided it was time to do something about the floor buffing mania that dominated our lives. Those buffer machines were stored in areas near the tunnel entrances. I proposed to my roommate, Mike, that we organize a team from each squadron in the Group and take all the brushes for those machines and hide them in the tunnel system.

The plan went perfectly, and our Group had no buffer brushes for our use that Friday night. We kept those brushes hidden for about six weeks. An amnesty was finally offered. No action would be taken against the cadets who took the brushes if they were returned in the next few days. Buffing of floors would no longer be a weekly priority item. We got the team together and used another night foray into the tunnels to return them to their rightful places.

I know I did pranks with Ron, Frank, and Jim too. But I seem to recall the ones with Mike now. Wing parades were the bane of our existence on Saturday mornings. Before we could escape for weekend partying, the whole Wing would march out of the Cadet Area on to the parade ground where we would stand at attention and listen to some ceremony or speech. We would then pass in review and bestow our salutes squadron by squadron on the VIPs hosted by the Commandant or Superintendent.

Our dining hall was staffed with waiters who wore white uniforms and hats. Mike and I got the bright idea to get out of one of those parades for a prank. I don't recall what we did to be excused, but we managed it. We were friendly with some of the waiters and managed to borrow two uniforms from guys our size. The dining hall supplied us with pitchers of Kool Aid and a couple of serving carts. While our compatriots were parading on this hot day we sauntered out to the area where the parades terminated beside the dormitory. We started getting in the way of the formations as we offered our heat-relieving beverages. At first our customers had no idea what was going on and didn't recognize us. Finally, someone did, and we had a crowd around us. I don't know how Mike and I got away with it, but we were never subjected to any discipline for our outrageous act.

◆◆◆

## JUNE 3, 1964
*Great Day in Air Force History: USAFA Class of '64 Graduates*

Finally, June Week 1964 was upon us! On June 3, 1964, we pinned on those treasured gold bars of a USAF Second Lieutenant!

In those days, graduation always occurred the first Wednesday in June. That week was called June Week. It was a time of great joy, graduation ceremonies, classmates' weddings following graduation, and fond farewells. For graduating cadets, it was time at last to enjoy the best view of the Academy from a new graduate's perspective: from the rear-view mirror!

Graduation was a time of great family celebration. My parents and siblings were present as were a brother and sister of my mother. My girlfriend from Iowa, Sandi, was there. She had finished her junior year at the University of Iowa. We had a great time together and stayed over a couple of days following graduation to attend some of my classmates' weddings. Cadets cannot marry, so there were many weddings that occurred immediately after graduation. Had I not met Patti Moss, I might have taken the plunge later that summer. Instead Sandi and I eventually went our separate ways, but we remained friends until her death in 2013.

General Curtis LeMay, Chief of Staff of the Air Force, was our graduation speaker. General LeMay was highly regarded and considered the father of Strategic Air Command, the nuclear bomber, and missile command. He had a reputation for being a real tough officer who never smiled. Not true. He had a daughter who lived on base at the Academy. I happened to run into him once when he was out for a visit. I was so shocked I forgot to salute. He made some joking comment and I about fell over. He seemed to get a kick out of it. I later learned that he had an affliction that resulted in partial facial paralysis that made it seem he was in perpetual scowl mode.

General LeMay handed me my diploma at graduation and I was a 1964 Graduate of the United States Air Force Academy. As they say, or at least we say, "None has done more than '64." The graduating survivors of the original 750 have compiled an impressive record in their military and civilian lives.

The Cadet Chapel was dedicated September 22, 1963, by Chaplain (Major General) Robert Taylor, Air Force Chief of Chaplains. The Class of 1964 had the first use of the chapel as a wedding venue. Five Classmates married following graduation ceremonies on June 3, 1964. I recall that the ceremonies were performed in the order in which reservations were made. A classmate reserved the chapel for his wedding right after BCT, probably in September 1960. This was well before the chapel was completed. It was also before he had selected a bride—now that is planning! He was first in line but did not find a bride in time. The order on Graduation Day was Richard Flechsig and Karla Kitt (daughter of the USAFA Wrestling Coach); George Hess, Jr. and Sigrid Ronnecker; Perry Lash and Sally Grimes; James Evatt and Thelma Pruett; and John Denko, Jr. and Shirley Paine.

I am very fond of the Academy and grateful for the opportunities it created for me. I was exposed to knowledge, issues, and people that I otherwise would never have experienced. I got to pursue my interests in aeronautics and astrophysics. I began to travel the world. I embraced the study of international relations, began to confirm my belief that good intelligence information is vital to operational success militarily and plays a critical role in preventing misunderstandings of other countries' capabilities and intent that could result in a catastrophic accidental war. I met impressive civilian and military people of other countries, cultures, and beliefs. Some became leaders of their country.

# 4

# Pilot Training

AFTER GRADUATION, I had a couple of months off which I spent in Milford before reporting to Webb Air Force Base, Big Spring, Texas, for USAF Jet Pilot Training. I had requested Webb because it had the new T-38 supersonic jet trainer and my class rank was too low to get a coveted assignment to Williams AFB in Phoenix, which also had the T-38. Webb was my realistic first choice. Not all pilot training bases had the T-38. The fighter version of the T-38 was the F-5. I got to solo in the T-38 in February of 1965. Living my dream! Twenty-three years old and roaming the skies of the Southwest by myself flying faster than the speed of sound!

I left Milford for pilot training a couple of days early so I could visit Austin, Texas and the LBJ Ranch. It was a good summer spent with family and Sandi. Sandi and I parted planning to marry after she graduated from Iowa in the spring and I had received my pilots' wings in September. We had a complication, her parents had never accepted me because of my Catholicism. They had made it very clear to me that I would never be welcome in their family. They had put a lot of pressure on Sandi to dump me and move on. To this point she had ignored them.

After Austin, I left for the unknown: Big Spring, Texas, the home of Webb AFB. By the time I approached Big Spring it was late night and very dark. I was totally unfamiliar with West Texas and its great oil resources. As I was approaching Big Spring, I noticed lots of lights on what appeared from a distance to be significant buildings forming a large city. But when I hit the outskirts of Big Spring, it seemed like the small city I was expecting. I realized what I had thought was a skyline was a group of oil wells with lights on their pumps or derricks.

I easily located the Webb Air Force Base gate and showed my credential to the gate guard. There happened to be a good-looking blond in a convertible who drove up beside me and offered to guide me to the headquarters building where I was to sign in and get my BOQ (Bachelor Officers Quarters) room assignment. I accepted her kind offer to serve as a guide.

She led the way to the HQ building and said she would wait for me in her car. I reported to the Officer of the Day who smiled and asked, "Did you by any chance happen to acquire a good-looking blond escort?"

"Yes, Sir, I did indeed!"

His smile broadened, and he said, "Watch out!"

When I came out, she was waiting to show me to my quarters. When we got there, she offered to help me move in. At this point, I declined further assistance! One of my wiser decisions I was to learn later. The next morning the new class of eager student pilots gathered. Several were talking about the blond that helped them get signed in. They had her phone number and were eager to get lined up with her.

The local newspaper came and took our individual pictures and ran them in the Sunday edition with our names and hometowns under each of our pictures—full page, yearbook style! Guess who reportedly had that picture posted on the inside of her bedroom closet door and was eagerly checking us off? I know for sure there was at least one she didn't get!

Pilot training was a wonderful time. About half the class of about 60 were Academy classmates. The remainder were commissioned officers from various ROTC units, and a few were commissioned from Air Guard units. We constituted the Class of 66B. For the Academy graduates, the newfound freedom was a real joy! It took time to get used to being able to do whatever whenever, so long as you met your military duty schedules.

Ron Growden and I roomed together again. Everything was going great. Then, after a couple of months I got a call from Sandi. She had met someone else. Her parents had never wanted her to marry me. The pressure increased after I left for pilot training. She was told she would be disinherited, and they would not allow her back in their home no matter how cute our children.

She wanted to date this guy, a friend of her brother. She wanted me to date in Texas. She wept, and I begged her to slow down and see a counselor. No dice, we were done even though it took me awhile to accept it. In a few weeks I realized it would be best if I accepted the situation. It was probably ten years before I saw her again.

The bachelor officers lived in a building with two-bedroom apartments. Ron and I lived next door to Mike Adams of the New Mexico Air National Guard and Al Trent, an Academy classmate. Mike introduced the three of us to Mexican food. I already had a great appreciation for Mexican music and was interested in learning Spanish. It didn't take long to also appreciate Mexican food. The best place to eat Mexican was in the "rough" part of town where most of the Mexican members of the community resided. The best Mexican restaurant was owned by a nice lady who took us under her protection. We never had a problem. She placed us off limits to the local thugs.

The class bonded together quite well, and contact is maintained to this day. We had a great reunion in Denver in the fall of 2013. The number one and two graduates in our class were an Iowa State ROTC graduate and a Texas Air National Guard product. I don't remember which finished at the top. Both were killed in jet aircraft accidents in the US within a year of graduation. Our neighbors, Mike and Al, among others in the class, were killed in the Vietnam war. Mike was killed in Laos and Al in Cambodia.

These four officers call to mind three stories. Permit me to skip ahead.

The Iowa State Grad, Roger Carr, was married to Karen. They had family back in Ames, Iowa. That Christmas I picked them up in Ames for the return to Big Spring. I don't recall how they got to Ames. I had delayed my departure to Iowa a few days to help Al Trent, who performed magic acts as a hobby. Al and I did a few magic shows for orphanages and nursing homes in the Big Spring area. Since Sandi and I were no longer together, I didn't mind giving the time to a worthy cause.

On our trip back to Big Spring I was driving through Leavenworth, Kansas, at about 2:00 in the morning. Roger and Karen were asleep in the back. Suddenly, I found us being pursued by several police cars with full lights and sirens. I immediately stopped of course. Several officers approached the car with guns drawn, including shotguns. My immediate fear was Roger and/or Karen would wake up and pop up in the back seat. I was sitting there with the driver's window down and my hands clearly displayed. I was yelling that I had passengers asleep in the back. The police officers checked our papers and quickly concluded we were not a part of the prison break that had occurred. They apologized for scaring us half to death and wished us well.

The Texas Air Guard officer, Graham Galloway, was married to Martha. Both Karen and Martha were good friends. They fed home cooked meals to us bachelors! A few years after Graham was killed, I was attending a class reunion at the Academy. Who should walk up and give me a hug but Martha! She had met and married one my classmates who had lost his wife to cancer. They make a great couple and I am very happy they got together. I enjoyed seeing them at our 55th class reunion this summer.

My next-door neighbors, Al and Mike, became my close friends. I was especially close to Mike. He had not finished college and did not have ROTC or Academy training. The academic part of pilot training was a challenge for Mike since he did not have the college engineering background part of those programs. I helped him with his academic problems, and we tended to party together too.

When flying the early shift, we went to the dining hall around 4:30 for breakfast and then on to the flight line for pre-flight briefings and training. One such morning Mike and I were walking to breakfast when he asked what I was doing that was waking him up at 3:00 in the morning. We had a common wall between our bedrooms. I assured him I needed all the beauty rest I could get and had no idea what he was talking about. I suggested his magician roommate would be a prime suspect for a practical joke. He said Al denied doing anything too. And he said he had been locking the door to his bedroom just to be sure.

A couple of weeks went by and I asked Mike whether he was still waking up at 3:00 AM. He said that he was not. But he didn't say anything else. I asked him what had been waking him up. He said he did not want to talk about it. That, of course, really made me curious. I persisted until I finally got him to tell me.

Mike said that he would wake up at 3:00 AM and feel a presence in his room. He wouldn't see anyone, but he had this feeling. After several occurrences he began to think someone was wanting to contact him. But there wasn't anyone there and he would go back to sleep. He then said that the last time he woke up at 3:00 there was a man in flight gear standing at the foot of his bed holding a pilot's helmet cradled under his left arm. Mike said he was not frightened by this apparition. In fact, he had a feeling of peace and comfort. The man did not speak. He just smiled and kind of waved with his right hand. Somehow, he communicated the thought to Mike that no matter what happened, everything would be just fine! He gave another slight wave of the hand and disappeared.

Bear with me as I make this out-of-sequence interjection. The rest of the story: my wife never met Mike. He would call our home in Tennessee to chat. When I was off somewhere, he would talk to Patti. Patti would tell me Mike had called while I was gone and update me on their conversations. Sometimes I would be gone for months at a time and they would have talked several times. Patti did not always know where I was or when I would be back.

I eventually got orders to Vietnam as a Forward Air Controller (FAC) in the fall of 1967. Mike called after I had gotten those orders. I was gone on another trip. Mike was excited to report to Patti that his guard unit had been called up and he would be going to Vietnam in F-100s. Patti told him that I was also going to Vietnam as a Forward Air Controller. We would both be arriving in Vietnam in April of 1968. He was hoping we would have an opportunity to get together in Vietnam, which we did. In fact, Mike put me on the plane to go home at the end of my tour. We planned to get together after I finished C-130 retraining. He had only one more mission scheduled before he was also to leave Vietnam.

I got back to the states and returned to Tennessee to requalify as a C-130 Aircraft Commander. I had been assigned to Dyess AFB, Abilene, Texas, upon completion of retraining. I had not received any word from Mike about getting together in Albuquerque. I had not given that much thought as he was aware it would be awhile before I arrived in Texas.

Once we got settled in at my new base in Abilene, Texas, I gave Mike a call. It is a call I will never forget. Thinking about it still brings tears to my eyes, even after fifty years. His grandmother answered the phone. I asked to speak to Mike. She paused, told me who she was, and then stated that Mike had been killed in Vietnam just before he was to have returned home.

I was in shock! I just didn't know what to say. I had lost a lot of friends in Vietnam, but I just couldn't deal with this one. In fact, I broke down and retreated to our backyard sobbing. I had let my guard down and I just couldn't handle it. To be honest, I still can't. Mike's family had attended pilot training graduation and did things with me and my family. But they wanted nothing to do with me after Mike's death and I honored their wish.

About seven or eight years ago, Mike's brother contacted me. I was really rocked. He was about my brother's age. He idolized his big brother. We talked at length and I could tell that he still suffered his loss. The conversation was very emotional for both of us. We wept together in our renewed grief. We communicated by phone and e-mail for a few years. He was enlisted in the Air Force and looking to retire in the not-too-distant future. He said he had trouble with alcohol and had failed at marriage. He eventually quit communicating and it has been several years now since we have talked. I have tried to contact him to no avail. I fear Vietnam has claimed another casualty. Prove me wrong and give me a call, Pat. I think of you and Mike often.

Patti became pregnant with our first child, Kathleen, shortly after we learned of Mike's death. The pregnancy proceeded normally. We were increasingly excited about the birth. I was again off doing my thing overseas. When I got back, Patti had a story to tell.

She would wake up hungry at 3:00 AM and go into the kitchen to get something to eat. One morning while passing through the living room, she noted a man sitting on the sofa. Believe it or not, she did not react. He just smiled at her and she did not feel threatened in the least. She thought he wanted to see me. This happened more than once. She described him and what he was wearing—chinos and a cardigan sweater. She had described Mike! She had never seen Mike or even a picture of him.

Our pilot training class had a yearbook with pictures of class members. I didn't say anything, but I dug out the book and showed her some group pictures. I asked her if she recognized her 3:00 AM visitor among them. She immediately pointed to Mike's picture!

Why did he appear to Patti and not me? Probably he knew I would have had a heart attack! I think he was passing along the message his 3:00 AM visitor had left with him: that things would indeed be just fine and not to worry.

Now, back to Webb Air Force Base, Big Spring, Texas for pilot training.

While pilot training was a lot of fun, it also was intense and stressful. All but three of us had a preliminary light plane training course before coming to Webb and its jets. We trained on two jet planes, both of which had versions that flew combat in Vietnam. The first we flew was the T-37 which was a sub-sonic jet plane made by Cessna with side-by-side seating for two. After flying that plane, we moved to the T-38, the new supersonic jet plane that Northrup built. It had tandem seats, front and back. It was a great airplane.

While we were at the Academy there was no on-site preliminary pilot training offered. There was a glider club and sky diving club established while we were there. Those who were going to pilot training after graduation were given light aircraft off-site preparation for Air Force Pilot Training. As cadets we got an introductory motivational ride in a T-33 two-seat jet trainer. We had a navigation course in which we navigated T-29 twin engine passenger-like aircraft. I cannot remember why now, but I was unable to take the introductory light plane training course prior to graduation. There were three of us in the same situation at Webb.

I was able to catch up to my classmates in the T-37, but my two friends who had no prior flight training were not. I thought it was very unfair as they could have been good pilots with a little additional training. I probably made it because I had worked at my small-town airport for some flying time when I was in high school. I was once again lucky!

Hot planes and green pilots lead to accidents. Fortunately, we did not suffer any fatalities in our class at Webb. We did, however, lose an instructor pilot. There were eight or so other pilot training bases. Some of them did lose contemporaries. I recall returning from a night solo cross-country flight in the T-38 when air traffic control contacted me and asked that I change course to look for fires—two planes from one of the other pilot training bases had run together head-on. I was not able to locate any wreckage. Being told later that there was not much left to find was not comforting!

In-flight emergencies were not rare for me. There is a saying: "There are old pilots and bold pilots, but there are no old bold pilots." Probably one of the best things that happened to me occurred on my first solo out of the traffic pattern in the T-37. I got together with a couple of classmates prior to takeoff. We determined to meet in the air over a certain town. I had the first take-off time and decided I would fly high into the sun over that check point and make a pass on my classmates out of the sun. Great idea for a genius with three solo landings under his belt! I got to around twenty thousand feet when I saw them. I started my diving roll-in on them when out of the corner of my eye I saw another idiot doing the same thing on a collision course with me. I don't think he ever saw me. I yanked the stick back and kicked a rudder pedal to avoid a mid-air collision. Pilot readers know what happened next: a high-speed stall that ended in a flat spin.

We were instructed to eject at 10,000 feet if we had lost control of an airplane and were unable to recover before passing through 10,000 feet. I was already worrying about what excuse I could come up with to satisfy the evaluation board! I fought for control. I could get the nose down, I couldn't get the spinning to stop. 20,000 quickly became 15,000 and at 12,000 I began to get control. But I still hadn't achieved controlled flight as I passed through 10,000. But at 8,000 I was sure I would get control. At about 6,000 I had control. Now my problem was to get out of the high-speed dive and control my airspeed before I flew into the ground.

The trick was to keep control of myself and get control of the aircraft while not panicking and pulling up so hard that I would go into a high-speed stall and hit the ground or pull the wings off with the same result. Ejection was no longer an option. I kept control of the aircraft and myself and I made a smooth recovery while bottoming out at 1,500 feet. I scared the hell out of myself in the process and I vowed never to do something that stupid again. I was very lucky!

I also was prone to some legitimate emergencies that were not self-induced. On my first night solo in the supersonic T-38 I lost power from both engines just after lift-off. Most jet fighter planes have "afterburners" that further heat and burn the exhaust stream coming from the jet engine. Extra power is gained (at the expense of higher fuel consumption) by using afterburners on takeoffs or in some emergency situations. They make a booming noise when engaged, and engine noise becomes quieter when they are switched off. I had built up a little extra speed on takeoff just in case something happened. A little insurance speed so to speak. Standard procedure was to "come out of burner" (switch off the afterburners) after taking off and reaching a certain speed and climb rate. I delayed just a bit and came out with extra speed and a faster climb rate. When I came out of burner, I lost all power from both engines. I immediately began the "relight (re-start) procedure" for one of the engines and then the other. No go!

I did this alternating between the two engines while preparing to eject as soon as I made it over the school located a mile or so off the end of the runway. It was looming ever larger in front of me. The unpowered T-38 has all the glide characteristics of a rock! It also had a new kind of ejection seat that would allow ejection just above ground level.

I was determined to avoid the school at all costs as the parking lot was full and I assumed the building was too. I was rapidly losing altitude while conserving airspeed necessary for control. It looked like I would be able to clear the school by a couple of hundred feet after which I could safely eject. I did another set of engine restart procedures and got a positive response on one engine just as I was going to pull the ejection seat actuator handles.

I staggered along on the one operating engine and managed to coax the plane up to a safe altitude. I was also able to get the other engine back on-line during the climb. I was too busy to even make a radio distress call. I climbed higher and burned off enough fuel to get to an acceptable landing weight. I then started a descent to the traffic pattern and called it a night with one landing. I never did find out why those engines quit! I was sent up the next night to get my other two required night solo landings.

The other incident, also solo in the T-38, involved a control lockup. In this case I was flying solo as number two in a four-ship formation when my throttles locked on me. I could not move them! I called out my problem and moved out of the formation. The instructors in the other planes offered advice. Try as I might, I could not get the throttle controls to unlock.

Luckily both throttles stuck at 82% of thrust. I knew from flying practice landing patterns that I could land a T-38 solo below a certain fuel weight using a normal landing pattern with a thrust setting of 82% without touching the throttles. I would focus on getting the engines shut down as soon as my main landing gear hit the runway. I wasn't sure I would have braking capability, but I really felt confident about getting on the ground in one piece.

This time I was using my radio to communicate with the control tower. Ground crews put runway end barriers in place in case I couldn't cut off fuel to the engines in time to come to a normal stop. Everything went as I planned. I was even able to turn off the runway and coast onto a taxiway just as the plane rolled to a stop. The airplane had recently undergone some major maintenance. Someone had failed to properly reconnect the throttle control cables.

Another pilot training story: my good friend and Academy classmate (and future General) Al Rogers and I were scheduled for one of our last training flights at about the same time. It was a beautiful day and we were to fly solo cross country. We were flying the same route. I had the first take-off and agreed I would stay in afterburner an extra few minutes and he would come out of burner at the normal time. This would guarantee separation between us. There was not a cloud in the sky and we were higher than anything else flying in the area. A great day to enjoy the scenery. I made a turn at a checkpoint in New Mexico. When I rolled out of my turn who was almost on top of me but Al! I don't think we missed each other by more than fifty feet. Al said he was enjoying the scenery and let his airspeed creep up without noticing.

Okay, one last pilot training story! We also did low-level solo cross country flights in the T-38. We did this in a remote area where other aircraft were prohibited when the airspace was being used for military purposes. The objective was to navigate manually (no GPS those days) and fly over a designated route to arrive over a "target" at a designated time after take-off. It involved mentally calculating and recalculating time and distance to target and adjusting airspeed as required. I was able to do that and hit the target within six seconds.

On one of those runs I was going over a hilly area in the desert towards a check point, an abandoned airfield. It was located out of sight until after cresting a hill a half mile or so out. I crested the hill going, I would guess, around 350 MPH at about 200 feet. That is moving along at more than 500 feet per second. I had four or five seconds to find the field and adjust my heading to pass over it. About two seconds out I saw a light aircraft that had just taken off from this closed field. He was coming at me from my left and a bit above me. I rolled hard to my right and passed under him. I leveled out and saw him in my rear-view mirrors rocking violently from my jet wash. Thankfully he recovered control, and I continued my run. I'll bet he never violated that federal regulation again! We missed by just a few yards.

We did a lot of partying in pilot training. Our commander was a partier and we kept the Officer's Club humming. I think he felt morale might be a problem if we didn't throw him in the swimming pool every month or so. I dated several local girls and settled into a good friendship with one of them. It never evolved into a big romantic relationship. I guess neither of us was wanting that. We did have a lot of fun together, though. She left West Texas before I finished pilot training. She was not sure where she was going. She was from Philadelphia and had a cousin who was a movie actress. She wanted to continue west to check out Southern California. Small world story: I was crossing a street in San Francisco a few months later and we met in a crosswalk! We had an enjoyable dinner and shared lots of laughs.

My dad had a good friend who was an oil company executive who lived in nearby Midland, Texas. He and his family invited me to dinner several times. I forgot something on one of my visits, and he had his secretary deliver whatever it was to me at the base the next evening. She was quite attractive, and we dated a couple of times. I suspect Dad's friend was trying a little matchmaking. Eventually she started dating one of my friends after I had introduced them.

# 5

# In Search of the "Real Air Force"

BY THE TIME I finished pilot training I had decided to select the C-130 Hercules troop carrier and cargo hauler as my aircraft assignment to the chagrin of my instructor who expected me to choose the F-100, a fighter aircraft. I knew C-130s flew combat missions in Vietnam as well as covert combat missions in other countries. I figured the C-130 would carry me to adventure all around the world after Vietnam was long settled. In the C-130 I could be flying covert combat missions while my F-100 friends would be flying boring training missions. Believe it or not, I had classmates at the Academy who were worried Vietnam would end before they had a chance to fly combat missions there. I had no such concern as I could see the war dragging on for quite some time. I wrote a paper in a political science course at the Academy explaining why I thought our strategy would not yield a quick or satisfactory result. The professor disagreed and my grade for the paper reflected his superior opinion! After all, he had a president and secretary of defense on his side!

I graduated from pilot training in September 1965. I passed the FAA examination for a commercial multi-engine civilian pilots license the next day. I had my orders to report to the SERE (Survival, Evasion, Resistance and Escape) School at Stead AFB located outside Reno, Nevada. My orders further provided I was to report to Seward AFB upon completion. Seward was located near Nashville, Tennessee, and was home of the C-130 Hercules training school. At the Academy, and occasionally during pilot training, we would complain about our situation and express our yearning to be in the "REAL" Air Force. In the REAL Air Force, we surely would be doing things more significant than marching in parades, cleaning our rooms for inspection, studying, and taking academic tests.

Stead was still an Air Force school operation, but the lessons taught were very serious. Some of us would be put to the test within a year or so of completion. The program consisted of a couple of weeks of intense academic instruction taught by people with expertise in survival, escape and evasion, and unarmed combat techniques. We were divided into groups of about 30 as I recall. Once in the field we were sent off in pairs for the escape and evasion (E&E) part of our training.

Another week or two of training consisted of being dumped in the mountains with a couple days of normal rations and given a week to escape and evade while traveling to a point where we would be "rescued." There were three marked spots that we had to find each day or so of our E&E. It was part of the challenge to find those spots where we would sign in. The procedure also had a safety purpose as well as a compliance check. If a team failed to timely sign in, a search and rescue operation would ensue. Or if there was a medical emergency a healthy team member could get help for the injured person. One of our group suffered a heart attack and was helicoptered out.

I was paired with an Academy classmate, friend, and future general. I will call him "Bob." Each two-man team started separately. We were instructed not to link up with any other team. We were released late in the afternoon on a cold wintry day. Stead divided its E&E courses into winter and summer treks. The winter trek was shorter due to the terrain and the impact of snow and ice. We were sent out on the last scheduled summer trek. Unfortunately, Mother Nature was not influenced by the training schedules at Stead. Only a blizzard might delay use of a scheduled summer trek.

Bob and I decided we would keep going after dark. We could put more distance between us and the "enemy." Also, the cover of darkness would decrease the risk of using patrolled jeep trails. That would allow us to cover more ground faster and further lengthen our lead. We were each given a heavy paper tag to wear. If our tag was marked by an enemy, it would result in a lower grade for the course. A couple such marks could lead to a repeat.

We discovered that evening that the cadre was not unfamiliar with our idea of continuing in the dark. We were making good time on a trail when an "enemy" spotted Bob and declared him arrested. The enemy was on the edge of the trail with his back to a downslope. He didn't see me. I managed to get behind him. I crouched down, and Bob pushed him over me, which sent him tumbling down into a small ravine. Bob and I ran like the devil into the dark as we could hear him reporting us over his radio. We were relieved to know for sure he was okay. But we could hear responders to his call for back-up. We could see "repeat" in our futures.

Bob and I covered a lot of ground that night! We were almost certain the enemy did not know who we were. We began to relax late that night as the sounds of pursuit began to fade. We had moved far enough they would not be able to pin our audacity on us even if we were found.

Then the snow started. It got cold and we were short on rations to begin with. We got cold and hungry in a hurry! The going got very difficult. The mountainous terrain was increasingly dangerous. The snow obscured hazards and navigation points. I was beginning to wonder if our E&E training course was about to become a real test of survival.

Sleep was necessary, of course. We were provided with some parachute canopy and harness materials with which to fashion a shelter. But we were clothed and equipped for the summer trek, not the winter trek. It was very cold the second night after a day of snow.

We eventually found our reporting sites and made it to our rescue point in the early morning hours of the fourth day. Our "rescuers" were to then deliver us after daybreak to a prisoner of war (POW) camp set up to replicate what would lie ahead for several of us in North Vietnam. We were in the camp for about a week. We arrived exhausted, hungry, and cold. They didn't have to soften us up. Mother Nature had already scored with her first shot at us.

We were subjected to the various interrogation techniques used by the North Vietnamese to include sleep deprivation through the use of noise and lighting, close confinement in small cells without room to lie down, and confinement in small punishment boxes when we were caught trying to sleep in our cells. The punishment boxes were so small that we had to assume a fetal position. We were wedged into the boxes by the guards. They pushed and shoved and finished by kicking as necessary to force us into the boxes. Just in case we were to fall asleep, oriental music and the sounds of crying babies were piped into our cells. No lullaby in the cacophony!

We went through interrogations by very convincing camp personnel with foreign accents who seemed to relish their roles. They used waterboarding, good cop/bad cop, physical abuse such as kneeling on broom sticks and variations of these kinds of techniques. We were to stick with the Uniform Code of Conduct (UCC). It allowed disclosure of only name, rank, and serial number. The Geneva Convention prohibits captors from seeking more than that.

I was foolishly proud of my effort to be a hold-out until the bitter end. They assembled us and pulled me from the ranks and drug me to a hole in the ground filled with water. It was a cold morning and there was ice and other even less desirable things floating in the water. This was a new kind of device. I was asked questions one last time. When I gave only my name, rank, and serial number I was shoved into the hole. I still resisted. I had noticed there was a hinged cover attached to a frame around the hole. They began to run more water into the hole.

Very cold water, of course. They then swung the cover over the hole. The cover was shut, and I was in the dark, the rising cold water almost up to my chin. The black hole was slightly deeper than I was tall. I soon realized this had great potential to get very bad real fast. I offered up some false information and they took the lid off and pulled me out of the hole. I was not allowed to dry off. I thought I would freeze to death just standing there at attention. One of my Academy classmates came up to me at a reunion 30 years later and remarked that he had never forgotten my holding-out and my morning in the hole. He said he was sure glad it was me, not him!

But I had my victory too! There was another reason I ended up in the hole. We were told at the beginning of the program that no one had ever escaped from the POW camp. If a successful escape occurred, the escapee would be given a certificate of completion of the course and a free steak dinner. He would not have to complete the course. When first put into the camp, I observed the guard routine closely and devised a plan for an escape. It would take three men to get one man out. One of my best friends from the Academy and a member of the 19th Squadron, Ron Bliss, was in an adjoining cell at the end of the cell row. We did not know the fellow on the other side of my cell. I knew he was not an Academy classmate, but what I had seen of him made me think he would be a good co-conspirator. We had learned in pilot training that there were indeed many truly outstanding ROTC graduates. I communicated my plan to each, and they agreed that it would very likely work. They recognized the risk. Woe be unto the two who were left behind! They were almost certain to be caught. We drew straws and Ron won. He escaped. The other fellow and I paid dearly!

There was an element of divine justice in the great escape. Ron was shot down and captured while flying an F-105 Thud fighter over North Vietnam the following year. He was severely injured ejecting when his 105 was struck by a ground-to-air missile while exiting the target area accelerating to supersonic speed. He never really knew whether he had initiated an ejection sequence or was just spit out as the airplane disintegrated around him. The North Vietnamese addressed his medical issues. He recovered and was enrolled in the extreme interrogation program. He was held as a POW for nearly six and a half years.

I think the unspoken educational goal of this training was to make us realize it was not practical to expect to be able to avoid giving up some information if captured. The trick would be to hold out for as long as reasonably possible and then save yourself by feeding useless information as necessary. That approach couldn't be officially taught, but it became obvious that everyone has their breaking point. I concluded that when the breaking point was near it was better to "break" while you still had some control and the ability to think and feed false information.

Well, maybe not everyone. Three men that I had the privilege of knowing were awarded the Medal of Honor for their heroic resistance in the Hanoi Hilton and feeder prisons. One of those men lived just down the hall from me at the Academy, Lance Sijan. Lance died in prison. I got to meet members of his family after the war. I will always remember his mother telling me it was wonderful that her son had been awarded the Medal of Honor, but she would much rather have her son back. Bud Day, an Iowan, was captured August 26, 1967 and repatriated March 14, 1973. Leo Thorsness was captured April 30, 1967 and repatriated March 4, 1973.

Following his release from Hanoi on March 4, 1973, Ron Bliss (captured September 4, 1966) called. He laughingly told me he had been given a lot of time to contemplate his future. He had decided he would like to become a lawyer. He had heard that I had been practicing law and asked my advice. He wondered if I thought he could hack it! I told him he would find law school a cakewalk after what he had been through. But I advised that he go ahead with his requalification as a jet fighter pilot and enjoy a year in which he and his wife and son would be able to accept the accolades they had earned while he was a POW. He took my advice and enjoyed his celebrity status and the opportunity to experience firsthand the admiration of the nation's leaders. He then enrolled in the University of Texas Law School. He graduated and was employed by the Fulbright Jaworski Law Firm in Houston, a nationally recognized firm. He ultimately became the leader of the firm's intellectual property department.

Ron had met Charlene while at pilot training near Lubbock, Texas. It was a couple hours' drive from where I was in pilot training, Big Spring, Texas. I made a few trips to Lubbock and met Charlie. She was the "real deal." Everyone liked her. She had a goodness about her. While Ron was in prison, many POW wives proved they also were made of steel! Charlene is a very courageous woman and a leader among POW wives.

Ron and Charlie were among the many POWs and wives entertained at a state dinner at the White House. He had packed the wrong color formal uniform jacket. He received a lot of good-natured kidding about that. But he said it worked to his advantage. They all remembered his name! He said he was with some clients in New York City when he ran into Henry Kissinger. His clients were very impressed when Kissinger recognized him and treated him like a long-lost friend.

At a Class of '64 reunion in Colorado Springs several years after the war had ended, a small group of us decided the scheduled party had ended too early for us. Our wives, having better sense, went to bed. We had more celebrating to do. We moved down the street to a nice little bar. I think there were five of us. Three had been POWs. After we had been there a while, a fellow walked over to us and asked if we had been POWs. General Ed Mechenbier spoke up. He said that he and two of the other fellows (Ron Bliss being one, and I think Kevin McManus the other) had been POWs and given the opportunity to serve their country in unusual circumstances. But he went on to point out, General Brett Dula and I had been denied that opportunity. The guy thanked all of us for our service and, shaking his head as he walked away, observed that he thought we were all a bit crazy.

Ron Bliss died of cancer after a long battle on February 8, 2005. He told me about his grim diagnosis, melanoma, early in the process and asked that I keep it confidential. We would talk by phone about his condition and the treatment programs available. It was a difficult secret to keep, but I kept it for five years. At our 40-year class reunion banquet in Colorado Springs, Ron wanted Patti and me to sit next to him and his wife, Charlie. I was the only man at the table who hadn't been a POW. While singing the Air Force Song, he put his arm on my shoulder and sang "Off we go into the wild black (instead of 'blue') yonder…" I told him he better knock it off—it was all I could do to keep the secret and avoid weeping! He just laughed.

Ron was willing to try any experimental treatment available. While he beat the time-of-survival predictions by years, he eventually recognized he had run out of options. Most of the Class of '64 members of the Playboy Squadron managed to meet in Houston for a farewell party for Ron about 10 days before he died. Mike Robbins had roomed with Ron at the Academy. He and his wife, Leslie, lived in Texas and worked to put the party together. I recall another 19th Squadron classmate, Jeff Gordon and his wife Karen, who lived in Houston also helped.

I called Ron about three weeks before the reunion to needle him about the outcome of a bowl game. He said he was looking forward to seeing everyone. At one point he remarked, "Lucky, I hope you guys didn't buy non-refundable airline tickets in case I don't make it another three weeks!"

My reply: "Ron, you know us all very well. We are all too cheap to buy anything else!"

He was a man of great character and courage. At the Academy we had taught each other it is never good to end a boxing match in a draw! We beat the pulp out of each other. The month before, I had to have sinus and nasal surgery. I had called him then to give him the blame for it. He laughed!

I will never forget walking to Ron and Charlie's door about three weeks later, ringing the bell and having him greet me with a hug saying, "It is so great to see you, Lucky! There is life before death!" It was a great weekend for all of us, especially Ron.

# 6

# Closing in on the "Real Air Force"

UPON COMPLETION OF SERE school, I was planning on taking leave in Milford. I was to have a couple of weeks before reporting to Nashville, Tennessee. But first we had to process out of SERE. The first night of freedom, we were bused from the mock POW camp to our quarters where we enjoyed a long shower and preparation for a celebratory party traditionally given by Bill Harrah of Harrah's Club fame. Bill Harrah hosted a great dinner, including all the adult beverages desired, for each class after they finished SERE school. It was a great party! Bill provided bus transportation both ways between the base and his casino. He also gave us each $50 worth of chips for gaming after dinner. Most quickly lost their $50 and purchased more chips as the night wore on. Bill was no dummy!

Not being much interested in gaming, I spent the time after dinner visiting with Bill. He seemed to enjoy talking about airplanes, the casino business, the SERE school, and my future. Years later this would pay off for me.

One of my law partners and I were contacted by Harrah's Club and asked to interview for the position of legislative counsel (lobbyists) for Harrah's Club in Iowa. We did the interview. Of course, I recounted my evening with Bill Harrah. I mentioned the reason for spending time with him rather than gambling. I have nothing against gaming as entertainment, I just found it boring. They allowed as how that was fine, they weren't hiring us to gamble! They didn't want to gamble on a tax issue, they wanted good honest legal representation capable of protecting their interests.

After the Harrah's celebration, I returned to my room and found a note under the door. I was to report to the duty officer. When I did, he handed me a new set of orders: my leave was cancelled, and I had four days to report to Nashville for training after which I was to be assigned to Taiwan for missions in Vietnam. HECKUVADEAL! This "Real Air Force" business was for the birds! I was not a happy birdman.

Nevada had no speed limit at the time. I set out, determined to make the most of my travel time. I was driving 100 mph plus across the desert heading for Nashville via Lake Okoboji, Iowa. After a couple of hours, I noticed a car slowly gaining on me. After another half hour, it began to get closer and I decided it might be a state trooper. I began to slow. Soon he was close enough to turn on his light bar and my suspicions were confirmed. I pulled over. An older-looking trooper walked up to the car. Looking me and the car over, he noted the Air Force gate pass sticker on the windshield. He asked if I was in the Air Force. I told him I was. He said he had been in the Air Force. He asked if I was in a hurry. I told him I was and why. He put down his ticket book and offered his sympathy, shook my hand and wished me good luck. He only asked that I keep it under 90 mph for the next hour or so which would take me out of his area of responsibility. I gladly agreed!

I managed a pit stop in Iowa. Driving towards Nashville from Iowa, I began once again to think about that girl from Paris who was presumably back home in Louisville, Kentucky. Louisville was on my route. We had exchanged cards over the years and I was sure I had a current phone number. At my next gas stop, I made the fateful call! We quickly arranged to meet and have dinner that evening. And after dinner we made plans to get together the next weekend. We married the following June!

# 7

# The Lockheed
# C-130E Hercules

I REPORTED TO the C-130 Hercules school at Seward Air Force Base, Smyrna, Tennessee, located just southeast of Nashville. The C-130 is a four-engine turbo prop high-wing aircraft used for carrying cargo and passengers. It was HUGE compared to anything I had flown. It was to become my magic carpet for exploration of every continent except Antarctica.

We had several weeks of classroom schooling learning the various aircraft systems and emergency procedures. The systems included flight control, communications, fuel management, electrical, hydraulic, navigation, oxygen, and pressurization systems. The C-130 is a very sophisticated and durable machine. I was fortunate in going right into training on the newest model, the C-130E.

The typical crew included two pilots, a navigator, a flight engineer, and a loadmaster. The two pilots sat side-by-side in the cockpit with a large control panel and throttle quadrant between them. The flight engineer sat behind that control panel. The flight engineer was responsible for a large ceiling control panel with all the engine, electrical, fuel and hydraulic systems control switches and circuit breakers. The senior pilot sat in the left seat akin to an airline captain. In the Air Force the position is called "Aircraft Commander." In training school situations, the student is in the left seat and the instructor pilot is in the right or co-pilot's seat. The navigator's position is on the right side of the cockpit behind the co-pilot's seat. The navigation systems and a work table are situated so that the navigator faces the right side of the cockpit wall while working. At the back of the cockpit area there is a bunk and seating space underneath. This area of the aircraft is referred to as the "flight deck." The loadmaster's position is in the cargo space separated from, and a few steps lower than, the cockpit.

To reach the flight deck, entry is made through a door on the left side of the fuselage with steps up to the cargo floor level. Once inside, there are steps up to the flight deck. The space under the flight deck and forward of the cargo area contains the aircraft's vital electronic and hydraulic system controls.

The pilots and navigator are commissioned Air Force Officers. The flight engineer and the load master are enlisted crew members with the flight engineer usually ranked as a "non-commissioned officer." Often a working C-130 has at least two loadmasters. The loadmaster oversees passengers, if any, and the securing of cargo and its placement in the cargo space. Proper placement influences the balance of the aircraft. An aircraft can be rendered unflyable with a relatively light load not properly located and secured in the cargo area. Though usually the lowest ranking member of the crew, the loadmaster's role is vitally important.

All members of the crew of a C-130 play critical roles that directly impact the success or failure of a mission. Crews become closely knit teams. The best teams, as in athletics, are imbued with a team spirit that recognizes accomplishment of the mission is THE goal.

The aircraft functions as a transport plane. Cargo can include combat equipment from ammunition, arms, to small vehicles. It can also carry approximately 100 passengers.

The aircraft also has various combat roles. It is used to drop equipment and paratroopers into combat areas. The aircraft is a mainstay of the special operations functions of our military forces. It is used to insert, support, and extract people from hostile environments. Later modes of the C-130 have been specially designed for active special operations and combat roles. It has evolved into a deadly weapons system, with some models equipped with canons and machine guns that can be controlled with great accuracy and devastating effect. It is also a rescue asset in natural disasters. The aircraft is still being manufactured with increasingly sophisticated enhancements.

As its special operations mission capabilities were recognized, and weapons technology evolved, the number of crew members correspondingly grew. It would not be unusual for a special operations C-130 to now contain two more officers: a fire control officer and an electronic warfare officer. There would likely be six more enlisted positions: a TV operator (for targeting and fire control), an infrared detection set operator, and four aerial gunners.

My first flight in the C-130 was intimidating to say the least. The plane seemed huge! The first task was the pilot's pre-flight inspection of the aircraft. Prior to that inspection the crew chief (responsible for maintenance and flight preparation) and the flight engineer had done inspections of their own. Everything relating to pre-flight and flight was done in compliance with checklists. The C-130E checklists were lengthy due to the many complicated systems.

I made the climb to the flight deck and settled into the left seat. We began the challenge/response checklist ritual in preparation for the flight. Eventually the crew and plane were ready for engine start followed by radio calls for taxi instructions and flight plan delivery and activation. Then the adventure began. Engines were started, doors were secured, wheel chocks were pulled, power was applied, the plane began to move, and the process of coaxing it onto a path towards the runway takeoff position began.

I was most intimidated trying to taxi it around on the ground. There were engine controls for each of the four engines, and you could use "differential engine thrust," braking actuated by foot pressure applied to parts of the rudder pedals and a dinky little nosewheel steering device on the left side of the left pilot's seat used to steer the plane while on the ground. Differential engine thrust means applying higher power settings to the engines on one side to cause the aircraft to turn in response. This aircraft also had the ability to apply reverse thrust and back-up. Most people have never seen a plane back-up under its own power. The maneuver is a crowd pleaser at air shows.

Taxiing the C-130 is a real strange experience the first time! Unlike any other in my flying experience. At the runway, more checklists are completed. The engines are run-up and checked at full power. The aircraft is determined to be in flying condition and properly configured for takeoff. The control tower is advised of readiness for takeoff. The control tower gives clearance for take-off with departure headings and a change to air traffic departure control radio frequencies.

Amazingly, the airplane flew much like the other airplanes I had flown. It had tremendous power and we were soon in the air—we were very light. We had no cargo or passengers and our fuel load was low as we were on a short training mission. I was much more comfortable with the plane in the air as opposed to maneuvering it like a beached whale on the taxiways. I quickly came to know that not only were the missions going to be interesting, so would be the flying itself.

My training soon progressed to practicing engine failure procedures. Easy when only one engine is shut down. Even two down isn't much of a problem if it's a matter of one out on each wing. You still don't have too much trouble controlling the flight path. Things get a lot busier if you lose two engines on one side. Then you must stomp on the rudder pedal for the side that had the good engines to force the nose to track the desired course while maintaining the required "minimum control speed." Failure to maintain that speed would result in disaster as the plane would role, stall, and spin out of control.

Things get downright scary if you have a heavy load and lose two engines on one side at liftoff. You are low and slow, and the rudder is less effective in controlling the flight path. There is a point where the laws of aerodynamics render an aircraft unflyable. Once an aircraft's airspeed deteriorates to a certain point, there is no ability of the flight controls to keep the aircraft under control. Thrust, speed, and weight are the determinates. If two engines fail on one side of a four-engine aircraft carrying a heavy load immediately after take-off when at a low speed and low altitude, the situation is immediately critical. The same failure at higher altitude allows the aircraft to be flown in a descent to gain and/or maintain the airspeed necessary for control. When that airspeed is established, the airplane is aerodynamically stable, and control can be maintained.

The C-130 is a great aircraft. It is even possible to fly it on one engine if it is not carrying a heavy cargo/fuel load and is in a position close enough to a long runway to allow the descent rate necessary to keeping flying speed. I admonish young C-130 pilots: "Don't try this!"

The variety of the C-130's capabilities also add to its appeal. We flew low level missions in formation. We dropped airborne troops, and pallets with cargo strapped to them. We flew all over the world delivering passengers and cargo. We operated it on 1,500-foot-long dirt strips at night with flare pots for runway lights.

I was assigned to the 61st Tactical Airlift Squadron at Seward upon completion of my training. I didn't have to make another move. By then I had grown to like Nashville, especially its proximity to Louisville and Patti.

I had been trained and checked out to serve as a new co-pilot on the C-130E. I entered service with the 61st as my first "Real Air Force" working duty assignment. As luck would have it, my orders to Vietnam were rescinded. I moved in with one of my best friends from among my 19th Playboy Squadron USAFA classmates, Harvey Manekofsky. Harvey was not able to pass the pilot's physical and had been serving as a 61st Squadron navigator. We lived in a duplex in Nashville. We enjoyed the freedom and the party atmosphere of

Nashville. Our squadron superiors were good officers and very willing to help younger officers develop as pilots, navigators, and Air Force officers. Our contemporaries were "good guys." On occasion Harvey and I were on the same aircrew together.

Nashville and service with the 61st were good times. Harvey began dating Sheila, and I Patti. The four of us remain close friends with over fifty-year marriages.

The duplex Harvey and I rented was on a hill. It included a steep driveway. When Patti and I got engaged, Harvey wanted to take us to dinner—after a few celebratory toasts of course. Harvey's car was at the top of the driveway, mine was second, and Patti's was third. Harvey managed to ding both of our cars while backing down the hill. Oh well, what the heck—we were not going to let a little thing like that ruin a good party! Luckily the damage was insignificant. The USAA (our insurer) adjuster was not particularly impressed! We didn't invite him to the wedding.

But there was a war going on, and I began to feel its impact. I knew it wouldn't be long before I would fly my first trip into South Vietnam. There was kind of a nervous excitement about it. I was looking forward to the adventure. Our Academy class and the one ahead of ours (Class of '63) were particularly hard hit by Vietnam. By January of 1966 I had flown my first combat mission in Vietnam. Combat experience for me started as supply and resupply missions into and around South Vietnam. Over time it evolved into special operations missions and combat time on three continents.

I had a great Aircraft Commander (AC). He was an excellent pilot with lots of experience and a supreme partier. He soon learned to trust me and let me do most of the flying. After takeoff, when we were established on course with the checklists completed, he would typically go back to the crew bunk at the back of the flight deck. I would be put in charge and instructed not to awaken him unless there was an emergency, or we were getting close to our destination. He would be recharging to be ready to participate in whatever party was available at our next destination.

On a typical Vietnam trip, we would leave Nashville and fly to the west coast where cargo was loaded for transport to Vietnam. Then it was on to Hawaii where we would spend the night at Hickam AFB. The AC would enjoy a night on the town and most of the rest of us would try to catch a meal and a movie before crashing for the night. Then it was on to Guam or Wake Island where we would spend another night. Finally, we would make it to Okinawa for another night. Then we flew people and supplies to bases in South Vietnam such as Saigon, Bien Hoa, Cam Rahn Bay, or Danang.

My first trip into Vietnam was to Saigon, arriving late at night. I remember flying over the coast at a higher than normal altitude and then steeply descending to the landing at Ton Son Nuit airport. I asked my Aircraft Commander about the occasional sparkles I noticed coming from the ground. He commented that it was someone with a rifle taking shots at us as we passed. He didn't appear much concerned. We were busy in the cockpit communicating with the air traffic controllers and preparing for our steep approach to the landing. I still recall my first exposure to enemy fire—even if it was uneventful. So, there really is someone out there who wants to kill me! Oh well, what the hell!

When I first saw Cam Ranh Bay it was a tent city in the sand! I remember the first night when my C-130 crew went to a primitive officer's club for dinner and drinks. Most of us went home having been more than adequately refueled. But Ed, our navigator, stayed behind. He said he could find his tent in the dark by himself. No sweat!

We got up in the morning and no Ed!! We were really very concerned when someone from one of the other units came by and asked if we knew a navigator named Ed. They had found him passed out in the sand and sheltered him. His flight suit pockets were full of sand. He had apparently fallen and crawled until he passed out. Aren't you glad I haven't used your full name, Ed?

I was getting lots of flying time making these trips on a regular basis. We would be gone from Nashville about four to six weeks each time. I was given responsibilities not normally entrusted to a pilot of my rank and experience (or perhaps I should say "inexperience!"). Once there, we flew resupply missions within Vietnam for two to four weeks. Those would take us to smaller airstrips and bases throughout South Vietnam. Several trips were made in 1966 and 67. They were challenging, but not regarded as terribly dangerous. However, in 1967 one of my USAFA classmates who was a fighter pilot in Vietnam asked if I thought it would be safe for him to catch a ride on a C-130 to another location in Vietnam. I told him it was a great airplane and a safe airplane. His fighter missions were probably more dangerous. He took the ride. The plane was shot down and all on board were lost, including my friend.

On one of the trips, we flew from South Vietnam to Okinawa. We encountered a critical emergency. It was a late-night flight and the route took us on a northerly heading to a point where we would make a right turn to head east to Okinawa. That turning point was called Point Bravo. As we were approaching Bravo, I noted most of the crew had fallen asleep, including the aircraft commander. The navigator and I were the only ones awake. This wasn't the first time I had observed that. I thought to myself it was a wonder that no one had flown through that turning point and on into China. China was in sight as we flew this route. I asked the navigator our position relative to that turning point. He said to standby, we were almost there, and he would give me the new heading in a few minutes.

I made the Bravo turn when he directed. We proceeded for about ten minutes when there was a big explosion. I turned in my seat and saw flames coming up into the cockpit area. I hit the alarm bell, told everyone to get on portable oxygen and fight the fire. I depressurized the plane (less oxygen available to feed the fire) and called Mayday on the oceanic air traffic control radio frequency. I declared our onboard fire emergency and position relative to Point Bravo, requested a block altitude clearance to avoid other aircraft that might be in the area, and an alert to air-sea rescue. I requested weather conditions at the nearest available airfields. I announced we were shutting down all electronics and I would call back when I could.

We had high explosive cargo on board. I wondered if I would even hear the potential big bang that would destroy us if the fire spread. The weather was terrible in the area. I did not want to have the crew bail out as survival chances would be slim. I was alone on the flight deck as the whole crew was engaged in getting the fire under control and assessing damage.

The flight engineer came back to the flight deck and told me he thought the fire was out. It was in part of the plane under the flight deck that housed the electronic systems. I asked if he could pull circuit breakers on one electrical system circuit to isolate a communications radio for use. He thought he could.

We turned on the radio. Usually there was a lot of radio traffic. I heard none, and thought the radio was dead. I announced our callsign and asked if anyone could hear me. The controller came back loud and clear and announced all other radio traffic had been transferred to another frequency. He told me the Air Force Command Post wanted to talk to me. I told him we were too busy for that now. We urgently needed weather information as we had to decide where to land as soon as possible. I advised our navigation computers and instrument landing equipment may be unreliable due to fire damage. The oceanic controller hadn't gotten the weather information he had requested for us yet. He had asked for present conditions and up-to-date forecasts. It was the kind of information that took time to gather and evaluate.

From our pre-flight weather briefing I knew the weather was bad everywhere. Hong Kong and Singapore were down, and Taipei was marginal. I was aware of a restricted airfield at the other end of Taiwan and asked about it. The controller advised it was not a reporting station, but that it might be better because of its location. He would try to get weather information and permission for landing there. Again, he said the command post wanted to talk to me. I again told him we were very busy and would talk to them when we made a decision on where to land. I said we would be shutting down again and I would call back in ten minutes. He said the command post wanted to talk to me. I told him there wasn't time yet and turned the power off.

Ten minutes later we got great news: the controller gave us a fairly good weather report for the restricted field and had obtained clearance for us to make an emergency landing there. We would be restricted to the aircraft when we landed, and armed guards would take us into custody. We made a quick decision that was where we would go, and the navigator went to work to determine our new course. I advised the controller of our decision. He again said the command post wanted to talk to me. I asked him to put me through to them.

The first words from the command post: "Sir, if you guys make it, will you be declaring crew rest?"

"You better believe it," I replied.

He said scheduling was concerned about when we and the airplane would leave for Okinawa. I told him it would be after the command post arranged for repair of our airplane and we had a good 24 hours off duty.

As a crew we had decided on that deployment to quit smoking and cut down on drinking. After we had landed, and the Taiwanese processed us and decided we were not a threat, they arranged for our lodging and a meal. By then it was morning. We were exhausted from our ordeal, but we quickly found a place that would sell us cigarettes and booze. So much for our health kick! We celebrated just being alive!! This recalls the Vietnam definition of an optimist: a pilot who worries about lung cancer.

Our Operations Officer, a Lt. Colonel, was killed. One of an Operations Officer's duties is scheduling flights. By then a First Lieutenant, I volunteered to fill-in until another Lt. Colonel was slotted into his position. I scheduled myself in and out of Vietnam on a regular basis. Each such trip would involve combat missions at the end of one month and the beginning of the next. That qualified me for the hazardous duty tax deduction every month for about a year. I also got extra hazardous duty pay for each month in which I flew combat missions. I was giving real meaning to the phrase "timing is everything." If I could manage the schedule correctly, I could get every month covered with six trips. I was not that lucky!

When we were home, we still did a lot of flying involving training to keep current on the different skill sets required for the various kinds of missions we flew. We also did three-month tours of temporary duty in England and Germany. From there, we did all sorts of hauling of people and cargo in Europe, Africa, and Southwest Asia.

My AC was a good teacher and soon had me to the point he felt I should be upgraded to Aircraft Commander even though I was still only a First Lieutenant. That was very rare. He arranged to have my co-pilot's proficiency check flight and evaluation conducted as an Aircraft Commander upgrade check flight. He didn't bother to tell me. Probably a good thing as I would have been a nervous wreck. It was the most grueling check flight I have ever flown, and I was taken totally by surprise. I didn't know I might finish the day as the newest and youngest Aircraft Commander in the squadron until the instructor pilot conducting the check flight told me at the pre-flight briefing-it would be an AC upgrade check. He really put me through the wringer. Thanks to my AC, I was prepared.

Soon after I joined the squadron, I became aware that some missions were not the normal cargo or passenger hauling missions. Select crews were flying what we would today call Special Operations missions. At the time, there was no Air Force Special Operations Command or a joint services special operations command. Select crews from Tactical Air Command C-130 units performed these classified missions requiring special capabilities. Eventually a joint services command was formed which carries on the tradition using C-130s and other aircraft that are specially designed and equipped for those missions. Three of the first four commanding generals of the Special Operations Command were friends, one of whom I instructed in the C-130E. One has remarked to me that he wished he could tell me about their mission capabilities—much, much better than in my day. Technology is a wonderful thing!

# 8

# Combat Missions in the Company of Friends

MY FIRST EXPOSURE to the Central Intelligence Agency was while I was a cadet at the Academy. When presented, I seized the opportunity to work with the Agency and its dedicated men and women.

C-130 special operations were often highly classified. Information about some of them has appeared in the public domain in recent years, but there are others that have remained secret. Some will remain secret long after I have gone to my reward. These missions were flown before and after my last Vietnam tour, which I served as a Forward Air Controller (FAC). More about that later.

An Aircraft Commander's or Mission Commander's judgment is especially valued and relied upon in the world of special operations. My first exposures were as a co-pilot. I was an understudy to top-notch Aircraft and Mission Commanders. Theirs was a responsibility that went beyond the normal concern for the welfare of their crew and mission completion. The highest command authority needed your best judgment and performance. A "Can Do" attitude was an important ingredient, but only one ingredient. There were times when it was a detriment. Requirements for success and odds of success were expected to be critically analyzed and stated. Not only were crew lives at stake, other lives often were also. The nation's reputation was often on the line. The possibility and consequences of failure needed to be assessed honestly and realistically weighed in making the final launch decision.

Fundamental lessons from the Academy were reinforced in this most practical of practical worlds: character, honesty, dedication, and integrity were demonstrably essential requirements for service in these risky and sensitive assignments.

My Academy classmate and friend, Retired Lt. General Bruce Fister, served as commander of Joint Special Operations. In discussing the role of honor and integrity in military leadership in the book *Unbreakable Bonds published by Terry Isaacson, 2019* (also a classmate and friend), Bruce stated at page 164:

"But one thing that should never change is honor. An officer's character should always be about 'doing the right thing, the right way, even when you are alone in the dark,' as my mentor from years earlier, the late Lt. Gen. Sam Wilson, would say."

He further states on pages 165, 66:

"Honor and integrity in today's war-fighting environment is much more than answering honestly when asked a question... It is about being honor bound to do what is necessary to make the right calls, even when the requirement to report or make judgments does not clearly fall upon one's shoulders. Today the code ... must take on the mantra of 'doing the right thing ... even when it is not expected, and no one may ever know the difference. Yes, honor and integrity are even more important today. The results of a misstep can be greater in a more complex environment and happen at a faster speed the we've ever seen before."

◆◆◆

*Carolina Moon Tragedy*

My first operational life-changing hard-lesson-learned involved Operation Carolina Moon, a then highly classified complex mission into North Vietnam eventually launched in late May 1966. The essence of this operation is now in the public domain. It is this test that I apply when discussing covert or special operations. If it is "out there," at least the exposed material is open to discussion here. While incomplete, internet versions are accurate enough to present the essence of this high-risk operation. What follows is available in the public domain.

Carolina Moon called for two C-130s dropping huge specially designed high explosive mines intended to bring down a heavily defended bridge. This bridge near the provincial capitol city of Thanh Hoa was a vital transportation link in North Vietnam. Several air attacks had been unsuccessfully launched against it. The first major effort was made in April 1965. The bridge was hit, but the munitions used did not inflict significant damage. There were other attacks made with similar results. Ultimately at least twenty-four American aircraft were lost in the effort to destroy it. It was finally partially destroyed on April 27, 1972 with the use of large laser-guided "smart bombs." The job was completed with another such attack on October 6, 1972.

In 1965, Carolina Moon was conceived using the cargo-carrying capacity and delivery ability of the C-130 to drop five large magnetic mines upstream of the bridge. These mines employed a new mass-energy focusing design thought to have the power to bring down the bridge when detonated by proximity to the bridge structure. The plan called for two aircraft making a night run at low level. I was selected to be the co-pilot on the C-130 from my squadron. Another C-130 and crew was supplied from our sister squadron at Seward.

We tested the concept and trained in Arizona and Florida for an expected launch in early 1966. However, the mission was delayed several times. I began to be worried about conflict with another important mission, my wedding was set for June 4, 1966. After a few more delays, I expressed my personal concerns to the top military operational commander. He asked me to brief in my back-up, Hal Zook, and make sure he could take my place if necessary. The decision to substitute for me was made in early May. The mission was launched on the night of May 30.

The mission was high risk and depended upon the critical element of surprise. Someone in the chain of command decided at the last minute to send only one airplane. The North Vietnamese were taken by surprise and all their anti-aircraft ammunition was expended in front of the aircraft which successfully made the drop. Unfortunately, one of the mines failed to detonate and the other four failed to significantly damage the bridge. Perhaps if the original two-plane mission plan had been followed, detonation of the added mines from the second aircraft would have succeeded in bringing down the bridge, or at least making it unusable. The fact that four of the five successfully dropped the first night detonated as planned and failed to produce the desired result was not known until later.

The following day it was decided that the second plane with my crew, commanded by Major Tom Case, would launch that night using the same run-in courses and altitudes, the same fighter-cover plan, and the same timing. My back-up and eight other friends were lost on that mission. An F-4 fighter with its two-man crew providing cover was also lost.

Carolina Moon tragically illustrated that it is unwise to permit last minute changes to complex plans that are high-risk to begin with. I often think about those men. Would I have made a difference had I been there? I would have felt it my duty to speak up against the change in plan. If one plane made it through the first time, so would have two. The mission depended on surprise. Did my crew protest the change? Tom was an outstanding Aircraft Commander. I think they most likely did. They were highly regarded professionals specially selected for this mission. But the fact is at some point orders are orders. Carolina Moon will haunt me forever. Not many days go by without my remembering the loss of these heroic friends under those circumstances. Survivor's guilt is for real. What follows was hard to write.

◆ ◆ ◆

*Hard Times for Families*

Another aspect of Carolina Moon: my bride knew the pilots and navigators lost and their families. When we married, she had no idea what special operations were or that her husband and some of her friends engaged in them. When we returned from our honeymoon trip in mid-June, I reported to the Wing Commander. He ushered me into his office and shut the door. He informed me of the time of the mission, the change in strategy, and the loss of my crew. I was required to keep the information secret. He said I was the only other person on base who knew. The other crew was not back yet. The families of the crew members had not yet been informed. What followed were terrible days for me.

We were at the Officer's Club swimming pool a couple of days later, where we were joined by friends: the wife and two sons of one of the navigators, Monty Shingledecker. The boys were wanting to do some stunt around the pool and their mother, Bev, advised that they should wait until their dad got home. It was all I could do to keep my composure. I made an excuse to leave the pool soon after.

The loss of these men was painful to my wife. When it was finally announced, she realized I had kept this secret. She said, "You already knew that day at the pool, didn't you?" I admitted that I had. I remember her stating, "I don't understand how you people can live this way!"

Had Patti Moss not chosen to become Patti Luchtel on June 4, 1966, you would not be reading this! We celebrated our 50th wedding anniversary on June 4, 2016, remembering also it was four days after the 50th anniversary of the loss of my crew. They are still on my mind and always will be.

◆ ◆ ◆

*The Value of Good Judgment*

Some months and operations later, I met with a White House

representative in a foreign country. He told me the president wanted a certain plan executed as soon as possible. I can't go into the circumstances and details. I consider the whole scheme no doubt is still highly classified (by then I was a Mission Commander and had a "name" clearance, a special category of Top Secret. The name of the clearance is itself highly classified).

Had the operation been attempted, it would have been a source of great international controversy and put the president and the country in an awkward position—that is, if it had succeeded. The consequences of failure could have been catastrophic! I suggested another option which I considered highly likely to produce the desired solution to the underlying problem without loss of life (theirs or ours) or risk of damage to the prestige of the United States. The Aide was adamant. The president wanted it done as presented! I explained why I thought even if what he proposed was successfully executed, the eventual consequences would overshadow the desired result. I expressed my opinion it was a hare-brained scheme.

I suggested we go to our embassy where we could use secure communications to explain my reasoning to his chain-of-command, including the president. He backed down and I never heard any more about the proposed mission. I still wonder just what his actual authority was. I eventually learned that my suggestion was implemented. A successful result was obtained without any loss of life or national embarrassment. I am very proud of my role in this matter and regret not being able to reveal more.

Recently I came across the following regarding resistance to a bad plan, Operation Giant II, from the book *Soldier: The memoirs of Matthew B. Ridgeway, as told to Harold H. Martin* 82-83 (New York: Harper, 1956):

"When the time comes that I must meet my Maker, the source of most humble pride to me will not be accomplishments in battle, but the fact that I was guided to make the decision to oppose this thing [Giant II]. I deeply and sincerely believe that by taking the stand I took we saved the lives of thousands of brave men.

"The hard decisions are not the ones you make in the heat of battle. Far harder to make are those involved in speaking your mind about some hare-brained scheme, which proposes to commit troops to action under conditions where failure is almost certain, and the only results will be the needless sacrifice of priceless lives."

Perhaps I was exposed to and influenced by General Ridgeway's statement while a cadet. If so, I don't recall it. But its recent discovery is welcome even though my applications of that philosophy are minor when compared to his.

# 9

# The Lucky Forward Air Controller

IN THE FALL of 1967, I got orders to serve a full year's tour in South
Vietnam as a Forward Air Controller (FAC). I was expecting
assignment to a Vietnam tour, but I had assumed it would be in C-
130s. A FAC tour was very high-risk! The loss rate was one of the
highest among Air Force units, second only to the F-105 Wild Weasels
flying into North Vietnam from Thailand against missile sites.

◆ ◆ ◆

*Fort Walton Beach*

My orders directed me first to the FAC training program at Hurlburt
Field, Fort Walton Beach, Florida. I was to report in January for
about two and a half months or so of ground and flight training. Then
I would have a week of leave before heading to the Philippines for
a couple of weeks of jungle survival school. Then I was to report to
the 19th Tactical Air Support Squadron at Bien Hoa, South Vietnam.

I would then be sent to Phan Rang for more training on the
airplane and the intricacies of directing air strikes in South Vietnam.

The classroom and flight training were interesting and
demanding. The danger of the FAC mission was enough to ensure
close attention to the lessons being taught. Our classmates had
varied experience in their previous assignments. Some were from

fighter squadrons and had been through Air Force gunnery training. Those of us from C-130s had not had gunnery training. We had extra training flights at Hurlburt in that skill and the role of the fighter pilots we would be controlling in combat. My gunnery instructor in the A-1 Skyraider was killed a couple of months later in North Vietnam while providing cover for a Jolly Green Giant (helicopter) rescue mission.

Patti and I found a nice apartment in Fort Walton Beach which we shared with our Weimaraner, Beauregard. Beau was a wonderful dog we raised from a pup. He was big and loved kids. There were lots of children in the complex as many of the families were in situations like ours. I recall kids coming to our door and asking if Beau could come out and play. They liked to ride him! And he loved it.

Academy friend and classmate Buck Sheward, and his wife, Ann, were at Seward AFB with us. He also drew a FAC assignment and they lived in the same apartment complex. We played par three golf a few times. Our wives didn't play golf, but they seemed to do very well against us!

FACs were essential in Vietnam because of the coordination of forces required and the indiscernible nature of most of the targets in South Vietnam. There was often heavy jungle canopy in target areas. There was also a necessity to use a low and slow airplane to avoid collateral damage. Above all else, there was the awesome responsibility to avoid friendly fire incidents. American and South Vietnamese troops in contact with the enemy and in need of air support were our highest priority. The South Vietnamese units almost always were accompanied by American advisors.

In 1968 FACs flew single-engine, Cessna-manufactured light planes, the O-1. It was known to the Army as the L-19 and used to direct artillery. It had tandem seating for two pilots. It was called the Birddog. There was also a twin-engine Cessna designated the O-2 which had side-by-side seating for two pilots. The O-2 was called the Super Skymaster, The Duck, the Oscar Deuce, and some other names. Although also qualified in the O-2, I almost always flew the

O-1 in Vietnam. While the O-1 had only one engine, it was more maneuverable and provided a better cockpit view because the seating was tandem.

As I was finishing my tour in Vietnam in 1969, FACs began flying the new OV-10 Bronco, an armored twin-engine turbo prop plane with machine guns and tandem ejection seats. O-1 and O-2 pilots sat on flak vests for protection. We also wore flak vests and carried handguns, grenades, and rifles for use if shot down. Some found they could also be used from the window of an O-1 in flight.

The FAC was the link between military and civilian higher command, the fighter aircraft and any involved ground commander. The FAC was the on-scene commander of an airstrike mission. An airstrike mission could involve preplanned missions or a response to a change in a tactical situation occurring suddenly without time for pre-planning.

The training program was very intense, but we had some weekends off. Patti and I spent one of our last ones visiting New Orleans. We got settled in and went to a revolving restaurant on the top of one of the hotels. Soon after getting seated, a group came by our table and one of the men tripped and dumped his drink on me! He was very embarrassed and apologetic of course. A few napkins later I was about back to normal when a bottle of champagne appeared courtesy of the spiller. We waved our thanks.

The spiller's group was older, and from what we could hear the men were professional people, including a couple of doctors and lawyers. There were about ten people altogether. They were leaving the same time we were finishing. The spiller stopped by to apologize again. I told him not to feel bad, that we appreciated the champagne. Anytime he had the urge to spill on someone, he should seek me out!

Someone in the group asked if we lived in the area. We told them we did not and that it was our first trip to New Orleans. We explained our situation and they wished us luck. There followed a conversation amongst the members of the group asking who could stay out late. A couple volunteered that they could. They came over and asked if we would like a tour of New Orleans. We eagerly accepted. We had a wonderful time with them. We got the royal tour and made several stops. We ended up having breakfast. We got to our lodging around 7:00 a.m.

After completing the FAC program, we moved to Louisville, Kentucky, Patti's hometown. She rented a house. I departed Louisville for Southeast Asia on April 5, 1968, the day following the assassination of Dr. Martin Luther King Jr. It was an emotional goodbye. We both knew it was not an easy road ahead for me. I knew I was an excellent pilot, but was I also a lucky one? In war, luck is necessary to survival, especially in high-risk assignments! I was by no means confident that I would make it back. But after leading almost 250 airstrikes, I survived! But not unscathed.

◆◆◆

*The Big Leagues – FACing in Vietnam*

After Jungle Survival we had further FAC training. I arrived in South Vietnam shortly after the 1968 Tet Offensive. I was checked out and briefed on tactics at Phan Rang Air Base, the home of the 35th Tactical Fighter Wing and FAC-U, Forward Air Controller University. One of the wives observed it was a good thing we weren't doing underwater work.

The training was more extensive than at Hurlburt. The training was supplied by instructors that had served in especially high-risk areas. They passed along everything they could think of that might give us an edge on protecting our forces and surviving the effort. It was FAC Graduate School.

As the system worked in the field, FACs received "Frag Orders" from a central command center in the evening listing preplanned targets and air support missions for the next day. Sometimes we would fly reconnaissance missions with no pre-set strikes. These orders would be studied by the FAC who would begin the mission planning process. FACs first surveyed maps of the target area, identified the targets, tweaked the attack plan, and ensured civil and military authorities with jurisdiction of the target area, approved the mission.

We flew to the target area first. We scouted the area before bringing the fighters in so that we could identify anti-aircraft threats and better plan attack run-in headings and pilot ejection and recovery areas. The best way to discover the enemy positions was to make yourself an inviting target and draw their fire. But obviously not too inviting!

A change in mission could result from new intelligence, an emergency need for close air support by ambushed troops in contact with the enemy or outposts under attack. FACs in South Vietnam were assigned areas of responsibility and became intimately familiar with the terrain and the tactical situation. A bomb could not legally be dropped in South Vietnam without the specific on-scene approval and direction of a FAC.

It was a high-risk mission. It had become obvious to the North Vietnamese and Vietcong troops that if you killed the little airplane, the others wouldn't know what to do. I would eventually learn from intelligence sources that I had been identified as a FAC and a price put on my head. I never went anywhere without at least a rifle and pistol.

I led US Air Force, Colorado and New Mexico Air Guard, Australian Air Force, and Vietnamese Air Force pilots during my tour. Many missions involved working with Army helicopters, for which I also had on-scene responsibility.

◆◆◆

*Tan An*

My first operational assignment was in support of an Army unit at Tan An in the northern part of IV Corps (the Delta) southwest of Saigon. The FAC group lived in a Military Assistance Command (MACV) outpost. The "V" represented the number of the MAC – 5th. I was to be there for only a couple of weeks. I would break-in and then go to Tay Ninh along the Cambodian border west of Saigon, the Wild West of III Corp. I would get my FAC PhD at Tan An.

I got a local check-out at Tan An and was on my own in my little two-seat tail dragging O-1. Things were off to a good start. I had noticed a potential problem transitioning from the C-130 to the O-1 way back at Hurlburt Field, Florida. The starter button on the C-130 was the same as the panic button on the O-1. You guessed it: I was on standby when a call came in for a FAC. I ran out to the O-1, strapped in, and hit the starter—whoops, the panic button.

Hitting the panic button caused the rockets attached to the wings of the airplane to fall off. Its purpose was to allow you to shed armaments in the event of an emergency on takeoff or other situations where it was urgent to lose weight and explosives fast. Needless to say, I was not off to a good start that day! I took a lot of kidding about bombing the air field. I had to laugh at myself too. But I was glad to move on to Tay Ninh the next week, even though it was a much higher-risk assignment! I should add that the rockets we carried were not armed until immediately prior to takeoff.

Years later I was to become close friends with retired Army Colonel Mike Treinen who was based at Tan An at the time. He is good enough to say he does not recall ever hearing of my panic button attack on the outpost. We don't recall ever meeting there. Army helicopter pilot Leonard Boswell, also from Iowa, served that area at that time. Leonard became a Democrat legislator after retiring from the Army. He served as President of the Iowa Senate before being elected to the US House of Representatives. Treinen became a lawyer and also lobbied at the statehouse. The three of us became close friends. Leonard died last year and one of his aides recently told me that Leonard often mentioned me, especially when he was flying.

◆ ◆ ◆

## Tay Ninh

Tay Ninh was a small city west of Saigon and close to the Cambodian border. It had a distinguishing asset. East of the city there was a large area dedicated to the Cao Dai Sect of Buddhism.

It was beautifully designed and landscaped—a Vatican of a different sort. The monks were friendly and had a very serene quality. They seemed at peace with everyone, and the war ignored them, and they the war. I was very impressed with them. Today I wear a Ying-Yang ring in remembrance of them and their dedication to peace and balance in all things. I was told at the time that they had their own trinity: Buddha, Victor Hugo, and John F. Kennedy. As I say, peace and balance in all things!

The religion is an attempt to form a synthesis of the beliefs found in Buddhism, Christianity, Confucianism, and Taoism. The organization seemed to be established using Roman Catholic principles. They had a resident Pope in Tay Ninh. I think they used JFK as an outreach to Americans! They did look to Jesus Christ, Joan of Arc, Mohammed, and Sun Yat Sen for guidance. You can't please everyone, but the Cao Dais at least make a sincere effort. They have my admiration.

There were also a good number of Roman Catholics in the area. There was a small church and school not far from the compound where I lived. I went to Mass there, armed to the teeth! We lived kind of a wild west existence. FACs never went anywhere without taking precautions. The people encountered on a regular basis were very friendly. I did venture to the marketplace occasionally.

As was often the case, the people were caught in a bind. They were not clamoring for the right to vote or a democratic form of government. They wanted to feed their families and educate their children. But a friendly market vendor I spoke to in the afternoon might be pressed into service with the Viet Cong that night to attack our compound. They really wanted to just be left alone by all sides.

We (MAC-V, FACs and others) lived in a villa in the city of Tay Ninh which was enclosed by a wall. Our next-door neighbors were Operation Phoenix and CIA Officers. We provided our own perimeter defense.

Our quarters were not bad, but they left a lot to be desired, like air conditioning! Our airplanes were maintained at Bien Hoa Air

Base near Saigon. It was a real treat to fly a plane over there and spend a night in air-conditioned comfort. I had fighter pilot friends there who would put me up in their quarters. They had all the amenities of home, including a good Officer's Club. I regularly directed them in air support missions, so we had a close relationship. I never spent any money. The usual greeting at the bar was: "Lucky, you're still alive!! (Fighter pilots are notoriously sensitive souls.) Great to see you!! Let me buy you a drink!!!" On rare occasion I would pay for my own meals. I am blessed with a frugal wife. We made every effort to take advantage of the special 10% interest rate savings accounts available to service personnel in Vietnam.

We provided air support for US Army Special Forces, CIA, MAC-V, and South Vietnamese Army forces. We flew from an airstrip adjoining a Special Forces Camp a mile or so away. We were attacked on the ground almost every other night. The North Vietnamese infiltrated through the area for the Tet Offensive of 1968. After Tet we did a lot of business with the North Vietnamese troops exfiltrating back to Cambodia and the Ho Chi Minh Trail that led to North Vietnam. Ammunition expended on us didn't have to be carried back to Cambodia. That may have influenced the significant number of mortars and rockets sent our way. A lot of our air strikes were in support of Special Forces camps and operations near the Cambodian Border. We also did reconnaissance missions, scouting for enemy troop movements and checking on activity in our assigned area of responsibility.

Immediately after my arrival at the Villa in Tay Ninh, I was told by the Army duty officer that I was commander of the bunker defending the northeast part of the wall surrounding the compound. I replied, "I am an Air Force officer, I don't know anything about commanding Army troops in ground combat."

In response, the duty officer stated, "You are an officer and officers command!"

I asked where this bunker was. The sergeant took me outside and pointed up on the top of a fifteen-foot security wall.

I asked, "Just how does one get there?"

"Sir, you take this ladder up to the roof which gives access to the bunker, and its three M-60 machine guns. You just have to run along the roof and jump over to the wall."

"Well, that is just wonderful, Sergeant!" I told him. "You have to be kidding, even an Air Force officer knows better than to silhouette himself running along a roof line during an assault!"

He just shrugged and observed, "They haven't lost anyone up there yet."

I then asked who was under my command. He gave me a list of about five soldiers and their sergeant. I found the sergeant and asked him to assemble the others. I wanted to meet them and lay down some standing orders.

When we were assembled, I told them, "I am your new FAC, an Air Force Officer without much knowledge about the M-60 machine gun, our bunker's primary weapon, or Army infantry tactics. When in that bulwark of freedom, your sergeant is to be obeyed without question. You are to treat his orders as if they were my orders. I will be distributing ammunition to your positions as needed and respond to anyone needing help. You are not to be shy about calling out to me for ammunition or any other need for assistance. We need to operate as a team up there. Don't worry about rank, just worry about our mission."

We got hit that first night and I managed not to fall off the roof. I was reasonably competent distributing the ammunition for the gunners. The attack was repelled, and I didn't lose any men. I got good at this job; we were attacked almost every other night.

However, later in my tour at Tay Ninh I had a different experience. Mortars started coming in near us, the usual Viet Cong announcement an attack was about to start. I scrambled up to the roof and made it across the roof to the bunker. I went about my duties noting that none of the others had appeared. To help them out, I took the coverings off the machine guns and got ammo canisters in place for the gunners. Still no one else appeared. I began to worry that they had been hit coming across the roof. I decided I had to cover that quadrant myself and began the process of readying one of the guns for firing. The missing sergeant had the radio I needed for communicating with the command center.

I had fired an M-60 at Fort Benning while a cadet. But that had been in daylight and several years in the past. I was not about to turn on my flashlight! I already felt very exposed! I fumbled around with an M-60 in the dark and managed to get the breach open. I only had to insert the ammo belt, and everything would be ready to go. Yah, right!

I got the receiver open, but I couldn't get the ammo to seat in the chamber! Try as I might, it just didn't seem to want to fit. I decided I needed to pull the charging rod back and hold it back to make room for the first shell in the belt of shells. Not an easy trick! I managed to get that done in the dark. I had the first shell in the belt seated in the firing chamber, closed the receiver, and let go of the charging rod. The gun started firing on its own!! I couldn't shut it off, so I just sprayed the area of the expected attack. I had visions of the barrel melting and blowing up in my face (I saw too many cowboy movies as a kid).

Soon I was joined by the detachment's Chief Master Sergeant. He rolled into the bunker beside me. He asked me if I had a real war going on. By then the belt had run through the gun and my ears were really ringing! I asked him if my men were okay. He said he thought so—they had been granted R & R (time off duty) and were enjoying Hong Kong. They had forgotten to assign other men to cover the bunker. The ground attack never materialized. The Chief Master Sergeant and I later maintained it was because of the withering fire from our bunker.

When accorded the "honor" of being chosen to serve as a FAC, I was told it really wasn't as dangerous as it was made out to be. I would find that the Viet Cong and North Vietnamese troops would be afraid to shoot at me because it would bring the wrath of God down on them unless they managed to kill me.

That didn't convince me, but it did relax me a little. After all, I had been shot at on C-130 missions. But I had more than a few friends killed flying C-130 missions. My first couple of FAC missions were milk runs, new guy flights. But after a couple of those, it was the real deal. The bad guys were not at all afraid to shoot at FACs, we were the center of attention!

After my first real hardcore shoot-out, I noticed my testicles were sore. I worried that I was maneuvering the airplane so violently as to damage it from excessive aerodynamic forces caused by my maneuvering. The next day was easier and my concern faded away. However, the next two days were tough, and they ached again! Being a new guy, you don't ask one of the old-timers if their nuts hurt after a dangerous mission! My worry about my violent maneuvers pulling the wings off the plane surfaced again, though.

I soon was involved in a very dangerous mission with lots of anti-aircraft and small arms fire directed at me. The FAC makes the first run on the target to mark it with a rocket to provide a reference point for use in directing the fighters. The white smoke from the rocket's impact gives the fighters an easy reference point. In the process of doing that, the FAC pulls the plane into a steep climb to kill airspeed to enable a steep dive onto the target line. When coming out of the climb the FAC uses his left hand to pull the throttle lever back and reach up to toggle a switch on the ceiling of the plane to select which rocket or rockets are going to be fired. The right hand holds the flight control stick which contains a trigger button which fires the selected rocket when it is depressed by the pilot after lining up the target.

I located on my target and positioned the airplane for an attack run on it. My left hand returned to the throttle control and moved it to idle as I killed airspeed with the climb. I reached up with my left hand and toggled the switch to select the rocket I wanted to fire. The climb at idle power allowed me to drop the nose toward the ground, letting gravity accelerate the plane. I then noticed for the first time that my idle left hand had abandoned the throttle and instead grabbed my family jewels with a protective squeeze as I hunched down to make a smaller target of myself. It suddenly dawned on me why my nuts sometimes hurt after a mission! I was unable to continue my run-in for laughing and broke off the attack. The fighters thought I had been hit. I told them I was okay and would brief them later. We then went about our grim business.

After the mission I landed at the fighter base. I walked into the bar and immediately heard, "Lucky, what happened up there? Did you get hit by a fragment or what? Why did you break off on your first pass? There was intense ground fire coming up at you! Did you see something we missed? No? What then?"

"Okay, guys, I want everyone to just think for a minute about whether they have ever had sore nuts after a mission." After some macho fighter pilot remarks, some admitted they had noticed that too. "Okay, guys, think about what you do with your throttle hand when the going gets really rough up there and those tracer rounds are coming at you in swarms."

There was a pause and then a lot of laughter began to break out!

The story has apparently made the rounds, as former POWs Senator John McCain and Medal of Honor Recipient Colonel Bud Day have each kidded me several years later about my making this discovery.

The area and the involved operations were deemed high risk. We usually had to have a waiver issued to fly more than the maximum allowable hours per month. I recall logging 120 combat hours one month. FACs were to be relieved after four months in heavy action areas. I ended up doing five months due to the lack of replacements and the loss of my replacement soon after his arrival. Shortly after I was replaced at Tay Ninh, my roommate there, Dale Dickens, was killed the night of October 17, 1968. When I left, there were five FACs serving the area that Major Jim Cooper and I had covered by ourselves. I was fried!

◆ ◆ ◆

### Life in a Tay Ninh Villa

The compound we lived in was shared with a unique collection of people. We contributed "dues" to a fund for upkeep and food service. Local women worked as our maids and cooks. Besides the FACS there were Army advisors, an AID worker, and CIA officers. It was not unusual to sit down to an evening meal and meet a stranger passing through. We didn't ask many questions. The meals were usually presided over by the AID worker, Debbie, who had a permanent seat at the head of the table. She was a nice young woman who was not afraid of much of anything. Her job put her at risk, all alone, in the surrounding villages. I think what she did was appreciated even by the Viet Cong as they never bothered her. We didn't bother her either! She was everyone's little sister and we took good care of her.

One evening I was late for dinner. I sat down and there was a stranger at the table. Debbie began to pick on me for being late. I kidded her back and the stranger was taking note of our banter. She made some comment about my mission and I made some ridiculously inflammatory statement about it or the war. The stranger reacted, and our hostess started laughing as she introduced him. He was a well-known reporter from the New York Times. Even I knew his name. I was shocked. The guy was well regarded and had ruined an Army Major with a story a month or so before. I figured I was dead meat! He saw my reaction and laughed too. He said something to the effect that he figured Debbie was playing both of us! He was a sharp observer, thank God.

The flying at Tay Ninh was interesting, to say the least. One very good friend and Academy classmate from the Playboy Squadron, Brett Dula, retired as a Lt. General (three-star general). He also served as a Forward Air Controller in Vietnam. Over dinner at our 50th Year Class Reunion I was kidding him about the privileges of a Lt. General. I asked him what his best duty assignment was. He replied that being a FAC as a young Captain was the best. We made dozens of decisions a day that had life or death consequences, we had command and control of ground troops while they were being supported by fighters over which we also had command and control. And we were only 26 years old! Rarely did anyone question the decisions we made. He said I wouldn't believe all the paperwork and second guessing that were part and parcel of being a Lt. General!

◆ ◆ ◆

## *Ranch Hand*

C-123s are two engine high wing aircraft that were used in Vietnam for two main purposes: cargo hauling and the Ranch Hand mission. Ranch Hand aircraft sprayed defoliant over areas where the Viet Cong and North Vietnamese troops used jungle foliage for cover. The defoliant came to be known as Agent Orange. One of our FAC missions at Tay Ninh was to provide cover for the Ranch Hands as they sprayed the defoliant. We FACs would have fighter aircraft in orbit above ready at a moment's notice to dive down and attack anyone shooting at the 123s. We were down in the weeds with the 123s. Ranch Hand missions usually involved a formation of two to six 123s spraying a pattern over the jungle. I think they operated around 600 feet. My tactic was to try to be a little below the Ranch Hands and off to the side. I would weave to alternate sides by flying under the 123s. I'm sure I flew through some of their Agent Orange in the process and probably inhaled my share of it.

For the enemy there was also a considerable and immediate risk of lead poisoning. Eventually the communists figured out the lead and napalm they got back (it is truly better to give than receive in combat) in reward for their efforts to kill aircrews was not cost effective. I found the ground fire incidents during Ranch Hand missions were decreasing. If they exposed themselves by shooting at one of our aircraft, they knew the retribution would be immediate and deadly.

I am on the Veterans Administration Agent Orange List of exposed veterans. By being on the List I am assured the VA will provide medical coverage for a whole host of diseases, the cause of which is presumed to have been exposure to Agent Orange. Thankfully, I have never experienced any health issues I would relate to Agent Orange. Not yet, anyway!

◆ ◆ ◆

## *Church Tragedy*

A tragedy occurred at the little Catholic church and school in Tay Ninh that will haunt me forever. It is painful to write about. I can't talk about it. I discuss it here for the first time. An attack was made on the church one Sunday. The attack was meant to kill me and a couple of other Americans–who attended Sunday services there regularly. It was poorly executed. Two small children were killed: a little boy and girl about six or seven. Their little bodies were mutilated. I found and killed the perpetrator. I have killed many in the line of duty. This was the only killing that I enjoyed. I regretted only being able to kill this guy once! Ordinarily there was no joy in it for me. You are killing someone's family member. He, or she, was important in the life of their family. I think back to the impact my uncle's death in World War II had on my family.

While going down this painful path, I will say that I regret one killing in another context. I also recall it vividly. I think it's possible he may have been a mistake. If he was a mistake, he was in the wrong place at the right time. He fit the description I was given, but I can still see his surprised expression. It's not that I think he was innocent, but I was struck none-the-less by his expression of surprise. He apparently didn't appreciate the consequences of where he was and what he was doing. I did. But it still concerns me.

While I am on this digression, I will offer this: I found the Vietnamese people to be very good people. I did not hate them. I even found some North Vietnamese soldiers to be honorable, as you will see below. Because most Vietnamese spoke some French, as I did, I would be called upon to act as an interpreter. I was usually acquainted with local leaders and grew to admire them. How many Mayors do you know who would serve at the risk of assassination? Our service staff were Vietnamese from the local area. They were good people who cared about the people they served. One woman who worked in our compound was distraught when one of us was missing. She was a nice lady with nice children. I hope she is alive and well with lots of grandchildren.

Also, the Vietnamese Air Force pilots were outstanding. Some of them had flown thousands of missions. I loved working with them, as they were very accurate with their munitions. With one exception, things always went well when I worked with them. There were some language issues, but not many.

I had the practice of accounting for every aircraft after completion of a mission. I didn't want anyone left behind. After a mission with significant exposure to ground fire, I was flying away from the area. I was counting my flight of four Vietnamese A-1 Skyraiders when I couldn't find the fourth plane. There was a lot of excited radio chatter in Vietnamese. I was in a turn looking for the missing plane when I saw an explosion on the ground which I knew was from a plane crash. My heart sank until I found the pilot descending in his parachute. I quickly called for rescue and arranged rescue support with nearby US fighter planes that still had enough fuel to loiter in the area where the pilot went down. Rescue choppers arrived, and he was picked up without any difficulty.

◆ ◆ ◆

*It Only Takes One to Save a Village*

There were two engagements where my decisions were questioned. One of the best and most important decisions of my life, other than picking Patti Moss, involved an order to divert an airstrike mission to a different location to attack a reported North Vietnamese Army command unit. Intelligence agents reported there was to be a big meeting of area communist leadership.

I was in the air and on my way to rendezvous with fighter aircraft being vectored to me. I was prepared to lead them to a pre-planned target. The command center called me by radio to tell me they had a new higher-priority target I was to attack instead of the planned target. I, in turn, called the fighters and instructed them to enter a high-altitude fuel conserving orbit and expect a mission change.

I copied the coordinates given to me by radio and plotted them. They centered on a small village in my area with which I was very familiar. I had flown over it earlier that morning. It was near the Cambodian border and its residents had a peaceful routine. They waved as I flew over that morning. Everything seemed normal. I radioed the command center and requested a check on the coordinates they had provided. The operator read back the same coordinates. I radioed back that the coordinates did not identify a valid military target. I said they plotted out to where a small village was located. I reported I had recently flown over the village and everything was normal. No valid military reason existed that would allow me to lead an attack on the village.

The operator asked me to stand by. A Major immediately took over the radio and told me the coordinates were correct and I had a direct order to bomb the location indicated by them. I again asked for a check and said I would not carry out the mission on those coordinates as they did not constitute a lawful military target. There was a pause. A Colonel came on the radio. He very bluntly told me that if I failed to carry out the order, I would be on my way to Leavenworth the following evening. I told him that the coordinates identified a peaceful village which was not a valid military target and therefore the order to bomb it was not a lawful order. I repeated my request that they check and verify their coordinates.

There followed a longer pause and the initial operator came back on the radio. He simply stated, "Sir, please stand by for corrected coordinates." I shudder to think about the damage to the Air Force and our war effort had I backed down and bombed that village! I became a real-life example of a lesson I was taught in a military law class at the Academy. There are responsibilities that go with being an officer which are sometimes difficult to fulfill. Sometimes orders are not valid. It is not easy to stand against authority, but sometimes it becomes a moral and legal obligation to be fulfilled respectfully and with integrity.

I did lead the fighters on an attack on the corrected coordinates.

They defined an area in the jungle. I never could see that we accomplished anything. I think the intelligence was incorrect. We did not encounter any resistance and there were no secondary explosions indicating we had hit a target where munitions or fuel could be found.

◆◆◆

*Could this Really Have Been Cambodia?*

Another decision which caused consternation and command level notice involved attacking a North Vietnamese antiaircraft gun site that had been established in a somewhat confused border area between Cambodia and South Vietnam. While leading a flight of F-100s on a strike to support an Army Special Forces camp, large caliber antiaircraft guns opened fire on me and the F-100s. Flak is never a good thing to share airspace with, especially when flying a light aircraft. I found the situation unacceptable, broke off the attack, and redirected our attention to the antiaircraft site. The fighters did not question attacking the antiaircraft site at my direction, and it was eliminated. We then dedicated the remaining ordnance to the protection of the Special Forces camp.

Several weeks passed. The incident was all but forgotten. Then one day there was a knock on my door and a CIA Officer from the Saigon Station asked to speak to me. The State Department was concerned about an allegation that a bombing raid had occurred on Cambodian territory. I asked what that had to do with me. Playing dumb comes easy to me. He stated their investigation indicated that I was the FAC in command in the area at that time. He asked to record an interview of me.

It was hard to lawyer-up in the boonies of Vietnam! I agreed to the recorded interview. I told him there had to have been a mistake. He asked why I thought that. I replied that the incident I was involved in was an attack initiated by an antiaircraft site firing upon me and my fighters. The border in the area is unclear and difficult to determine even when one is not being shot at. I said it should have been safe to assume they were on the Vietnamese side of the border as Cambodia was a neutral country. He laughed, turned off the tape recorder, stomped on the cassette, and said, "That's pretty good, but I think we can do better than that!" After a bit of instruction, another tape recording was made by both of us.

I'm not sure how he handled the matter, but I never heard anything further. I think it paid to have CIA and State Department friends from my special operations days. Also, I spent time with the CIA Officers with whom I lived and worked in Tay Ninh. By the time of that airstrike, I had decided there were no targets in South Vietnam worth a pilot's life other than those necessary to the defense of troops in contact with the enemy. I was not going to stand idly by and allow that antiaircraft site to take out one of my fighters or prevent us from giving needed support to the Special Forces troops. If we hadn't taken it out, I don't know how we could have supplied that camp by air. The local CIA contingent agreed with me.

Ken Quinn is a friend who worked for the State Department in Tay Ninh Province at the time. We did not meet until years later in Iowa. He served as Ambassador to Cambodia from December of 1995 until July of 1999. Ken recently retired again, this time as President of the World Food Prize Foundation headquartered in Des Moines. Ken was a high school classmate at Dubuque High of Terry "Ike" Isaacson, my friend and fellow member of the USAFA Class of '64. Ken said he was most familiar with Ike's back—they ran track together. I recently discussed the matter of the anti-aircraft site incident with Ken. He had no recollection of it, but he probably wouldn't have any reason to know about it in 1968.

◆◆◆

*Primary Mission: Protecting the Guys on the Ground*

For a FAC in South Vietnam, providing effective support to ground troops was the primary mission. It was not unusual to get a call for help from an army unit in trouble. Those calls would necessitate an ad hoc response using whatever fighter support could be scrambled to the area. There usually wasn't significant wait time for fighter arrival and the turnover of command and control to the FAC. The wait time that was available was consumed establishing communications with the ground forces, learning their situation and deployment, redirecting their deployment if necessary, arranging alternative methods of communication such as flags, panels, smoke bombs or flares, and arranging for helicopter evacuation of casualties and after battle extractions. You were never bored as a FAC! When the fighters arrived, the FAC assumed responsibility for briefing them on the ground situation. That entailed briefing them on the location of our troops; target descriptive information including elevation, wind velocity and direction, run-in headings, ground fire potential, flight obstructions, conflicting operations; and, the best ejection area in case of a shoot-down.

I got an emergency call one afternoon that involved the ambush of a reconnaissance platoon by a large North Vietnamese force in a jungle area. They indicated their situation was very dire. I got the basic identity information from them and asked them to standby briefly while I contacted my command center to divert fighter resources to their area. I contacted the command center and requested a change in the rendezvous point for my inbound fighters for a troops-in-contact mission. I next requested the launch of additional staggered scrambles of four flights of four fighters each to rendezvous orbit points in the vicinity with high altitude fuel saving orbits and assigned altitude separation. It looked like it was going to be a long afternoon.

I re-established contact with the ground commander, helped identify a location where he could consolidate his forces, and established a defensible perimeter. He reported they were continuing to get heavy concentrations of fire. I noted the areas from which that fire was originating. I was also taking heavy fire. The fighters began checking in with me after hand-off from the command center. I briefed them on the urgency of the situation. I began bringing them in on target one flight at a time, starting with my diverted fighters. The North Vietnamese held their ground and I ordered more fighters. I don't recall how many flights of fighters were needed that day, but there was hardly any jungle cover left when we finished as evening approached.

I had Army helicopters in orbit nearby and directed them to a peaceful pickup. The ground commander reported that he had accounted for all his men but two who he thought were killed in action. He asked me to bomb a wider area between the site of the battle and the Cambodian border. I asked if he knew where his missing troops were and if he knew for certain that they were dead. He did not. I told him I was going to cease air operations until it was determined both missing were dead. I suggested we put an operation together for the morning to check the area for the missing.

The following morning, a platoon was inserted and quickly located one of the missing, a lieutenant. He had been wounded in the legs and could not walk or stand. He said the North Vietnamese commander directed his medic to tend to his wounds. He also directed his men to dig a bunker for the protection of the lieutenant in the event artillery or airstrikes were applied to the area. They left him food and water, medicated his wounds, and retreated to Cambodia. Medication was a scarce commodity for those North Vietnamese troops. The lieutenant reported that the other missing man, a major, was not injured. He was last seen being marched off with the North Vietnamese troops as a POW.

Years later I learned that the Major, Ray Schrump, had made it all the way to Hanoi. He was captured May 23, 1968 and repatriated February 12, 1973. He lived in Wisconsin. We have communicated but have never met. While visiting the Reagan Presidential Library thirty years later, I was amazed to see a bracelet on display that he had created while a POW.

It is easy to regard the enemy as less than human. And in many cases, they are! The "less than human" approach serves to make the dirty business of killing easier. This incident and some others taught me that even in war the human nature of combatants is worthy of recognition.

◆◆◆

*Most Beautiful Operative or Whatever She Chose to Be*

The preceding operation earned me the gratitude of a very beautiful woman. My air support saved the life of her lover, the ground commander. The ground commander was a friend, so it was through him that I came to know her. She was a unique person. An actress daughter of a Vietnamese father and French mother, she was stunningly beautiful. She was a success as an actress and singer in Vietnam and France.

She carried a huge burden. When she was a child of about eight (the exact age escapes me) her father was a village official. The Viet Minh, the communist insurgent predecessors of the Viet Cong, were initiating their reign of terror against the government of South Vietnam. They called upon her parents one night. Her father refused their demands. He and his wife were disemboweled. Their children were forced to watch.

Why was this beautiful creature in the boondocks of South Vietnam? She visited between gigs as an actress and singer to participate in operations. She hated the communists and was a deadly operative. She had great courage and sought any opportunity to avenge her parents' deaths by killing communists.

Our relationship never went beyond the professional and a personal friendship. Her lover trusted me with her. He was a senior Army officer and I worked closely with him. She learned to trust me too and depended on me as a best friend. When he had to be gone, he would ask me to look after her. That was the one support assignment from him that I enjoyed! I took her to a USO Show on one of these occasions. She didn't think much of the performance and asked me if it would be okay for her to offer to perform. Her offer was accepted, and she brought the house down.

In an emotional state over the near loss of her lover she wanted to "reward" me for saving him. She said he agreed before leaving for a command meeting at another Army base. I declined the offer, but accepted a hug and a kiss on my cheek. I sometimes wonder what happened to them. They were two of the most interesting people I met in Vietnam. I have not been able to trace either since the war. He is American, but I never knew either of their real names. I can only hope they both survived. I think it likely that they did. They had the skills needed to operate in high risk situations.

By the way, it was not unusual for special operators in Vietnam to have Vietnamese wives and children. Some had been in Vietnam for many years and could speak the language. There were a variety of unusual living arrangements that seemed to work out.

◆◆◆

## Trolling for Ground Fire

One of a FAC's responsibilities is to reconnoiter the target area and locate and assess threats to an air operation. We called that "trolling" the target area. We would offer ourselves as a target to invite ground fire that would allow us to locate threat areas. Having done that without drawing fire near a Special Forces camp in preparation for the arrival of a flight of F-4s, I began the process of briefing them upon their arrival. I gave my usual pre-strike briefing emphasizing the threat environment and ejection recovery areas. The establishment of the run-in headings and breakout areas was based on threat minimization, balanced with the need for attack effectiveness.

During this mission to support a special forces camp, I witnessed an outstanding display of cunning and courage—by two North Vietnamese soldiers. After briefing the fighter pilots on mission details and receiving an acknowledgement from each aircraft, I made the first pass on the target and fired a smoke rocket to mark it for them.

All four fighters acknowledged seeing my mark. I gave them an adjustment from the smoke location and cleared the lead aircraft to attack. He set up and turned onto the run-in heading I had given. I then cleared him to make a "hot" run (drop and/or fire weapons), which initiated the strike. As this was going on, I was flying perpendicular to his track to establish my orbit point, from which I could view the entire scene and direct adjustments if necessary. As he was reaching his release point, I was rolling out of my turn so that I could see his results and adjust for the next fighter.

As he neared the release point, his wingman began his run-in. Standard tactics called for him to be spaced so that he could see the lead aircraft's attack and, with me, observe any groundfire the lead was drawing. He would be back far enough to engage a ground threat to support the lead. Both the wingman, the lead, and I saw tracers (one out of seven to ten rounds fired were tracer rounds that gave off a glow that made them visible so that the gunner could see how his rounds were tracking and make aiming adjustments as needed). The tracers were fired at the lead aircraft coming from the left of his run-in heading and to my left in my orbit. The fire was coming from somewhere between me and the lead fighter. I made an adjustment to the run-in heading and cleared fighter number two, the lead's wingman, in "hot." He made his run and came through clean. The other three fighter pilots and I were focused on trying to locate the source of the ground fire. Numbers three and four followed with their attacks as I cleared them in "hot." None of us saw any fire directed at two. Lead, two, four, and I observed number three draw heavy fire as he closed in on his bomb release point.

I initially was not able to locate the source of the fire aimed at the lead. I was able to determine what I thought had to be the source of the ground fire directed at three. It appeared to have come from the middle of an open field of tall grass clear of jungle cover, a most unusual location. The gunners alternated aircraft. They would shoot at lead and three but skip two and four. Two and four would have the best opportunity to locate the source of the fire and vary their attack to focus on the gun site.

The third time the gunners fired, I was able to spot them. They had cleverly established a position. They were firing from a foxhole only big enough for the two of them and their anti-aircraft weapons. It was concealed by a removeable cover. I saw them remove the cover, fire at an attacking jet, and return the cover. I kept the general location in sight, quickly rolled in (a sharp banking and descending turn) towards it, selected and armed a rocket. I fired the rocket, which hit near to the spot where I thought the gunners were concealed. My rocket gave off white smoke I used to direct the fighters in an attack directed at the gunners. I can still picture those two men removing their cover and concentrating their fire on the approaching fighter until the fighter's napalm canisters were dropped and exploded on them. I had to admire their courage.

◆ ◆ ◆

## Getting Tagged

I was very lucky in Tay Ninh. The missions were almost always demanding and intense except for an occasional reconnaissance mission. However, on Flag Day of June 14, 1968 it was just such a reconnaissance mission where I managed to get myself, and the Army intelligence officer in my back seat, shot down. I had taken him up to check out some locations along the Cambodian border when we got tagged. "Shot down" may be a bit melodramatic as I don't recall the actual impact. But I knew the engine was failing. We routinely flew too low to manage a bailout. Also, with the intelligence agent aboard a bailout was out of the question anyway. Capture with him would have resulted in a horrible death for both of us.

I managed to nurse the plane almost all the way home. I recall thinking I had it made, but something went wrong. I don't remember the impact or what exactly happened. I remember being told someone or something pulled onto the short runway I was trying to make. I didn't have enough power to go around for another try. I had to crash land nearby. I got banged up some but did not suffer loss of consciousness, serious bleeding, or broken bones. I suffered some cuts on my right leg and I was bruised in several places. My passenger was unscathed. I ended up flying again the next day—in a replacement aircraft. However, I really wanted to go home— preferably by boat!

After recovering from the shock of being shot down, I

remembered that I had stuffed a small American Flag in the right leg pocket of my flight suit. The flight suit was torn up and tossed in my waste can. I retrieved it and found the blood-stained flag intact.

Mac, from Scotland, you will recall I met in Denver, had sent me the flag. His parents were very pro-American. They sent the flag to him from Scotland and asked to have it flown on a combat mission in Vietnam. I got the letter and flag from Mac around the first week of June. It occurred to me it would be neat to fly the little flag with me on Flag Day, June 14. I sent the flag back with a note that it had indeed been on a combat mission—and the blood was mine. Years later, I met Mac's son at our 55th Reunion. He knew the story and still had that flag given to him by his grandparents.

After the shoot-down I was stiff and sore with bad back problems. I had pain in my right leg. Over time the situation seemed to improve. Then I began to experience tingling in my legs after being in the air for an hour or so. That gradually worsened to the point that my legs would go completely numb in flight. The O-1 has a throttle control on the left which is actuated with the left hand.

The stick for elevator and aileron control (one controls the up/down control surface on the tail and the other the roll control surfaces on the wings) is actuated with the right hand. This control is called a "stick," probably because it looks like a stick. The rudder on the tail is controlled by pushing on foot pedals. Flying an airplane involves the coordinated use of all three: elevator, aileron, and rudder controls. When my legs would go numb, I would set my throttle and push with my left hand on the knee that needed to move the rudder in the desired direction. I still deal with numbness in my right leg. I occasionally injure it without noticing. That sometimes results in bleeding which then brings it to my attention that I have injured it somehow. I have full use of the leg.

◆ ◆ ◆

### Saving Ambushed Troops

A mission that stands out as having taxed my skill and cunning involved a heroic US Army enlisted man. He was a radio operator who had seen his officer and NCO killed in an ambush. He was desperately calling for help as I happened to be flying nearby. I responded to his call and turned towards his location a few miles away. I then called the command center and ordered fighters to be sent to a rendezvous point for turnover to me.

I then directed my full attention to the very young sounding soldier. He obviously needed to be calmed and know he had support on the way. I helped him gather the survivors of the ambush and establish a parameter that could be defended. Some Army Cobra helicopters had also heard his call for help and responded. They checked in with me. They were just what was needed at that point. Heavily armed Cobras were great to work with. They were small helicopters with two-man crews which were very effective in these situations. They maneuvered in close and kept the enemy pinned down until the bomb-carrying fighters arrived. They stayed on scene and together we worked in coordination with the fighters to gain control of the situation.

Our combined efforts allowed the rescue of the surviving ground troops by troop-carrying helicopters. The young enlisted man pulled it together and did an outstanding job of salvaging what initially looked like an impossible situation. He was probably 18 or 19 years old and managed to save what remained of his unit with the support of coordinated Army and Air Force air power. It was a great team effort.

◆◆◆

*LRRP Team in Trouble*

One of the most amazingly skilled and heroic exhibitions of combat flying I witnessed involved a similar encounter with an army unit in trouble. This mission required creativity under extreme stress with limited resources. Long Range Reconnaissance Patrol (LRRP) teams were small groups of about six to eight highly trained soldiers who were inserted into enemy areas to do reconnaissance, assist in rescuing downed pilots, collect intelligence, and harass enemy units.

They depended on stealth and maneuver. They operated in radio silence except for brief periodic transmissions at specific times.

I happened to be flying over one of the areas where they were operating when I received a call for help from one of these teams. They had been discovered by the enemy and one member had been wounded in a brief firefight. They were trying to escape in an area of dense triple canopy jungle. They could hear me, but not see me. They were on the move and the enemy was gaining on them. The wounded man requested to be left behind so the rest of the team would have a better chance to escape. The other team members refused to abandon him.

The LRRP team leader asked for help. I was his only link to the outside world. The team was in desperate need of extraction. They asked that I direct them to a pickup area and obtain available air support for their escape. I radioed the command center and ordered up some fighters and an LRRP team extraction helicopter. The LRRP team vectored me toward them using my engine sound. The jungle prevented visual tracking. However, I was soon able to locate their pursuers from the muzzle flashes of their weapons. I was then able to locate the LRRP team through signal mirror flashes. A flight of F-4s was being vectored to me. They checked in with me. I directed them to the target area, gave them the requisite target area briefing, and set them up on 20-millimeter cannon (6,000 rounds per minute) strafing runs.

Their strafing of the pursuers bought time for me to find a clearing somewhere in that triple canopy jungle suitable as a landing zone for the rescue extraction. There wasn't much to choose from close enough to the team and safe enough for the helicopter. Marginally suitable would have to suffice! The rescue chopper and two Cobra attack choppers checked in with me. Working with the chopper pilots, one small clearing surrounded by very tall trees was chosen. I steered the team toward that clearing.

The gap between them and the enemy was decreasing. I was very busy! I was directing the ground troops, the rescue chopper, the

Cobras, and the strafing F-4 fighters. Two more flights of F-4s were vectored to me, which added to the mix. Mid-air collision potential was a real concern! The helicopters were used to working together, so I asked them to coordinate their activities on their own radio channel in a designated area and altitude block. I asked that they advise me of any change of location or altitude and that they monitor my fighter strike frequency.

The LRRP team's pursuers were separating into two groups. That made it even harder to target them, defend the pickup area, and keep control of the aerial circus. I got the fighters organized and assigned to altitudes and orbit points. As the battle got closer to the pickup point, coordination of the strafing fighters and the Cobras was critical. I devised a visual coordination and separation plan for them. I was concerned about the fuel situation of the strafing fighters as they were working low level and maneuvering such that their fuel burn rate was high. I advised them I would release them soon so they could make it to a tanker being vectored towards them.

I then turned my attention to the two flights of orbiting standby fighters for the actual extraction. I brought the helicopters back onto my frequency and briefed everyone on my plan. I arranged visual coordination between the two four-plane flights of orbiting fighters. I asked everyone to visualize playing Tic-Tac-Toe, with the pickup spot being the center square. I told the fighters I would bring them down from their orbit points as the team began to enter the pick-up square. I wanted them to set themselves up to run passes on the edges of the square on cardinal headings (North, East, South, and West), using napalm when I gave the order. I would coordinate the low passes of each flight.

Timing was essential as the fighters had to avoid colliding with each other as they crossed paths entering and exiting the target area. They also had to communicate clearly as the rescue helicopter was going to be setting up over the square to get to the ground for the rescue. They also had to avoid firing on or hitting the Cobras who were working over the enemy so that the LRRP team could get into the square unmolested. Altitude restrictions alleviated most of the risk other than friendly fire.

It was a real test of skills for all involved. A chance to be Thunderbirds! Every fighter pilot's dream. And a chance for the Cobras to really show their stuff too! The LRRP team was getting close to the square. I directed the strafing pilots to let everything go (napalm and cannons were all they had left) on one last run and fly away from the area. I directed them to climb out on an assigned heading for their trip home or to the refueling tanker aircraft if they deemed it necessary to tank. I then had the standby fighters descend from their orbit point to substitute for their fuel hungry friends.

Their Tic-Tac-Toe napalm runs kept the enemy at bay and created a smoke screen. The Cobras filled any voids that developed while avoiding separation issues with the fighters crossing back and forth. The rescue helicopter pilot had to be able to descend through the turbulence and reduced visibility created by the napalm. I was very concerned about the possibility of a disaster should the helicopter strike a tree on the way down or up, get disoriented in the smoke and turbulence, or not be able to generate the lift to come almost straight back up through this chimney-like opening in the dense jungle.

The Army rescue chopper pilot performed the most heroic feat of combat aviation I have seen. He did not hesitate. He sized up the situation quickly, and courageously proceeded to do what had to be done to save the LRRP team. His communications with me and the team were clear, concise, and indicative of a superb professional performing at the highest level despite the extreme risks willingly accepted. The LRRP team commander and his men, the fighter pilots, and the chopper pilots and gunners were all outstanding. I was a very lucky FAC to have had them to work with.

All members of the LRRP team were rescued. The wounded man was treated on the chopper which made delivery of him to a medical facility their top priority. He lived to fight another day! I had the best the Army and Air Force had to offer that day.

◆ ◆ ◆

## My Own POWs

It seems ridiculous to say this, but there are lighter moments in war. One of them involved my "capture" of two Vietcong soldiers. They were a part of a unit I had finished leading a fighter attack against. They managed to escape and were running across a large open area like a big Iowa pasture. They would run for a while and hide and then run and hide again. I happened to catch their action out of my peripheral vision. I radioed for helicopter support and swooped down on them when they were in the middle of the large open area. I assumed Army Intelligence might be interested in these guys. As I began to chase them, they threw away their weapons and ran. I doubt they had ever run faster or further. Eventually they stopped, exhausted, and raised their arms in the air and waited. I made a few low passes and circled them, but I was not able to obtain a helicopter to pick them up. I chose not to use any rockets on them and made a low pass alongside them, waved, and returned to base. I hope they made it through the war!

◆ ◆ ◆

## My Day of Glory

Another mission I will always remember and be the most personally proud of, similarly involved a scramble to save troops in big trouble. A company-sized unit had been ambushed at a road intersection in a small city south of Tay Ninh. I had F-100s due in the area for a pre-planned airstrike when I received the Army unit's call for help. I called the command center to delay the F-100 departures and advise the pilots they would be diverted to assist troops in contact with a significantly sized North Vietnamese Army unit.

I proceeded to the area of the ambush. The weather was deteriorating, causing concern about bringing the fighters into the area. I was in contact with the ground commander who briefed me on their situation. His unit of around seventy men had been ambushed on the outskirts of the city. He had moved his troops to a relatively safe area and broken off direct contact with the enemy. But in that process, six of his men got cut off from the main body. The six were isolated in a house near a main road intersection. There had been very heavy fire back and forth between the main army unit and the North Vietnamese unit.

The Army commander stated that the main body of enemy troops had pulled back from the road intersection, no longer a direct threat to the six soldiers. However, an enemy component remained in a house between our soldiers and the road. Our soldiers were in a house furthest away from the road. There was a house between the one they were in and the one the enemy occupied. Neither main force could move toward the site due to opposing fields of fire.

The enemy component appeared to be trying to move to ultimately position themselves next to the house sheltering our troops. An assault on our troops appeared imminent. Our soldiers included wounded who were unable to move. The weather continued to deteriorate.

I called for release of the F-100s. There was one mountain, Nui Ba Den (Black Virgin Mountain), in the vicinity. It is just north of Tay Ninh and was aligned with the road. The mountain peak was about 3,000 feet above surrounding terrain. When the fighters arrived, the ceiling (cloud level) had dropped below their strike minimums. I asked their lead if they could assemble over the mountain (the top of which was above the clouds) and make run-ins on the road's compass heading away from the mountain.

I wanted them repeatedly coming in and out of afterburner, commencing after descending to 800 feet and 60 seconds from the mountain, for three 15 second intervals at 250 knots. I figured the noise from the afterburners would intimidate the enemy troops enough at minimum risk to the fighter pilots who would be protected by the clouds. At least some of the enemy would seek cover. That would diminish the fire I would take on my run-in below the clouds.

The clouds were at about 500 feet and it was raining. I had a mix of high explosive and marking rockets that I intended to use in attacking the enemy houses. To be effective, I had to get those rockets into each house through the windows. My plan was to run in just below the 500-foot ceiling and try to take out the enemy soldiers closing in on our troops in one desperate pass.

The Army commander thought the plan was too risky. But he agreed my plan was the only hope for his stranded men. I refused to abandon those soldiers. I knew I faced long odds, but such is the luck of war. Sometimes you just do what needs to be done even when you know the odds are against you. You become a victim of circumstances. You do what you gotta do!

The fighters agreed to be my noise-making diversion. On my command they started to make their runs, generating noise with their afterburners that I hoped would create confusion among the North Vietnamese troops and take attention away from me.

I thought of my wife and family and that I might never see them again. I then started my run. A calmness settled on me and things seemed to happen almost in slow motion. It was not the first time I had experienced that feeling of slow motion in bad situations.

There were mortars exploding below me. I told the Army commander to cease fire. He reported that everything I was seeing was being fired by the enemy. They were throwing everything they had at me, even mortars. Looking through my windscreen it seemed like there were at least 20 cigarette butts coming up at me. Those little red things were tracer rounds. The tracers looked like fixed objects because they were coming straight at me. If they don't appear to be moving, it is because they are headed right for you. I knew I was exposed and maneuvered as much as I could while still maintaining a line of attack on the houses. I ignored the tracers and concentrated on putting those rockets in the windows of the houses. If I sustained a mortal wound, I would try to stay conscious long enough to fly into the enemy-held house closest to our men.

As I began to close on the houses, I was descending which took me out of the line of sight of several enemy positions firing at me.

To my amazement, I got all my rockets through the windows in the two enemy occupied houses. I banked hard left, then hard right and dropped almost to the surface of the highway. By doing that I took advantage of the buildings along the highway to screen me from the enemy's fire as I made my escape. The enemy soldiers in the houses were killed. Our guys were rescued, and I lived to fight another day. The airplane had only one new hole in it. They don't call me "Lucky" for nothing!!

Later there was talk I would at least get the Silver Star. Eventually I got two Distinguished Flying Crosses. One was for outstanding aerial achievement (my creative use of the F-100s and Nui Ba Den mountain?) and one for heroism. There was no ceremony or explanation—they just showed up in the mail pouch. The "achievement" one showed up first. I wonder if the "heroism" one was in place of a Silver Star. I heard that the Army documentation had been lost/delayed but I would be getting a Silver Star later. Still waiting!

I am often asked what it is like to be in combat. Is it scary? You bet! Heroes are people who act despite the natural fear they feel. I know many and I don't think there are any that didn't feel the fear that went with their actions. Think about it: if there was no fear there would be no heroes! I had excellent training for the role of a combat pilot and leader—in the air. By the time I had my FAC assignment I had been shot at while flying the C-130. But I wasn't trained in ground combat and my fear level was very high when placed in that position at Tay Ninh. But I soon learned what I needed to know and adjusted to that environment.

The training for aerial combat was excellent. FACs were a primary target of the enemy. Minor issues can rattle me just like anyone, but in combat a calm would come over me and I became absorbed in the mission. I knew I could take a hit at any time, and there were lots of close calls. But I knew the fighter pilots and the ground troops needed steady guidance. I couldn't let my fears show in my voice or actions. I had to do what I was trained to do. I owed it to them and to myself.

In-flight emergencies in non-combat situations seemed to plague me. I encounter several while flying solo in pilot training. I was able to respond calmly and earned the nickname "Lucky." While writing this, I have been working with a friend from my lobbying days, Wayne Ford. Wayne is a former legislator and a leader in the African American community. Over lunch recently someone mentioned my having been a pilot in Vietnam. He looked at me and exclaimed, "That explains it!"

I asked, "Explains what?"

"We always wondered at the legislature how you remained so calm when there was a legislative battle going and everyone else was riled up. You calmly went about doing your job."

I also had a philosophy: people look at death as though they will be their own best mourner. If it happens in aerial combat it will be swift, and you may not even know what hit you. So why worry about it? I worried about the impact on my wife and family, but not about me. In combat I worried about providing the best support possible to our people on the ground and getting my fighter pilots home or rescued safely.

The heroism of our soldiers fighting on the ground demands mention. There death is up close and personal. It is often not so immediate. Cradling a dying buddy on the field of battle has to be agonizing. It is no wonder that some of those emotional scars can last forever. I have great respect for them!

Also, note that in the air and on the ground, it is my observation that combat is an exhausting experience. I have never been a good sleeper, except in Vietnam. I think I was exhausted most of the time! I think the adrenaline was pumping during battle even though I didn't realize it at the time.

◆◆◆

*Reassignment and Replacement*

All good things come to an end. When I was chosen as a FAC it was supposedly because of my experience and exposure to combat in C-130 special operations and in Vietnam. I had become an Aircraft

142

Commander ahead of my contemporaries. My skill and cunning were supposedly rewarded by my being specially selected to become a FAC.

I got the word that once again a replacement was on the way to Tay Ninh. I was excited. I was exhausted from the routine that involved flying several hours a day and then fighting on the ground every other night for a couple of hours. I was concerned about keeping focused. Mental lapses can be fatal in combat—especially in an airplane.

My excitement waned when I found out my replacement was right out of pilot training. He was being sent out as a FAC from initial pilot training as his first duty assignment. NO WAY! I couldn't in good conscience just introduce him, fly him around our area of responsibility a couple of times, and leave. I spent an extra two weeks teaching him everything I could think of to keep him alive. He was becoming frustrated with me. He was an excellent pilot, having graduated pilot training as first in his class.

But he didn't know about flying into and out of short and slick runways with minimum fuel remaining during a rain storm or what it was like to be the target of enemy gunners or have one of your fighter planes in trouble or how to respond to calls for help from troops in trouble. I tried to get him up to speed on these kinds of eventualities so I could leave with a clear conscience.

When I thought he was ready, I found an easy mission on the roster and I told him he was ready to go into battle on his own. He was immensely grateful and excited. We planned the mission together the night before, and I helped him the next morning. FACs at Tay Ninh City flew from a short PSP strip at a Special Forces camp. PSP is a system of interlocking perforated steel planks. It is very slick when wet. In that climate it was wet and slippery a lot!

I helped with the pre-flight inspections, helped him strap into the plane, and watched him takeoff. I got into the jeep, lit a nervous cigarette and headed back to the Villa. I was walking towards my quarters when a man from the radio room came running towards me.

He told me my man had been shot down. He said rescue choppers were on their way.

We hurried back to the radio operations room. The duty operator told us choppers were arriving on scene. He said it did not look good. The plane had impacted a building and exploded. The pilot was presumed to have been in the plane at impact. We feared the worst. The chopper was lowering a man to the scene. Soon the helicopter pilot came on the radio and announced the pilot had been found alive but badly burned. He reported that the plane had crashed into a communal outhouse. The impact tore the pilot from his seat and propelled him into a trench full of you-know-what up to his nose. He was barely conscious and was badly burned about his face and ears. And he smelled very bad! They said they were flying him to Saigon where he would be airlifted to the burn center in Japan.

About a year after my return from Vietnam I was in Frankfurt, Germany, waiting for approval of my flight plan. I was back in the C-130 business. The Germans processed filed flight plans at a large counter. They paged pilots as the filing process was completed. I heard them page my young pupil from Tay Ninh. I walked up behind him wondering if it was the same man. It had to be: he had badly burned ears and it looked like his scalp was very scarred. I held my nose with one hand and tapped him on the shoulder with the other. He turned and I asked him if they had gotten all the ---- cleaned off yet! He recognized me, gave me a hug, and we laughed together. He said he hoped he would run into me again someday. He also said he hoped what happened would be our little secret. His squadron mates all thought he was a real war hero! I don't know where he is today, but his secret is secure with me. And he is indeed a genuine war hero in my opinion!

Eventually I was replaced at Tay Ninh by a young man with great qualifications like my first replacement, but also lacking experience. Jim Cooper and I paid even more attention getting him tuned up and ready to go. He blossomed into an excellent FAC. He was luckier than my first replacement! Jim, by the way, spent most of his tour at Tay

Ninh. We went from the days when it was just Jim and me to, I think, five FACs after I left. He was a good boss and married to a Louisville lady too! As the boss he had a lot of responsibilities, some very unpleasant. There was a lot to like about Jim Cooper!

We were hit the last night I was in Tay Ninh. I no longer had a ground combat role. When the attack started, I just went back to bed.

I left Tay Ninh for Phan Rang, where I served as an instructor pilot training new FACs. A few days after that, my roommate at Tay Ninh, Dale Dickens, was killed. Dale was one of the best men I have known. He was a little older, out ranked me as a Major, and was a great roommate. He was devoted to his wife and children. He also had a strong religious faith and never cursed, smoked, or drank. He was a good off-set to me!

I wrote "the letter" to his widow. She wrote the most beautiful letter back to me. It was grounded in their faith, and I treasured it. Somehow, I lost it in Vietnam. I finally found it fifty years later going through some old documents while writing this book. It still brings tears to my eyes!

*19 November 1968*

*Dear Captain Luchtel,*

*I am so glad you wrote to me. It means so much to receive a letter from someone who was with my husband at Tay Ninh.*

*I was extremely shocked to hear of Dale's death. I never doubted that he would return in January. I was so in love with him; I could never imagine living without him.*

*All my memories of him are happy ones. He was a joy to live with – a wonderful example for our three sons – and for me. I admired and respected him above all others I've known.*

145

*I remember that Dale wrote that one of the FAC's was leaving Tay Ninh. I hope that Phan Rang is a better assignment for you.*

*Dale seemed to think he had made the right choice about getting a flying job and therefore, I do not regret his decision. I do not try to understand his death. I do find some comfort in knowing he died in the service of our Country.*

*I sincerely appreciate your thoughtfulness and sympathy. My prayers will be for your safe return to your family.*

*Sincerely,*
*Louise Dickens.*

When I got home from Vietnam, I tried to connect with her. I had never met her, but Dale had told me they were from a town in southeast Missouri where she was living while he was in Vietnam. I found one of Dale's cousins in the area who told me the family wanted me to stay away.

I later heard that Dale's widow did not think the remains returned to her were Dale's. I eventually found an address for her and established contact with her. We corresponded for a while. She did not want me to call or visit. I told her all the details about Dale's time with me and how we lived. She asked me if I thought it was his body that had been returned. I told her I was quite certain it was. I also told her that when the boys got older, I would be happy to tell them about their dad and how much he loved them and her. The offer still stands. Not the first time a good family has suffered greatly from the consequences of war. I hesitated to include her letter. I decided to include it in case Louise, one of Dale's sons, or other relatives would see it and contact me. Dale Dickens was a truly great man—they should know why I say that!

# 10

# Combat Instructor/Test Pilot

PHAN RANG AIR Base was a very nicely located base. The facilities had changed for the better since I had passed through the school as a new FAC. There were beautiful beaches nearby. It was a very scenic area along the coast and south of the major air base in the area, Cam Ranh Bay. It was a real base with an officer's club and motel-like quarters with air conditioning. And it flew the American Flag! I really grew to miss seeing those stars and stripes while I was in Tay Ninh. I was in Hog Heaven. It would have been a great place to buy some undeveloped beachfront property, but I figured I would have had to go to Moscow to find financing and title insurance!

I had less interaction with the local Vietnamese population. I rarely went into the city, but my general observation was that these were good people like in Tay Ninh. I did have a friendship with the local police chief and his wife. She spoke French and we would sometimes work together to iron out difficulties that occurred involving base personnel and Vietnamese employees. I attributed most of the problems to the differences in cultures and language. Her husband was a good man and appreciated solving problems, not exacerbating them. I think of them and hope they didn't suffer too much from the ensuing debacle. The communists didn't have much mercy for people who had held positions of responsibility.

I was assigned to an Air Force detachment made up of FACs who had also survived in very hostile environments. Our mission was to give advanced training to pilots who had been through the FAC training program at Hurlburt Field. We trained them on the latest techniques and situations they could expect to encounter. We taught a kind of this-is-for-real combat survival curriculum! The unit was known as FAC-U or Forward Air Controller University.

Those of us who flew the O-1 emphasized the fundamentals of flying a tail-dragging light airplane in combat to the new O-1 pilots. "Tail-draggers" are aircraft with a wheel at the tail end of the aircraft. It is an obsolete aircraft design and unfamiliar to most Air Force pilots. They are tricky to fly and require special training. Others with O-2 experience trained the new O-2 pilots. Most of the O-1 instructors were deemed qualified to fly both the O-1 and the O-2. O-2 instructor pilots, while initially qualified in the O-1, did not fly them.

We strove to teach both groups the combat tactics that would afford them the best opportunity to perform their missions and survive. The training involved academic training in the operation and maintenance of the aircraft, the command and control communications systems, the responsibilities of the FAC, the necessity of intimate familiarity with the terrain and expected activity in their areas of responsibility, and the enemy tactics they could expect to encounter.

We also provided ground school classes for each aircraft. I taught a class on operation of the aircraft with special attention to emergency procedures and engine issues.

This work with our students was an awesome responsibility. Our instructor cadre was dedicated to getting them to their highest achievable level in order that they might give the best possible support to the troops dependent upon them.

Our students were an interesting lot too! They had outstanding records and it was still considered an honor to be selected for FAC duty. We had New Zealanders as well as Air Force and Air National

Guard pilots as student FACs. We also had some Nationalist Chinese and Korean students. The Chinese were not deployed in Vietnam and only received familiarization training. The Koreans were good pilots and did well in the program. They deployed in support of their Korean infantry units that were fighting along with us in Vietnam.

We bonded with our students and worried about teaching them everything we could think of that would give them an edge on survival. They would need everything we could teach them. There was a documentary film on television a few years ago that focused on the role of the FAC in Vietnam. The title of the documentary: "Suicide Mission."

Language was an issue with the Chinese and Koreans. They were good pilots, but sometimes the language problems were significant. Our squadron commander happened to be the son of Chinese immigrants. When we first got a small group of Nationalist Chinese students, he called me into his office. "Lucky, I am assigning you to be the lead instructor for this group. You are to personally instruct their senior officer. I am depending on you to keep the guy from killing himself on my watch!"

"An easy promise to keep, Colonel. After all, I will have a vested interest in his flying, since I will be sitting right behind him on all his flights! Not to worry, Sir!"

Instructors flew in the back seat of the tandem two-seat airplane. We couldn't see much of the instrument panel. We could only see basic flight instruments in the back seat. Shortly after a take-off with my Chinese student, we had a problem. He reacted correctly, or so it seemed to me. I couldn't see the instruments and couldn't understand what he was trying to tell me. I advised the control tower we were declaring an emergency and needed to stay in the traffic pattern with clearance for an immediate emergency landing. That generated questions from the tower about the nature of the emergency and the requirement for crash rescue assistance. I explained that I had no idea what the problem was except the engine was running rough. The student flew a tight close-in pattern and made a good safe landing. He probably had as much or more tail-dragger flight time than I had.

◆◆◆

## The Rowdy Tenants

We were "tenants" on the base which was "owned" by the 35th Tactical Fighter Wing. An Australian Canberra (B57 to us) squadron and a Colorado Air National Guard F-100 Squadron were also tenants. We formed great friendships with the Aussie and Colorado pilots! We each had a single-floor, motel-like barracks building which had a large center area which, guess what, the pilots converted to a bar. Surprise, surprise! There was competition amongst the three groups about who had the nicest looking and best stocked bar. We also competed over who could beg, borrow, or steal the most steaks from the Navy. The Navy always had the best steaks! It was a matter of finding them. And we each had jeeps stolen from the Army that we kept in good condition. We were a wild bunch of outlaws when we all got together!

The Aussies were beyond a doubt the best partiers. They really knew how to make the best out of anything that involved the use of consumable alcohol. We had some real wild times just doing goofy things to and with each other. More than once I would wake up their passed-out Wing Commander in our bar and drive him home on my way to the flight line early in the morning.

We would occasionally get a bit rowdy. That would sometimes lead to flight suit fights! We would end up tearing the flight suits off the members of the other two groups. My wife didn't believe grown men would engage in something that goofy. I showed her pictorial evidence of just how goofy we really were. One picture of me at the end of an evening has me in my undershorts and flight boots wearing the remnant of a flight suit, the waist band. In the picture it looks like a belt.

◆◆◆

## *Christmas with the Aussies*

We spent the Christmas of 1968 with the Aussies. There was an airline crew that had landed at Phan Rang for some reason and were stranded Christmas Eve. Somehow the flight attendants ended up at the Aussie quarters. The Aussies threw a big party and invited the pilots from FACU and the Colorado Air National Guard. The flight attendants were the highlight of the party. They were very personable and attractive. They were also very married and exceptionally adept at fending off lonely warriors. Eventually everyone relaxed, and we had as merry a Christmas as possible under the circumstances.

◆ ◆ ◆

## *The Tacos of New Mexico*

One of my students was a Taco—a member of the New Mexico Air Guard, call-sign "Taco." Instead of flying the F-100 in Vietnam, Wilson Patrick (Pat) Hurley was to be a FAC. He was a Major and a great fellow. He was born April 11, 1924. Despite the age difference of nearly 17 years, he became a good friend. He also was a friend of my good friend and pilot training classmate, Mike Adams, to whom you were introduced earlier. Mike, you will recall, was flying the F-100 in Vietnam. Pat and his father were both West Point graduates. His father had been a Deputy Secretary of War during World War II.

Pat also was an artist. While enjoying a beer with him one evening, he offered to do a sketch of me. I thanked him for the offer, but suggested I was good for one more beer and then to bed. When I got back to the states, I learned from my art collecting uncle that Pat was a very famous southwestern artist. He had recently sold a painting for $50,000. I think this was in 1969. Pat and I stayed in touch for several years. He gave me a print of a painting he did of a space shuttle launch which I display in my office. Pat had studios in Taos and Albuquerque. He passed away from ALS on August 29, 2008.

You will recall that my close friend Mike Adams was killed in

Laos. I had two other friends in the New Mexico Guard who were killed in Vietnam, Major Bobby Neld and Lt. Mitch Lane. All three were flying the F-100.

After completing his tour, Pat did a commissioned painting named "Missing Man Formation," honoring Bobby, Mike, and Mitch. Pat was not allowed to make prints, or he would have given me one. I understand it is displayed at the New Mexico Air Guard Wing Headquarters in Albuquerque. One of these days I will call down there and ascertain its exact location. We go through Albuquerque on our way to and from San Diego every other trip or so. I hope to stop and see that painting sometime.

While instructing, we were still operating in combat conditions and participated in combat operations beyond our instructional role when called upon. It was good experience for our students when we got a call for assistance.

One of our FAC aircraft was shot down while I was there. The instructor and student were rescued. They were flying our newest FAC aircraft, the OV-10, which had ejection seats. They successfully ejected and were located and rescued after an hour or so on the ground. I am sure it seemed like years to them! It was getting dark when we got them picked up. We put up three or four FACU birds to search for them. It is a wonder we didn't have a mid-air.

◆◆◆

## A Real Thunderbird

One of the most challenging students I instructed had recently been a Thunderbird pilot. Obviously, he was an outstanding pilot, or he would not have been flying with the world-famous Thunderbird Team. But there is a world of difference in flying a T-38 jet and a little, light, tail-dragging O-1 Cessna FAC bird! The O-1 is real stick and rudder flying where a gust of wind can be significant. Instructors had flight controls in the back seat which we could use to demonstrate maneuvers to our students or assume control when necessary.

My Thunderbird was sure he knew more about flying than God.

Also, he was a Major and I was a lowly Captain. I couldn't get him to follow my instructions on landings. I gave up nagging him on his landing deficiencies for a couple of days as we worked on other critical skills on which he was making great progress. I then asked if he wanted to work on his landings. He replied that he did. He said that he thought he had it all figured out now.

We returned to the base. He was doing good when suddenly we picked up a crosswind and he ignored my coaching on how to handle it. He apparently had a better idea. He took us into an almost unrecoverable situation. I yelled, "MY AIRPLANE—GET OFF THE CONTROLS!!" I was able to get the plane back under control a few feet above the ground and made a safe landing. I taxied the plane from the back seat in silence except for my radio calls to and from the control tower. We parked. I got out and looked at him. "Do you know how damned close that was, Sir?!"

He could tell I was very unhappy with him. He was crestfallen. He looked at me. "I apologize, Lucky! I have been a jerk. You have my full attention now!" He turned out great once he opened himself up to instruction. We finished his training as good friends.

◆ ◆ ◆

*Ejections*

I never ejected, but I have many friends who have. I have participated in rescues of pilots who ejected in combat. Unfortunately, I have seen an unsuccessful one.

A successful one occurred immediately following an air strike I was controlling near Tay Ninh as discussed above.

In Texas I had a friend eject at low altitude who didn't get out of the ejection seat. He impacted in swampy ground still in the seat with his parachute undeployed. We were trained to try to manually "beat the seat." The seats had a belt mechanism that automatically snapped tight upon ejection to expel the pilot from the seat as a part of the ejection sequence. When ejection seats were first used, it was learned that some pilots literally got a death grip on the seat. We were trained to try to "beat the system" by manually acting to ensure seat separation without waiting to be expelled by the belt system. I don't think it was possible to be faster than the belt when it was working. If it wasn't, we would beat the seat manually and be on our way anyway. When my friend hit the swampy ground, he was still trying to do this. When he succeeded, he pushed out of the seat and promptly fell flat on his face. Both ankles, which extended beyond the protection of the seat frame, had fractured on impact. Other than that, he escaped injury!

I also saw the successful results of one in Germany. The weather was terrible, but I had managed to land. While I was walking from my plane to base operations at Ramstein, I saw a pilot descending out of the snowy low ceiling in his parachute. I think he may have run out of fuel or the weather had gotten so bad he couldn't land.

I was involved in a tragic ejection incident at Phan Rang. I received a call for assistance from a flight of F-100s returning from a strike mission. I set up a rendezvous with them over a safe area as they were approaching the base. One of the four aircraft had sustained battle damage and was losing its hydraulic systems. Flight control was becoming tenuous. His flight leader and I discussed the situation and agreed he should not try to land at the base. It was too risky to the pilot and to the base itself should control be lost at the last minute. The other three pilots concurred, including the one with the damage. I went down to near ground level to scout for any enemy presence and found none. The vegetation was thin and more like small bushes than trees. I knew it would be an ideal place for an ejection.

The flight leader read the ejection check list as I was climbing back towards them. Everything was set up perfectly in terms of weather conditions, air speed, and flight angle. It was a textbook ejection. I had a rescue chopper on the way. I watched the F-100 pilot safely come out of the plane. I then did a steep dive down and away. When I looked back his chute had deployed. Everything looked perfect. I was busy on the radio to the rescue chopper guiding them to the location where he would touch down. I also vectored the fully armed and fueled backup fighters on their way to provide cover for the pickup if necessary. The chopper was several minutes away. I dropped down to about fifty feet above ground level looking to ensure the area was still clear of any enemy activity.

I did not watch him land. I saw him on the ground right after he landed. I refined my guidance to the rescue chopper and fighters. They gave me an update on their arrival time. I checked-in and coordinated with the incoming fighters to arrange an orbit point where they could hold until needed. I was also making calls to the downed pilot on his survival radio channel. I noticed as I passed over him, he seemed not to have moved. I could not raise him on the radio. He was still in his chute. I also noticed his ejection seat was not very far away.

That was unusual. I dropped down nearly to ground level and flew right over him. I made more radio calls. No response, no movement. I could see his radio on the ground near him. Also, there was no emergency beacon emitting a radio signal either. It should have activated when he separated from the ejection seat. I advised the chopper he was not responsive and was exposed in an open area. I assumed he must have been knocked out upon landing. I continued to ensure there was no enemy presence. I secured my cockpit for a landing in the unlikely event it became necessary to land and protect him pending rescue chopper arrival.

The chopper arrived. A para-rescue specialist was lowered down to the pilot. There was a period of silence as we waited to hear what was wrong. The rescuer reported that the pilot was dead. He surmised that the ejection seat had hit him on the head. I assume the seat hit him while they were in the air as the seat should have accelerated past him on the way down. The wind was calm, and he wasn't very far from where the seat impacted.

I encountered another similar situation while at Phan Rang that ended successfully. I had no direct involvement, other than to back up the resources already supporting the ejection and subsequent rescue of the pilot.

### ◆◆◆
## *Lucky the Test Pilot*

While I was at Phan Rang, a request was made for volunteers for a classified flight test program. It was to be flown at the base as a part-time duty. I was one of two volunteers selected (it wasn't too clear what we were to do, so we may have been the only two dumb enough to volunteer).

I had always wanted to be a test pilot. I heard about a test program offered after I had graduated from pilot training. It was of short duration before I was to report to my next duty station: SERE School. I eagerly applied and was one of about eight that were selected. After reporting to the desert test site, we learned we were going to test what is now known as a parasail.

Understand, I am afraid of heights. I know that sounds crazy, but it is not that unusual among pilots. If we are strapped in or enclosed in something that flies or glides, we seem to be just fine. But I wasn't yet convinced that would include a parachute harness. Fortunately, it did. The Air Force was experiencing high injury rates from ejections due to pilots not making good parachute landings. There is an art to it! Even with a fully deployed parachute you still come down at a fast rate. If you don't "relax" and roll upon ground impact, injury can result. An injured pilot is less likely to successfully escape and evade long enough to be rescued. It was decided there had to be a better way to train pilots about how to land after ejection.

The test required that we be harnessed in a fully deployed parachute spread out on the ground behind us. Then we were attached to a jeep by a very long rope. The rope was secured to our parachute harness at mid-chest level. It had a quick release mechanism that could be used should something go wrong. It was also used to initiate the test while in the air. The jeep would drive away, and we would run behind it. The chute would fill with air and we would be lifted off the ground. The jeep would accelerate. As a result, we would end up in the air a few hundred feet (determined by the length of the tow rope). On command we would release the rope which would initiate our descent to the desert.

We had Army paratroopers training us on how to land and roll. They had bullhorns to use to communicate to us if they thought we were doing something wrong during our descents. The main lesson for the first drop was to look only at the horizon and never look down. We were told if we looked down, we would likely freeze up and not make a good landing. Well, guess what! I remember my first drop. I just had to look down. It was just too interesting to resist. Wow, the ground was really coming up fast! I tensed up and hit like a load of bricks. I thought I had broken every bone in my body, including maybe my teeth! Turned out I wasn't really injured at all, but it sure seemed like it at the time.

After getting a real chewing-out by the Army instructors, we were harnessed up again and away we went. This time I became a real student of the horizon and meditated on my land-and-roll impact procedures. Much, much better this time.

By the time we did the last of probably six to eight drops, we were landing and rolling back up to a standing position. Nothing to it. I don't know if the Air Force made use of the program. Beach entrepreneurs certainly have!

Years later I was at Lake Okoboji, Iowa, on my birthday. We were on the beach watching parasailers. The boats would raise them and lower them and eventually let them settle into the water at the end of the ride. My Uncle Marvin said he would pay for my ride if I would do it. I think he was quite sure I wouldn't. He was very surprised when I agreed and took his money. I told the boat crew that I had made parachute landings on land and wanted to see what one was like in the water. I ask that they signal me at the end of the ride at which time I wanted them to take me to max height and release me. They agreed. I came down in the water and was amazed at how deep I went!

The Phan Rang test flights were trickier, but nothing compared to the adventures and achievements of friends who were the "Real

Deal." But I enjoyed this experience and my time as a C-130 Wing Test Pilot. Both were more fun than actual risk.

The Phan Rang project tested a system devised to keep an O-1 engine functioning at reduced capacity in flight under circumstances where it had sustained damage that would normally result in total engine failure. Everything had been bench tested and the engineers were sure it would work in actual flight conditions as they existed in Vietnam. If it didn't, it was possible the system could explode.

I did the first test flight after going through a final detailed pre-flight briefing and inspection with the test team. I think I had to sign my name on about 50 sheets of paper in that process (this process repeated many times is why my signature is basically illegible).

The test protocol was to climb up to 6,000 feet above the base and shut down the engine by cutting off its fuel supply. Then once glide and airspeed criteria were established, a toggle switch on the instrument panel was to be actuated. It would implement the alternate system being tested. I still remember hesitating briefly before throwing the switch the first time. I reviewed my procedures for a quick bail out if an explosion occurred.

Things worked almost as advertised. The airplane didn't have full power and airspeed and my descent rate had to be modified to make an acceptable landing. The system provided power to stay airborne long enough to enable a pilot to avoid having to make a dead stick landing in the middle of hostile territory. After we did a dozen or so test flights, the system was fine-tuned and installed in operational aircraft in Vietnam. The other test pilot and I flew-test flights on each of the first few new installations. Too bad my plane at Tay Ninh didn't have this installed!

◆◆◆

*Phan Rang Duty Officer*

Even though we were a tenant squadron on the 35th TFW base, we pulled our share of base duties. One of those was being the duty officer of the day at Wing Headquarters. I found that rather interesting. You never knew what would come up. Two interesting experiences come to mind.

We were in a monsoon stand-down during one of my duty officer shifts. There was just me and a couple of staff assistants at Wing Headquarters. Nobody else was doing anything as the weather conditions were awful with heavy rain and high gusty winds. Visibility was very limited. The cloud ceilings were low. The insurgents surely had to be suffering! At least they weren't moving around causing trouble.

On my shift, a forecaster in Hawaii called to report we should be experiencing the ending of what had been a three-day weather rage. Not long after that, some genius in Seventh Air Force HQ in Hawaii decided it would be a brilliant idea to have a FAC do a recon flight in the Phan Rang area and report back on existing conditions! My duty phone rang, and the order was given. I laughed and told them they were crazy. They also didn't have a sense of humor. The more I resisted, the more insistent they got. I gave them our existing conditions and told them it would be impossible to launch a FAC aircraft. They insisted that in two hours it would be okay, and I better see to it that a FAC was launched.

I called our squadron and ordered up a ground crew to prepare an O-1 for take-off in two hours. They protested mightily. They were warm and dry. It was still raining heavily, and it was very windy. I related my experience with Seventh Air Force. They acquiesced. Who was going to fly? I said I would, unless someone else wanted to do it. They offered to deliver my flight suit and gear to Wing HQ.

At the appointed time I called Seventh Air Force HQ. I reported our conditions, as somewhat eased, but still not safe for launch. They were certain conditions would be rapidly improving. They insisted I find an instructor pilot and launch him. I told him they were speaking to him and he was not recommending flight. "GO!" they said.

"Yes, Sir!" I said. It's a good thing they couldn't see my one-finger salute.

I changed into flight gear and was taken out to the plane which the soaked ground crew had ready. They told me as soon as I got out of the revetment area, I would be subject to out-of-limit wind gusts. I said I understood that. I told the ground crew they were to stay clear of the aircraft no matter what. I would be solely responsible. I didn't want anyone injured. I got the plane started and the crew untied the plane and removed the wheel chocks. I began to taxi. As soon as I got into the open area, a gust blew me into a revetment. I shut the engine down and the damage was minimal. We got the plane back into our revetment and tied it down and put in the wheel chocks. I returned to the headquarters building duty office and made my report. They were not happy in Hawaii. Guess who didn't care!

◆ ◆ ◆

## Spy Catcher

I spent a lot of time with the intelligence folks at Phan Rang. They had a great photo lab. I was given twenty-four hour a day access to it. I have always been interested in photography and enjoyed the use of their high-tech equipment to work on my films. That put me in contact with their intel "customers."

I had been told by one of the intel types that there was a security breach involving the identification of some code names and identities, including mine. It was not a huge deal, but it required more frequent changes of code designations and identifications. I was familiar with the security arrangements at the headquarters building and the storage location for that compromised information. On my next duty officer shift I paid attention to the treatment and handling of those materials. I was especially interested in the custodial personnel who would be able to gain access to the information should it be left out unattended. I became suspicious of one of the custodians and left bait on my desk—a copy of a routine letter that I had stamped "TOP SECRET" in big red letters. I announced I was going to lunch. I did not leave the building. I moved to an area where I could see the exposed letter. I caught my spy!

I confronted her. She broke down and confessed that she had been stealing documents. She explained that her husband had been "drafted" into the Viet Cong and was "encouraged" to have his wife provide information. I don't know if that was true or not. I knew she lived alone in humble circumstances, had poor English and French skills, and always seemed stressed. But that would describe most of the Vietnamese custodial staff.

There were lots of people caught in a bind in South Vietnam. They had relatives in the North who could be leveraged, or they had relatives, like she said she had, in the South who were under the thumb of the Viet Cong. These were basically unsophisticated people who were susceptible to pressure tactics. She begged me not to have her arrested. I was glad to have discovered the source of the leak, but I wasn't eager to turn her over to the Vietnamese Security people either. I told her I would report her the next morning as absent. Later that afternoon I would announce that I suspected her of stealing classified documents. It was noon, so she would have a good start on escaping to wherever she was delivering the documents. I did report her absence and noted that her work was unsatisfactory anyway. I told only our security people the rest of the story. She was just another victim and I hope she survived the war.

Years later my wife was teaching English-as-a-second-language classes to refugees in Des Moines. As a drill she asked them to tell the class, in English, what they had done before coming to the United States. One lady replied that she shot at airplanes in Vietnam. Patti informed her that her husband was flying those airplanes. The lady quickly ascertained that I was okay. She then said, "We friends now, okay?" She showed up with eggrolls for me at the next meeting.

◆ ◆ ◆

### Last Bunker Hunker

Phan Rang was a relatively safe base. We rarely experienced a ground attack, which had been almost a normal occurrence at Tay Ninh. There was, however, a highly organized raid on the base late one night. The sirens went off, rockets and mortars were exploding, and there was lots of gunfire. The parameter had been breached.

I grabbed my helmet and flak vest, some weapons and ammunition, and ran for the nearest bunker. It was a fair-sized bunker and there were other men there ahead of me. Most were armed like me, except for three chaplains. The three chaplains had never experienced anything like this. They were really shaken. I told them to relax, as we probably wouldn't be attacked in the bunker. What if we were? I explained that some of us would position ourselves at the entryway and be prepared to shoot anyone who tried to get in. At all costs we had to prevent someone from getting in far enough to throw a grenade through the entryway and into the main area of the bunker.

They asked why I thought the bunker wouldn't be attacked. I stated my theory. The communists went after our planes and equipment. Since they didn't have much of either, they placed a high value on the materials of war. We, on the other hand, were into body counts as we placed a high value on human life. They had more people than they could feed. And we had materials of war we didn't really need. It was but another aspect of what I was becoming more convinced was a crazy, but not unnecessary, war!

# 11

# To Be or Not to Be

WHILE AT PHAN Rang I made the decision to resign my commission. My back situation was not getting any better and I knew it was just a matter of time until it was observed by someone in authority or discovered on a flight physical. I had to act while at Phan Rang to avoid getting a service commitment for whatever training school I would be assigned to upon my return home. The Air Force had promised FACs that they would never have to do that mission again. This promise was made because of the danger of FAC duty. The Air Force was prone to giving returning pilots new duty assignments requiring training that, in turn, extended their service commitment. But if you had a termination date established before you finished your Vietnam tour, they could not extend your commitment. I was committed to four years for my Academy schooling plus one additional year incurred for a year of pilot training. I was eligible for separation in July of 1969, as things stood, when I left Vietnam in April of 1969.

Sure enough, a Colonel noticed I needed help getting out of my airplane one day and approached me about it. I tried to shrug it off, but no such luck. He arranged for me to see the Flight Surgeon (Air Force Medical Doctor with specialized training related to flight fitness) the next day. The doctor happened to be a friend. He told me he was not going to ground me unless I wanted to be grounded. I did not. He said I probably would not pass my next flight physical.

While I was at Tay Ninh our airplanes were maintained at Bien Hoa Air Base near Saigon. That afforded the opportunity to experience air conditioning, good showers, and an uninterrupted night's sleep. I met an Air Force lawyer at the Officer's Club bar on one of those trips. Air Force lawyers are known as JAG (Judge Advocate General) Officers. I was exploring the idea of becoming a JAG Officer. I couldn't envision being in the Air Force and not being a pilot. But I was also interested in the law and public policy. He encouraged me to take the law school aptitude tests required for admission to law schools. We met a few more times when I was on the base. He was very helpful and my plan for the future began to take shape.

Skipping ahead, I eventually ended up being a civilian private practice lawyer, not a JAG Officer. A few years after I had been in practice in Des Moines, I went to Washington D.C. on a client matter. On the Chicago to Washington leg of my flight I was seated next to a lady who noticed my Air Force Academy Class Ring. She asked me if I was in the Air Force. I told her I had been a pilot but had gotten out of the service and now practiced law. She told me her husband was a JAG Officer. I told her I only knew a couple of JAG Officers, one whom I had met in Vietnam who had helped me decide to go to law school.

We visited about her husband's Air Force career, and it developed he was the Major General in command of all Air Force JAG Officers. I was impressed! We continued to visit the rest of the flight. As we got close to DC, I gave her my business card. She gave me one of her husband's. I was shocked. It turned out he was my friend from Vietnam!

We were both amazed at the coincidence. She asked if anyone was picking me up at the airport. I told her I was just going to take a cab to my hotel. She told me her husband was picking her up. They would take me to my hotel. She couldn't wait to see her husband's reaction to seeing her with me. It was a lot of fun to watch when he pulled up and saw my smiling face standing at the curb with his wife! We had a great mini-reunion.

# 12

# Return to the Land of the Big BX

THE END OF a tour in Vietnam was always cause for celebration. There were "last-flight jitters" with typical radio calls such as "Ascot 13, SHORT TIMER, on final, final approach for landing." The practice was for squadron mates looking forward to when they made their "final, final" to gather and meet the end-of-tour pilot as he deplaned. A bottle of champagne was tendered and a fire truck appeared to hose down the celebrant. A picture of this event in my honor hangs in my office and inspired the book's cover (you have to strain to see the bottle of champagne in my right hand). I didn't leave the next day, but I left a few days later in April of 1969. I had survived! I considered myself very lucky! The number "13" had been appended to my unit's callsign, "Ascot," which made my radio callsign "Ascot 13." The number 13 was not in use and I thought it fitting for my nickname, "Lucky."

I was surprised by a visit from my good friend, Mike Adams. He celebrated with me, and the next morning, poured me onto my departure plane. He had only a couple more missions scheduled before he would also be heading home. He was looking forward to returning to Albuquerque. We were especially excited about my assignment to Dyess Air Force Base, Abilene, Texas. He agreed he would call me when he got home and settled in. We planned to meet in El Paso and celebrate. He was looking forward to meeting my wife, Patti. She was also excited about meeting him. They had talked several times on the phone when he would call, and I would be off "somewhere."

I was very excited boarding the plane taking me to Seattle via Tokyo! I was not alone. It was an exuberant bunch! And the stewardesses shared our joy. It was a long, but wonderful trip back to what we longingly referred to as the "Land of the Big BX" (Base Exchange, the military department stores located on Air Force bases).

Much has been said of getting home and walking through a civilian airport and getting spat upon by fellow Americans. We were advised to change out of uniform as soon as we could to avoid any incidents. I followed that advice. I personally did not experience any open hostility before I changed in a restroom by my departure gate. But nobody thanked me for my service either!

I do recall being thanked by my Republican United States Senator, Jack Miller of Sioux City. He served in the Army Air Corp in WWII and attained the rank of Lt. Colonel. He was in the Air Force Reserve and ultimately attained the rank of Brigadier General. We met when I was a cadet at the Academy. He later treated me to lunch in the Senate Dining Room on one occasion and took me to meet with some of his colleagues in the Senate Cloakroom. He was interested in my special operations and Vietnam experiences.

We were very well acquainted by the time I was assigned to Vietnam as a FAC. I was comfortable with him. I had always given him honest answers about my perspectives whenever asked. He also asked questions of me that came from President Nixon. In late 1972, I was invited to attend a ceremony at the White House discussed below. President Nixon thanked me for my service and shook my hand.

Other than that, friends welcomed me home of course, but nobody thanked me "for my service" as is commonly done today. Some were awkward at first. Some were opposed to the war. That was fine with me and I didn't take it personally. I wasn't too wild about it myself! I believed it was in our national interest to oppose the spread of communism in Southeast Asia, but I thought our strategy could not succeed in Vietnam. We dominated militarily, but we did not have enough public support for the time it would take to establish a feasible post-war system of governance. I thought it was a war that the circumstances of that era made necessary to deter other communist aggressions. I do think the "domino theory" was valid. A military response to aggression would be required somewhere, sometime.

◆◆◆

*Homecoming!!*

I traveled to Louisville, Kentucky, Patti's hometown. Patti had started working on her Master's Degree in English Literature at the University of Louisville before we married. She was able to take two graduate classes at Middle Tennessee State University in Murfreesboro while I was assigned to Seward AFB. When I went to Vietnam, she moved back to Louisville and rented a house. She finished her Master's at the University of Louisville where she had obtained her Bachelor of Arts Degree with an English Major. Patti's dad had retired, and her parents lived fairly close to her rented house.

Patti's best friend invited us over for dinner the day after my return. It was a fun evening! I had to laugh when Martha served a rice dish! I thought I would never eat rice again after a year in Vietnam, but Martha's rice was excellent! And I enjoy rice to this day, Martha. Thank you!

I felt like a fish out of water after my return. No one around me knew what it had been like over there. I had trouble sleeping, had nightmares when I did sleep, and was very restless. I had some leave I could have taken, but I didn't feel up to returning to Milford. My sister was graduating from college later that spring, but to my regret I wasn't ready for that either. I am very proud of her. She had paid for her college education and graduated in four years with a degree in education.

I was not prepared for my reaction. I expected to live in a bubble of joy and relief. I had experienced periods of high stress in special operations. I had been in combat before this last tour of duty in

Vietnam. I had a few months at FAC-U that were not nearly as stressful as the daily combat grind at Tay Ninh. But I saw death there too. I slept better in Vietnam than I have ever slept in my life, before and since. Life was quite simple: you got up, flew several exhausting stressful hours leading airstrikes, wrote a letter home after dinner, prepared for the next day's strike missions, and went to bed. About every other night at Tay Ninh you would awaken and respond to a ground attack. That became part of the routine too. You survived another day. You would keep on surviving as long as your luck held out. Not much you could do about it. Worrying about it would just reduce your effectiveness.

Friends in Murfreesboro had located a rental property for us. We arrived at our new home late in the day and there were bugs everywhere! A window must have been left open. Our return to Seward was less than glorious. But we were both excited about seeing the few old friends that were still in the area, including Air Force friends at the base.

Our new home was a mile or so away from a railroad track. Patti said I would be startled by every train on that track all night long! I would react but not wake up. But I would wake her up! It was hard for her to get back to sleep before the next train. Other C-130 pilots with Vietnam combat experience were in my training class. The camaraderie we provided each other was very helpful. We helped each other recover.

A recurring nightmare I suffered with was based on ground attacks at Tay Ninh. The Viet Cong or North Vietnamese soldiers were coming over the wall, and we couldn't kill them fast enough. The last time I had that dream they were dressed as American Indians coming over the wall wearing war paint and feathered head bands and shooting arrows. We were cavalry troops fighting them off with rifles. How ridiculous! I woke up laughing and have never had a recurrence of that dream. I was beginning to settle in, but as I would learn later, I was not cured.

◆ ◆ ◆

169

## *C-130 School Again*

The C-130 school was easy duty as I was able to pick up with the C-130 about where I had left off. My instructor, J. D. Kennedy, was from Spirit Lake, Iowa, nine miles from Milford. He had graduated from the USAFA with the Class of 1963, a year ahead of me. We often drove back and forth between Colorado Springs and home. He had a Corvette. I sacrificed and did most of the driving. While at the Academy I had introduced him to his wife, Corinne, a friend I had met through Ruth.

While at Seward the four of us did a lot together. It was a good decompression period for us as a couple.

# 13

# West Texas Here We Come!

WE MADE THE move to Dyess AFB, Texas, upon completion of my training at Seward. We had a dog, a Weimaraner, that we really loved. He was our second Weimaraner. Patti had wanted a Great Dane when we married. When she went to get the Great Dane she had agreed to purchase, the seller jacked up the price. She left in disgust and ended up buying Beauregard, the Weimaraner, instead. He was a great companion for us, especially for Patti when I was gone. On one of my overseas trips Beau was struck by a car and died, despite the attentions of our friend across the street who was a veterinarian.

We found Beauregard II, who lived with us for 13 years. Patti got interested in dog shows and Beau II competed in several in the area during our first assignment at Seward and while I was in Vietnam. While traveling in two cars to Dyess at Abilene, Texas, we stopped one night in Little Rock, Arkansas. It was a beautiful evening and we were walking Beau. We sat by the motel swimming pool and Beau did some exploring. I was watching him as he wandered over towards the pool. He seemed interested in something. The next thing I knew, he just walked into the deep end of the pool. He apparently thought the lit pool was a hard surface of some kind. He sank like a rock, but quickly surfaced. We had to fish him out. That was not easy, as he weighed about 100 pounds and was panicked! Luckily there was another fellow nearby who assisted me. Everyone but Beau thought it was very funny!

We made it to Abilene and checked into the base. We were assigned a house on base, the first time we lived in Air Force housing. It was a nice house and the neighbors turned out to be great. The movers arrived late in the day. Our next-door neighbors, Major Shelley and Marian McConnell, came out to greet us when we showed up with the movers. Shelley was excited when my golf clubs appeared and invited me out to golf the next morning. I don't remember why Shelley wasn't deployed, but we were glad that he wasn't. They became great friends.

The squadron to which I had been assigned was deployed. I didn't have much to do other than get moved in and play golf with Shelly. I learned he was an excellent golfer. No wonder; he had been a major league baseball player with the New York Yankees. He had served in World War II, which interrupted his baseball career. After the war, he went back to the Yankees, where he played a utility role for a few years before being called up for the Korean War. After Korea he decided he would stay in the Air Force until he could retire.

We once again had neighbors who liked Beau, especially the children. Speaking of dogs, aircrews were often referred to as "crew dogs." We settled into Dyess and quickly adjusted to life in base housing. We had a nice house and enjoyed the close-knit little community. With my squadron on deployment, I had little to do other than check in. I read up on squadron regulations and local base procedures. I found a small civilian airfield nearby and checked out in their rental Cessna 150 light aircraft. Patti and I did some touring of the local area by air.

Our Tactical Air Command (TAC) squadron was a tenant unit on a Strategic Air Command (SAC) base. SAC was much different culturally than TAC! TAC was always on the move and involved in operations all over the world. SAC was a more stable existence for the crew dogs, not that they didn't also participate in deployments and serve weeklong standby alert duty in specially constructed isolated alert quarters when home. The command leadership attitudes differed greatly. SAC was much more "military" in terms of adherence to an abundance of rules and regulations. Somewhat to my surprise I found the SAC command elements and squadrons good to work with. They were highly trained professionals with the burden of always being prepared to deliver a nuclear response at a moment's notice.

On July 20, 1969, I took my first Dyess Aircraft Commander flight check (check ride). The squadron advance elements had returned from deployment and it was time for me to assimilate and get to work. My check ride was only the first historic event of the day. It ended (I passed) in time for me to get home to watch the first manned lunar landing and hear Neil Armstrong's report of his history making first step. I think the whole base was glued to their TV sets that afternoon and night.

I was in a kind of limbo state. I had submitted my resignation before I left Vietnam and was theoretically eligible for out-processing at a time of my choosing. I had made it through my flight physical when I got back from Vietnam. I don't think my medical records were completely updated from Vietnam. Nothing was said about my back. The Air Force was short of pilots, especially pilots who could serve as Aircraft Commanders, instructor pilots, and test pilots. It was not long before I was serving in each of those capacities at Dyess.

My squadron commander asked if I would commit for another year, to which I agreed. I wasn't sure what I wanted to do. I was interested in trying to convert to an Air Force lawyer in the Judge Advocate General (JAG) Corp. I still thought my pilot physical-qualification time was about up. I had the symptoms I had in Vietnam, but I didn't mention them during my flight physicals. They were less problematic as a C-130 Aircraft Commander's seat is much more comfortable than an O-1 pilot seat! And I could get up and walk around. I didn't seek treatment. I was still thinking of myself as a career Air Force officer. I was also considering the CIA, but I quickly decided I couldn't subject Patti to that life. She had waited and wondered at home long enough enduring my spook absences! I was not the only one suffering from stress issues.

Another factor in our decision to stay at Dyess for at least another year was Patti had become pregnant! The Air Force was a great place to have a baby. All expenses were covered, and Patti had lots of supportive friends on the base. Kathleen Elizabeth joined us on May 19, 1970, which just happens to be Ho Chi Minh's birthday. If you are wondering, Ho was the communist leader of North Vietnam. Usually his birthday was observed by shelling or attacking any South Vietnamese or allied troops available. So, I was familiar with that date, having been on the receiving end of a couple of those "birthday parties." Kathleen is my Ho Chi Minh revenge! She was also a real bargain: $8.75 hospital bill for the rental TV in Patti's room (I like to tell Kathleen "you get what you pay for!").

◆◆◆

## C-130 Crew Dog Again

I settled into the C-130 routine, which soon involved a lot of travel to interesting places. My special operations experience was noted. It wasn't long before I was flying C-130 combat missions in areas other than Southeast Asia. It was interesting and, compared to the FAC duty, it didn't seem all that dangerous. The operations were in different locations than those done while at Seward, for the most part. There was some overlap, but it was interesting to operate in some other parts of the world.

I also did a solo mission while with the Dyess group which involved going to an area as a tourist to check for a certain kind of activity. In preparation I learned some fundamentals of the local language. Upon arrival in that country, I obtained a room at a small hotel. I then went to the location of interest and had dinner with two other guys who had no idea of my real purpose.

I got a table where I could see the other diners. I noticed three guys I thought I had seen before that day. They seemed to be interested in our group. They were seated so that only one could see me without turning his head. The other two would look away when I was looking in their direction. I could watch them without turning my head. I overheard a comment that made me feel they had tagged me.

It all may have been my imagination, but to be safe, I put money under my plate and asked the fellows I was with to pay my bill for me if I didn't return from the restroom. The restroom provided an exit that couldn't be seen from the dining area. I used it to leave the restaurant and get back to my hotel room. I picked up some supplies along the way and holed up there for the next day. It appeared to me that I had worn out my welcome (usefulness) in that country! The following morning it was non-stop to the airport and let's get out of here! My foray was successful as I had managed to get the needed information.

Over time I had become acquainted with intelligence agents from other countries. It was not all that dangerous, although I was once asked to get the body of another country's agent who had been killed and return it to her home country. We sometimes worked together or in support of each other. To me it was a fascinating group of people. I became used to having different identities, even different nationalities. I saw spooks as playing an important role in keeping the peace.

To this day I have the habit of sitting in bars, restaurants, and the like where I can see the doors and other patrons. I get kidded about it, but it's a habit I share with a friend who had worked for the CIA whom I often see. When we go out, he gets first pick of seats—he's bigger than me!

A Dyess C-130 special operation that I commanded probably remains classified to this day. It is the one of which I am most proud. It was directly controlled from the Pentagon and/or the White House. It involved extracting people in danger in a hostile nation. While we were in route, I received a coded message indicating our embassy in the target nation reported unusual fighter aircraft activity near the pickup area. The message gave me the authority to make my risk assessment and declare a "go" or "no go."

I called the crew together on the flight deck and advised them of this message and the authority granted me. I told them as we got closer, I would get more information, but that I was still in "go" mode. We were still more than an hour out before our low-level entry into the target country's airspace. I thought the fighters were probably just on a training mission and would have used their fuel and landed by the time we arrived.

One of the enlisted men asked me whether there was a contingency plan. I advised that Navy fighters would be launched from a carrier as we got closer to the pickup point. The Navy pilots did not know the full mission, but they were appropriately armed and briefed generally. They would be holding off the target country's coast available for vectoring to our assistance if needed. He looked at me, thought for a moment, and asked whether our "passengers" were already moving to the pickup point and exposed to danger as a result. I told him that they were. He looked at me and said, "Sir, then let's go get 'em." The others cheered. The mission went off perfectly. No hostile action occurred. No Navy fighters were needed. I will always be especially proud of my crew that day!

I was involved in two other covert operations that remain classified. Both required a new identity and one also included a change in nationality. One was not fully implemented, but the other was very successful. Both required a lot of time and had the support of other nations. I think the circumstances continue to require confidentiality. I hate to disappoint, but when writing and considering what could be revealed, I recalled consoling the widow of a CIA Officer who was outed by an irresponsible reporter. He was killed in her presence in front of their house after they returned from a dinner. My experience was that we had people around the world who helped the US at great risk to themselves and their families. I choose to do nothing to increase that risk.

◆ ◆ ◆

## Eagle Claw

One last C-130 story which doesn't directly involve me. I left the service in 1970. You may remember Operation Eagle Claw. It was a very complex attempt to snatch American hostages taken from the American Embassy in Tehran. It involved the use of combined Air Force, Army, Marine, and Navy personnel. The C-130 Mission Commander had been a trainee of mine at Dyess. Hal Lewis and his crew were killed in the desert staging area in Iran. A helicopter struck his 130 while maneuvering during a sandstorm. The C-130s and helicopters traveled great distances to rendezvous in the Iranian desert. The helicopters were to fly to a pickup point in Tehran. Operatives in Tehran were to free the hostages and transport them to the helicopter pickup point, a soccer stadium as I recall. The helicopters were to then transport the hostages to the C-130s which would refuel the helicopters and fly the hostages to freedom. This is an abbreviated and simplified version.

Whoever came up with the KISS (Keep It Simple Stupid) rule knew what he or she was talking about. I think that rule should be applied generally to the planning of any large organization, especially governmental and corporate. Over-complication costs time and money, and in this case, lives! No doubt you can think of your own examples. When there is an attempt to execute overly complicated plans with several possible failure points, the possibility of failure increases almost exponentially.

Another of that excellent young Dyess group, Charlie Holland, became a general and the third of my friends who became Commanders of the Special Operations Command at Hurlburt Field, Florida. I had the privilege of serving with some truly outstanding people. It was those associations (and the free sunglasses) that I really missed when I left the Air Force.

◆ ◆ ◆

## Adventures in Dentistry

When Shelly retired, the McConnell's moved and we had new next-door neighbors. He was a newly-minted dentist. They were younger, and a very nice couple.

Before I left for Vietnam in '68, the dental clinic had insisted I have my four impacted wisdom teeth removed. I had never had a problem with them. They said I should have them removed as a precaution. I resisted and asked, "Are you telling me we don't have any dentists in Vietnam!?"

"Of course we do, Captain. But we are short of oral surgeons. If you have an impacted wisdom tooth problem, you will need an oral surgeon."

"There must be some," I replied.

"Sir, you will always be able to get treatment, but you might have to go to Tokyo for it."

"I'm sorry, but that is not a convincing argument to me! It would probably mean missing three or four days of getting shot at! That's a risk I am more than willing to take!"

"But Sir!"

"No way, not gonna happen!"

I never had any problem with my wisdom teeth in Vietnam. My first awareness of them was at the dentist-neighbor's Christmas party. I suddenly experienced sharp pain in my jaw, which my neighbor diagnosed as a wisdom tooth issue. During the holidays he wasn't very busy and invited me to his office the next day for treatment. He confirmed I had a wisdom tooth that needed to be removed and started the process. He was doing fine. Then it appeared he was encountering problems. He began to sweat and asked if he was hurting me. I told him not to worry, just take a little break and finish. If I needed more Novocain, I would tell him. We proceeded. After three hours in the chair the tooth had been broken up and removed. I thanked him, got my pain meds, and went to the squadron. The squadron commander took one look at me and asked what had happened to me. He said I looked like death warmed over! I told him about the wisdom tooth. I felt okay, but my mouth seemed to be swelling. He sent me home!

I got home and collapsed on the sofa to watch TV. I noticed

discomfort and took my pain medication and got an ice bag. As time went on, more pain and more pain medication. The discomfort turned into agony. I asked Patti to have our dentist neighbor come over as soon as he got home. He seemed shocked at my condition and immediately left for the base hospital pharmacy to get some narcotic pain meds. I was so sick and weak that I spent three days camped out on the living room sofa!

After a few more days, the squadron needed me to fly a few special missions. An Aircraft Commander had been injured or gotten sick. My jaw was beginning to feel good, but it still bothered me. But duty called, and I ended up in another part of the world and flew a couple of those missions with the stranded crew. I knew them (they were from Dyess) and we had a good time working together. On about the third day I woke up to prepare for our usual pre-dawn departure. Everything seemed fine until I went to shave. It was like I had a golf ball in my mouth when I looked in the mirror! I could barely open my mouth! I couldn't even talk. I had to wake a neighbor and have him call the secret number and give them my cancellation code. The crew was stranded again! I had a bad infection and could not fly for a few days. I was seen by a dentist who put a needle in my jaw and sucked out what seemed to me to be a large syringe full of puss. I also got antibiotics and pain medication.

I eventually made it back to Dyess and thought I was fine until I started to notice numb spots on my face. I began to lose feeling in my jaw and was referred by the base dentistry office to a civilian oral surgeon in Fort Worth. He was unable to diagnose my problem. I figured it would go away—it didn't.

While my dental adventure was building, I was applying to law schools, taking the standard Law School Admissions Test (LSAT), and talking to the Personnel Office about the JAG program I was going to enter. We were making moving arrangements. I had good LSAT scores and I was admitted to the University of Denver Law School and Drake Law School (Des Moines, Iowa). I was favoring Denver. It was near the Academy and would allow me to remain more connected to the Air Force. Everything was lining up and I was looking forward to law school. I thought service in the JAG Corp would be interesting. I would be unique in that I would have pilot's wings and medals awarded for combat. I would come out of law school a Major with good prospects for further promotion.

◆ ◆ ◆

## JAG Officer? Not So Fast!

As I was winding down my flying career and getting ready to make my law school move, the base personnel officer called and asked me to come to his office ASAP. I walked in and I could tell he had a problem and I was it! He had found out that congress, in its wisdom, had put an obscure subparagraph somewhere in the authorizing legislation for the JAG program that disqualified service academy graduates. I suppose the thinking was that enough federal dollars were spent on service academy graduates without adding to it by making them lawyers! (As I write, the service academies now have programs that allow a limited number of graduates to go directly to law or medical school upon graduation from their service academy.)

"Okay, so now what do I do?" I asked my friendly personnel officer.

He was embarrassed and upset. "I've looked at other options. There are no good ones that end up with you becoming a JAG Officer." Intelligence agency options came up for discussion, but that would be asking too much of Patti, especially since we had baby Kathleen.

He told me the Air Force considered me a high-value officer. They would give me any assignment I wanted so long as it was non-flying. I could get an advanced degree and teach at the Academy. Also, I could resign my commission and go to law school. They would take me back into the Air Force as a JAG Officer upon graduation from law school. They would even give me a promotion to Major in the process. But I would have to go to law school on my own dollar. HECKUVADEAL!

I went home and broke the news to Patti. We discussed our options. We both favored taking the risk of going to law school without Air Force support. We had built up savings. While I was traveling around the world, I was getting good travel payments. While I was in Vietnam, I could live on about $60 per month. FACs were the rock stars of Vietnam. We couldn't pay for a meal or buy a drink. The Army troops loved us, and the Air Force pilots put their lives in our hands. The little I spent was paid into our room and board kitty at Tay Ninh and Phan Rang. Patti lived frugally too as she worked on completing her Master's Degree at the University of Louisville. I put everything I could into a federal program for Vietnam servicemen that paid 10% interest. When necessary, we enhanced that by dipping into our pre-existing savings to maintain our high level of investment in the 10% program. I think that program was limited to 100% of base service pay. We thought we were in good shape when we left the Air Force.

◆◆◆

## *Wilford Hall, San Antonio, Texas*

My dental issue was also unresolved, and the numbness was becoming more significant. Patti expressed concern about the possible impact on us if it got progressively worse after I was out of the Air Force. Good point! So, I went back to the base dentistry office and asked if there was some other dental specialty that could help me. They decided I should be seen at the oral surgery department at Wilford Hall, the Mayo Clinic of the Air Force, in San Antonio, Texas. Time was of the essence as I was going to be starting law school in late August. They got me an almost immediate appointment. San Antonio is about 240 miles from Abilene, and I drove down a day or so later.

I was awed by the facility that is Wilford Hall. It is huge and staffed with outstanding providers. It even has a golf course adjacent to a wing of the hospital. I found the dental clinic and was soon being examined by the chief oral surgeon, a Colonel. They had the most modern X-ray equipment available, according to the Colonel. He seemed confident he would be able to diagnose my problem. The machine whirred. Films were produced. The Colonel called in two other oral surgeons, also full Colonels. They huddled around my films and arrived at a consensus diagnosis and treatment plan.

I was asked if I had any plans that fall. I told them that I did indeed—I was going to start law school in a month. They told me that was not going to happen. And they wondered why a combat pilot was going to law school anyway. I went through the whole story with them. Another Colonel huddle resulted. They broke from the huddle and asked if I had to go back to Abilene that evening. I told them I did not, and that I had no duties left to perform.

They had a plan. I had osteomyelitis of the jaw resulting from a severe infection that developed following removal of my wisdom tooth. They said that the infection was destroying the surrounding jaw bone and causing nerve damage which produced the numb spots on my face.

The remedy was surgery that would remove the infected part of the jaw bone. They said this would be done as oral surgery from inside my mouth. But before they could do the surgery the infection had to be terminated and the necrotic bone limits defined for removal. Prior to surgery I would need massive antibiotic infusions intravenously in the hospital.

They expected they would not be able to do the surgery for two to three weeks and that a week recovery period would probably be necessary. If everything went well, I should be able to be back in Abilene in time to move to Denver or Des Moines for law school. The Colonel would call my commander and get it cleared. I agreed to the plan and was told to go to the Base Exchange and buy whatever I thought I would need for my hospitalization. I was told to report back by 1600 hours (okay, 4:00 PM) for admission to the hospital and the start of my intravenous treatment.

I called Patti and outlined the plan. She observed that it looked like she would have to make yet another move without me. And with a four-month old baby. But we were both thankful she had insisted I not just ignore my dental problem. (I recently read that my condition untreated could lead to a fatal brain infection!) Then I did my shopping and reported back to start my treatment.

Being an officer, I had a private room at the hospital. It was adjacent to the general oral surgery ward for enlisted servicemen. I was feeling well, and it was not long before reading and watching television became very boring. I found out there was a hospital movie theater, and that I was free to walk around using a portable rack for my IV bag. I made the acquaintance of the enlisted men in the ward (I was the only officer), ditched the "Sir stuff," and enjoyed their friendship. Several were from West Virginia and had joined the Air Force as their best opportunity to better themselves and establish a career. To their disappointment, they encountered trouble passing their final physicals when they arrived in San Antonio for basic training. They had jaw problems too and oral surgery was required.

The necessary surgical procedure was explained to them. They were given the choice to proceed or revoke their enlistment and go home. Their surgeries were going to be longer and more painful than mine. They asked my advice. I advised them to go through with the surgery and stay in the Air Force. They seemed intelligent and motivated enough. The Air Force afforded them an opportunity that they otherwise would not have. It would offer them training and an education that would serve them well. They all decided they would go for the surgery. My Colonel friend "counseled" me as it hadn't taken long for him to figure out what had happened! But I could tell he was amused and agreed with my advice.

After a couple of weeks of dragging my device around the hospital, it was determined that the infection had been terminated. It was time to excise the parts of the jaw bone that it had killed. I was very concerned about the surgery, as I had suffered greatly by that time at the hands of several dentists. I assumed they would put me under general anesthesia. Not so! I was in a dental chair, given Novocain injections into my upper left jaw, and hooked up to an IV.

I don't recall what was in the IV, but it must have been good stuff! A surgical drape was put around my face and over my eyes and the fun began. I could not believe the pain—there wasn't any! I have had teeth cleanings that hurt more than this procedure.

They had opened my jaw and removed the piece of infected bone and sutured the jaw, leaving a hole for direct insertion of antibiotics and other medication to the bone surface. This was done by insertion of what looked like a short length of shoelace saturated with antibiotic medication. It was about three inches long. It was to be pulled out and replaced at regular intervals. I did not feel any pain as they stuffed this medicated ribbon into the hole in my jaw. The Novocain was still working. The initial "stuffing" seemed, to me, to involve a lot of prodding and pressure.

I was told that when I started to experience pain that evening, I should call for the duty nurse. She would inject me with a narcotic painkiller. I figured I could handle pain, and I didn't want to risk getting hooked on drugs. I decided to tough it out! The next morning the oral surgeon stopped by on rounds, looked at my chart, expressed surprise, and asked if I had turned down pain medication. I told him I had. He asked if I had pain. I told him I hurt like hell, but I didn't want to acquire a drug habit. He laughed at me and assured me that was not a risk in my situation. He said if I had actual pain, taking the medication would not create a drug habit. He called in the nurse and it was added to my IV. I finally got some sleep!

I was soon able to walk around with my IV again. I had my golf clubs in the trunk of my car and yearned to get out of that hospital and play some golf. I begged the doctor to let me do that. I could see the beautiful course out the window and I really felt I was getting well enough to play. Eventually the IV was discontinued and permission was granted to play golf. I was very excited—and I lasted half a hole! I was really weakened. I hit a weak shot to the downhill hole. I made it to my ball, which I picked up. I struggled back up the hill, got my money back, put my clubs away, and went back to my bed!

A couple of days later I was discharged to go back to Abilene with a hole in my jaw which required at least daily re-packing with the medicated shoe lace. I was given follow-up instructions to deliver to the Abilene dental clinic for them to follow. My treatment was outstanding at Wilford Hall. I am very grateful for what they did for me, and the extra effort made to expedite my treatment.

At Abilene I began the process of resigning my commission and reverting to civilian status. That entailed a discharge physical. I had decided on Drake Law School. The Air Force referred me to the Des Moines Veterans Hospital Dental Clinic for follow-up treatment of my jaw. I was also authorized VA physical therapy services for injuries sustained in Vietnam.

In late August Patti, Kathleen, and I arrived in Des Moines. I checked in with the VA Hospital for the re-packing of my jaw. I started law school the following morning. I had to report to the dental clinic every other day for a couple of weeks. Then I was instructed on repacking my wound myself, until weekly follow-ups indicated healing was complete. The VA then removed my remaining three impacted wisdom teeth. I cannot say enough good things about the VA and the treatment they gave me then, and the treatment they continue to provide today.

We began a new chapter in our lives. In the first nearly four and a half years of our marriage, we were together about 18 months. Patti maintains the one-year Vietnam tour was the easiest; she at least knew where I was, what I was doing, and when to expect me home. Those who have not served in the military do not realize the demands made on service families. Upon reflection, I have come to realize the burden on the family may well be bigger than the burden on the service member.

# PART III
# THE LAW:
# STUDENT AGAIN

# 1

# Drake Law School: Des Moines, Iowa

I WILL NEVER forget my first day of law school. This was late August 1970! The anti-war movement was in full bloom. No one thanked anyone for their service! Vets just learned to appreciate not being harassed or spit upon. Having never attended a "real college," I didn't know what to expect. I assumed that since law school led to a professional occupation, one would be expected to dress like a professional. Another bad assumption! The first gathering of the law school class was in an auditorium. I don't recall how many we were—probably around 100. I walked in and was amazed. I looked like the nerd. I guess I was in comparison to my classmates! I looked around and observed the majority uniform of the day: dirty looking jeans, peace symbol tees (almost clean) and peace symbol jewelry, along with flipflops, sandals, or gym shoes.

I surveyed the scene. I saw another short-haired, clean shaven, professionally dressed nerd on the other side of the auditorium. I quickly made my way to him. I introduced myself and learned Ralph Nelson had been a Marine pilot a few short weeks ago. I confessed to having been an Air Force pilot and asked him where he parked. He looked at me like I was nuts! He asked what difference that made. I replied that I wondered who parked closest. I suggested we put our jackets and ties in the closest car, try to look a little scruffy, and find out where these jerks drank beer. He asked why I would care about that. I told him that we needed to beat them to the joint, pull some tables together, and buy some pitchers of beer to see if we couldn't make a few thirsty friends. If we didn't break through at some level to these folks who would obviously consider us to be baby killing monsters, we were going to be in for a miserable three years! He smiled in agreement and we executed our plan after the Dean welcomed us. We also were at an age disadvantage. We were about six years older than most of them. There was one woman about our age who was also well dressed. We introduced ourselves to her and invited Linda Archibald to participate in our plan. She readily agreed.

◆ ◆ ◆

### Law School—Another World

Law school was an interesting grind, but a grind for sure. It involved a lot of reading of course. Figuring out what all those words meant and how they fit with the ones from the night before was a constant struggle. I resolved at the beginning to never fall behind in the reading and research projects.

My other priority was finding housing for us. We initially accepted the gracious offer of high school classmate David Wood and his wife, Cathy. We then located a motel that was near Drake and rented for extended stays. Keeping up was difficult at the beginning as we were living in a motel with a baby. We soon found a small but nice apartment to rent. The apartment house was managed by a friend or relative of a fellow in the class a year ahead of ours, Pat Payton.

We hadn't been in that apartment too long before I got a letter from the VA setting forth my veteran's benefits. I was found to be 60% disabled and entitled to free books and tuition. Talk about mana from Heaven! I knew I was entitled to some care from the VA, but I didn't anticipate payments! We were suddenly as well off as if we had been sent to school by the Air Force. What a country! I was entitled to compensation for my dental condition, my back injury, and the damage to my hearing when a cockpit canopy failed at high altitude leading to incurable lifetime traumatic tinnitus (continuous buzzing or ringing noise in the ears). What a relief a government check is! We began to think about renting a house.

◆◆◆

## Homeowners at Last

We looked at houses and explored the Des Moines area. There were not many for rent. But we got lucky and found a nice three-bedroom house in West Des Moines for sale by owner. We began talking to the owners and, with a loan from Patti's dad, put together an offer which they accepted. The transaction was handled by Dan Stamatelos, a West Des Moines lawyer who was the seller's attorney. Dan took a liking to us. And we to him.

◆◆◆

## The Routine of Law School Life

After the closing, Dan asked if I would like a job as his law clerk. I didn't know for sure what a clerking job entailed, but I assumed it would be in his law office, with an educational component. He asked if I had ever done any tax returns. I told him that I had always done my own and had established a practice of making myself available to help enlisted Airmen do theirs. I was what he needed! He had a lot of clients who needed to have their tax returns prepared. I would go to the office when I could and bang out tax returns. After tax season I was introduced to the legal issues faced by small business people, the laws of failed marriages, and recovery for injuries to our clients due to the negligence of others. This two-person law firm did a lot of interesting business.

Law school was a different experience in more ways than one. For example, grades in most classes depended on one final test at the end of the semester. There were usually no mid-terms nor, except for rare instances, were there quizzes or consultations about the professor's perception of you as a student. There was a lot of back and forth during classes, and lack of understanding or preparation stood out.

I can still visualize our first final exam. Ralph and I walked out of the testing room together. He turned to me and suggested we go have a beer. I readily agreed. One of our younger classmates looked at us like we were crazy. He asked how we could go drink beer after what we had just been through. The Marine looked at me, looked at him, and walked a few steps back into the classroom. He looked around and came back out. He told the classmate that he hadn't seen anyone dead or wounded in there, so what was the big deal! Some of the others standing around had a good laugh, and we all adjourned to the tavern together. Note: by then we had managed to make many friends and overcome the baby-killer image. I think those younger people learned a lot from us, as we did from them. We began forming friendships that bridged wide differences in political philosophy which endure to this day. Remember: if lawyers don't have anyone to argue with, life has no meaning!

Life as the spouse and daughter of a law student is not easy. The spouse really is the one who has the task of holding everything together. I would come home from school or work, play a bit with Kathleen, eat a quick dinner, go down to my desk in the basement, and prepare for the next day of classes. We did have fun with neighbors and other law students on the weekends. Playing bridge, grilling hamburgers, and drinking beer was high living and a lot of fun. Sometimes Patti and I think those were some of the best times we ever had.

Kathleen was a beautiful baby. I loved showing her off. I had a bicycle and mounted a child's seat on the back fender. It would flunk any safety inspection today, but we had a great time bike riding when time and weather permitted.

I attended summer school which made law school practically a full-time job. That allowed me to graduate in less than two and a half years. But it meant a constant, disciplined grind of work and study. By the time I finished, Kathleen was talking, and she and Patti started calling me "The Phantom who lives in the basement."

I found law school to be very interesting and did well. I studied religiously and kept up with the readings and case briefings. I did indeed spend a lot of time at that desk in the basement with a heater in the foot well, an essential in the winter months. The areas of law that evolved from the English Common Law were easiest for me. From my perspective, they were based on common sense that had developed over hundreds of years.

The areas of law built upon statutory allocation of legal rights and responsibilities were more difficult. They were newer and less tested. The application of common sense in conjunction with code provisions addressing a problem did not always lead one to what I viewed as the correct conclusion. These legislatively enacted codes and their subject matter address issues unique to modern society. Even though they are usually influenced by and grounded in common law concepts, they often involve new and relatively untested applications. These codes are needed to address modern complex issues that spring from the increased speed and complexity inherent in continuing development and advances in economics, commerce, communications, and data management.

Law School was a real education in more ways than one. I made many new friends from various backgrounds. I was closer in age to some of the professors than I was to most other students. I had a lot of adventure in my life and experienced a lot of violence before law school. I had traveled in all continents except Antarctica. I was used to performing in very stressful situations accompanied by risk of life and limb. The stress of law school was not difficult to manage. It seemed relatively low level. Law school taught me how "things work" in this country. The law is the fabric of society that holds it all together. It establishes the boundaries of commercial risk and reward necessary to the establishment and maintenance of a modern society and the legal environment necessary to sustain its survival and continuing development.

We did manage to have fun along the way. The faculty had its share of very interesting, and often entertaining, folks. One of my favorite stories involves a very hard-nosed professor and a very beautiful young lady student. The professor had a good sense of humor, and I enjoyed his combativeness. The young lady was really an outstanding student and very quick witted.

The professor tormented us with a snap quiz on a Friday morning. On Monday he came in and chewed us out for our poor performance on the quiz. He really was on a rampage! He told us that there was only one "A" test paper and the rest of us, mostly because of his generosity, got "Ds" with a few "Cs." He ranted and raved and finally called on the young lady. He told her she had gotten the only "A" and asked her to tell the class how she had gotten that "A."

She promptly stood up, looked at the professor, looked at her shoes, and shyly looked up and stated, "But, Professor, you promised me no one would ever know how I got my "A." The class went nuts and the professor was stunned into silence. He just stood at the podium not knowing what to say or do. The continuing waves of laughter dominated the room. He finally closed his book and walked out of the classroom.

The young lady finished high in her class. She was a budding star in the firm that employed her. Just a couple of years after graduation, she tragically collapsed and died while giving a presentation at a continuing education seminar for practicing attorneys.

Another tyrannically-inclined professor ran a very tight ship that sailed not so merrily through very turbulent waters. The lessons were usually complex and the legal concepts not always apparent. He loved to embarrass students whom he suspected were not very interested in the subject matter or came to class unprepared for the day's lesson. He called on one of my friends who made the mistake of trying to ramble his way through a problem. It was apparent he had no idea where he wanted to go with it—he just kept talking. The professor finally interrupted him and exclaimed, "Mr. _____, I can usually hide the ball from most students, but you take the cake! I don't think you even realize that there is a ball!"

The professors were good teachers and cared about their students. The faculty at Drake Law School included some outstanding lawyers who had practiced law before entering the teaching profession. Most had courtroom experience. They were very orientated towards the practical application of what they taught. They instilled respect for the law and the professional obligations of intellectual honesty, courtesy, and respect. It is not always easy to preserve the necessary civility when engaged in heated argument and significant conflict. We benefitted from the practical experience of these professors and their reverence for the law and respect for colleagues, even though sometimes philosophical opposites.

There were some students that, sadly, were just not cut out to practice law. There was a sadness when a classmate struggled, especially when the logical conclusion was he or she was not suited to the practice of law. We lost some very good people along the way, most of whom distinguished themselves in other careers. Unfortunately, there also were a few that made it through who were not cut out to practice law and turned out to be anything but a credit to the profession.

The law school had an honor code, but I was to learn it was rarely, if ever, applied. After one of our first-year finals, I noticed two students, friends, who continued to write for a few minutes after the "stop" order was announced by the proctor. I thought I had an obligation to report it and did. I explained to the Dean that I thought that was my duty. But from the reaction I received, it appeared I had created an exceptional problem. I stated I did not hold any animosity toward either student, I considered them friends. I told him I planned to talk to them about the matter. I would explain that in my background I was governed by an honor code at the Air Force Academy that was strictly enforced, and failure to report an observed violation was itself a violation. I suggested that since the law school code had been rarely enforced, it would be unjust to impose it on these two students for a minor infraction. I surmised the two didn't even think their finishing an answer constituted a violation. Apparently, there was no precedent for such an interpretation. No action was taken, but student awareness was raised. Thus, it was resolved, and the two students accepted my explanation. One of these students went on to have a distinguished judicial and academic career. She gave me a special peck on the cheek as I congratulated her after her first judicial swearing-in ceremony. Our friendship survived the incident.

# 2

# Law School and Politics

I HAD LOTS of friends who were prisoners of war, having been captured by the North Vietnamese or their allies. They were imprisoned in horrible circumstances and subjected to prolonged periods of abusive interrogation. Our government tended to treat their circumstances as a secret to be withheld from the American public. I was determined to bring attention to the plight of my POW friends. I thought becoming involved politically would provide a path that would lead to public recognition of the issue. About that time the country began to wake up to the situation—thanks to the increasing activities of POW wives. The military had advised a low profile for these women, but when it became apparent that was not leading to any benefit for their husbands, they became a force to be reckoned with. They became the heroic spouses of heroes!

I became very active in Republican politics. In that process I became acquainted with Governor Bob Ray and First Lady Billie. They were very good to me and Patti. He was a very popular and successful governor who served several terms. J. B. Morris, an attorney and the editor and publisher of The Iowa Bystander, was a member of the first African American officers class that served in World War I. He was an active Republican and interested in the POW issue. A friendship developed that lasted the rest of his life.

Through him I became acquainted with other African American leaders in the community.

I also established some good Democrat friendships. The treatment of POWs was not a partisan issue. While the Democrats were burdened with their far-left nuts like Jane Fonda, I found the Iowa rank and file Democrats embarrassed by the antics of folks like her and Joan Baez. I mention Joan Baez because, over time, I grew to respect her. While she remained very anti-war, she also became a critic of POW mistreatment. I still haven't found anything to respect about Jane, not that I am looking very hard.

In the fall of 1972, I was contacted about going to the White House to meet President Nixon. All expenses were to be paid by the Republican Party. It was the thrill of a lifetime! The president was to sign a new veterans' bill and wanted to have two decorated Vietnam Veterans from each state attend the bill signing ceremony. Another veteran from Iowa and I flew to Washington and checked into a nice hotel. The next morning the two of us were provided with an extra treat. We had breakfast in the private office of the Director of the Veterans Administration, Donald Johnson. He was a fellow Iowan and we were given royal treatment. We were picked up at our hotel by a limousine and driven to the VA offices. Mr. Johnson was very nice to us. After breakfast he took us to the White House in his limousine. It was a wonderful experience! I had been to Washington before and had met President Johnson. But I had never been delivered in VIP style to the White House.

President Nixon impressed me as very reserved. I think, though, that he enjoyed our company. He was very friendly and thanked each of us for our service to the nation. But there was a shyness about him that struck me. One of our number was an American Indian from the southwestern part of the country. He lost his eyesight when he was wounded in Vietnam. The president got down on the floor of the oval office with this veteran and took his hand and guided it around the seal of the United States that was inlayed in the carpet in front of the president's desk. He explained the features of the seal as he guided the soldier's hand over the carpet.

After the bill-signing ceremony in the East Room of the White House, we were given presidential pens. I was able to get one for my parents too. It was a great day!

I was very disappointed in President Nixon when the Watergate scandal brought him down. It is a mystery to me why he would become involved in such a stupid venture at a time when he was assured re-election. I wonder if he was so affected by the loss to President Kennedy in 1960 that he was paranoid about what dirty tricks the Democrat Party leaders might stoop to in the 1968 election. Some attribute his 1960 loss to voter fraud in Cook County, Illinois. Having such a belief, even if not true, would certainly influence the loser's perspective towards future races.

By the way, my parents mounted their pen on a plaque which they proudly displayed. After the president resigned, I was visiting my parents and noticed they were still displaying that pen. I went over and idly examined it. I removed the cap and noticed the tip of the pen was corroded. Yes, indeed, there was corruption in the White House!

# 3

# Terry E. Branstad

TERRY BRANSTAD IS one of the most determined and purposeful people I have ever known. He was a year behind me at Drake Law School. He had served as a military policeman in the Army. To say he was very interested in politics too, is a great understatement. Not long after I met Terry, we were taking a break in the student lounge. I asked him what he wanted to do as a lawyer. He was from a small town in northern Iowa. He informed me that he was going to be Governor of Iowa. I chuckled and observed there were probably a few more in the lounge with the same ambition. I wished him good luck. It didn't take long before I grew to realize he was not kidding!

We started out on what I learned were different ends of the GOP spectrum. Terry was very conservative. I thought I was too, until I met him. Governor Ray was more moderate, as was I. I came to be considered a moderate "Ray Republican."

Terry wanted to lead the Drake Young Republican Club to conservative glory. I was asked to run against Terry for the office of Drake Republican Club President. I agreed, and we battled it out. It is the only election Terry has ever lost, thanks primarily to the efforts of my campaign manager, Dennis Jontz (Dennis was very bright and had a successful legal career in New Mexico where he became President of the New Mexico Bar Association).

My goal was to keep things on an even keel during the upcoming election campaign. Conservative demonstrations and publicity were not thought to be helpful to the cause by the party leaders of the day. As a result, Terry and I were placed in opposition at nearly every club meeting. Terry and his loyal band of conservative followers were determined to garner publicity and have the club gain prominence. Barry Goldwater was their hero. He was a Reserve Air Force General and pilot, so he was mine too! He had visited the Academy while I was a cadet. I was warned in 1964 that if I voted for Barry, I would end up fighting a war in Vietnam. They were right, I did—and I did!

The President of the Drake Republican Club had an ex-officio position on the State Republican Central Committee. I attended the meetings when able and met Republican politicians at the local level from around the state. I was seated as a delegate at the State Convention. After law school I continued to be active in the party, and for many years served as a precinct committeeperson and state convention delegate. I met very interesting people of both parties through these activities, many of whom have become long-time friends. The attorney I clerked for was a committed, active Democrat. It was through him that I initially made lots of Democrat contacts and friends.

In the 1970 Iowa gubernatorial election, Bob Ray was elected to a second term by a vote of 51% to Bob Fulton's 46.6%. Bob Fulton was Lt. Governor when Harold Hughes was governor. Harold Hughes resigned in January of 1968 to take a seat as a US Senator, leaving Bob Fulton to serve a few days as Governor Fulton. Bob Ray's first term followed Bob Fulton's. This occurred while I was in Vietnam, so I really didn't know Bob Fulton until several years later, when we were paired in a golf tournament in Waterloo, Iowa, which we won. It was part of a political fundraiser. He is a very nice fellow and I enjoy his friendship. We proclaim our golfing victory whenever we get the chance!

◆ ◆ ◆

## *Representative Branstad*

Terry ran a successful campaign in 1972 for the Iowa General Assembly House of Representatives, representing the district in northern Iowa where he was raised. He also ran a successful campaign for the hand of Chris Johnson, who he married on June 17, 1972. These accomplishments occurred while he continued with law school and helped on the family farm. There isn't anyone that can outwork Terry Branstad!

He began his legislative career as a state representative at age 26. He served his constituents well and continued with law school and work on the family farm. He finished law school in the summer of 1974 (the summer of 1974 was a great year for us too. Daughter Kristina was born on July 22).

Terry won re-election to the Iowa House of Representatives by increasing margins in 1974 and 1976. In 1978 he won a three-way primary race for the position of Lieutenant Governor of Iowa. He was elected in the general election. He was re-elected in 1980.

I began lobbying in 1981, and it was very helpful to have a friend who was Lt. Governor. In those days the Lt. Governor presided over the Iowa Senate. He made the point of assuring me, on my first day, that I was always welcome to stop by his office for coffee.

I recall visiting with him in his office after conclusion of the Senate's business on a Friday afternoon. We discussed weekend plans. Mine were simple. He was off to give a speech somewhere that evening. Saturday morning, he was speaking at a breakfast somewhere else followed by a dinner at yet another location that night. I asked when he would get home to Lake Mills to see Chris and the kids. He said he would get home late Saturday night and be home until Sunday evening when he would head back to Des Moines. He was laying the groundwork for a gubernatorial campaign. I remember saying, "Wow, what a schedule! Better you than me, my friend!"

He replied with a question. "You mean you aren't interested in running for office?"

When I replied in the negative, he smiled and said, "Good!" He knew that Governor Ray had been trying to get me to run for the legislature.

In February of 1982, Governor Ray announced he would not run for another term. He assumed Terry would run in his place and become a successful governor. Terry immediately announced his intent to run for governor. After Governor Ray made his announcement to GOP leaders, Terry and I were together at a GOP fundraiser at a private residence about four doors down the street from my home in Clive. We were sitting together on a sofa, and he seemed unusually fidgety. I asked him if the governor had publicly made his announcement. Governor Ray had talked to me about it a couple of days prior in confidence and said his announcement was imminent. Terry said that he had. My memory is that it hadn't been made public yet. Recently we reminisced about that evening. Terry was sure it had been made public. It may have been, and I hadn't heard it yet. But I don't recall it being a topic of discussion at the fundraiser. Regardless, he was eager and prepared to seize the opportunity! He was elected governor in November 1982, by a margin of 53% to 47%. He won re-election in 1986 (52/48), 1990 (61/39) and 1994 (58/42). He chose not to run in 1998. He left office as Iowa's longest-serving governor.

# PART IV
# THE OLDEST
# YOUNG LAWYER

# 1

# Finding a Professional Home

BECAUSE I WENT to summer sessions, I graduated from law school in December of 1972 and passed the bar examination in January 1973.

I had been clerking with the small firm in West Des Moines for almost two years. It was a very good experience, and very helpful as I began making the decisions that I hoped would lead me to a successful legal career. Originally, I thought I would like to practice in a small firm in a small town. My father wisely advised that I probably should look beyond that kind of practice. He pointed out the problems of establishing oneself in a small town, even one's hometown. Perhaps, especially in one's hometown. I also had the counsel of some of my law professors. They urged me to make applications to larger practices they recommended in Des Moines. I began to see the benefits of a large practice, which would allow me to develop specialty skills while having partners who could best serve my clients when they had problems outside the scope of my expertise.

I really thought highly of the attorney that I clerked for while going to law school, Dan Stamatelos. Although older, we were friends, as were our families. His daughter, Kim, now a successful attorney, babysat for us. Law school friend Pat Payton had joined the firm upon his graduation the year before. It was a very difficult conversation when I told Dan I had decided I wanted to look at other options, despite his generous offer to practice with him. He was very gracious about it and did not pressure me. To the contrary, he was very helpful as I weighed my options. He was especially helpful when it came time to make my final decision.

I was primarily interested in Nashville, Tennessee, and Des Moines. I also considered an aviation law firm in Chicago.

The Chicago firm offered me a huge starting salary of $50,000, an almost unheard-of amount for a starting lawyer in those days. I was 31 years old, an Air Force Academy graduate with an engineering education geared to aeronautical engineering and astrophysics, a jet pilot, a combat pilot, a test pilot qualified in single and multi-engine aircraft, and a new member of Who's Who in American Aviation. I assumed that for that amount of money they would expect extraordinary effort. I had heard horror stories about starting out in large city law firms from friends who had done it and returned to Des Moines. Also, the thought of commuting to work in Chicago did not appeal to me. I discarded that opportunity early in my decision-making process.

I had a very interesting offer in Nashville. I interviewed with a well-regarded mid-sized firm that was open to hiring a Yankee. One of its members was a veteran who had served in Naval Intelligence. He took a liking to me and wanted to hire me to help him in his growing music law practice. He represented an up-and-coming talent by the name of Dolly Parton. They made me a fair offer, but not as good as the ones I got in Des Moines. Yes, I do wonder "what if?" I made two trips to visit the firm. Patti accompanied me on the second trip.

On the second visit I spent most of my time with the Parton attorney, and met some of his other clients. I was not a country music fan, but I had met some country music entertainers while living in the Nashville area. When with the attorney and a group of people he represented, I had no idea who might be a star, or an agent, or what have you. The attorney informed me that they liked me and thought I would be a good addition to his practice.

After these sessions I would report on the events of my day to the friends we stayed with, JD and Corine Kennedy. They knew the country music scene and were impressed with the people I was meeting. I was thinking that litigation was where I would be most successful. But I was very seriously considering the music field after my meetings with the Nashville firm. I didn't know how a Nashville jury might react to a Yankee accent, but apparently the entertainment folks didn't mind it.

I also met nationally known attorney Jimmy Neal while I was in Nashville. He had just finished a complex trial involving union leader Jimmy Hoffa. He was in solo practice and wrapping up from the Hoffa case when I met him. He had an office that I noticed while walking to my car from my first Parton firm interview. I decided to drop in and see if he would talk to me. I gave his receptionist a copy of my resume which she took to him. He invited me into his office and we had an interesting visit. He was very friendly and encouraging. He was not going to be hiring anyone soon, but he said he would seriously consider me if I were available when he began to rebuild his firm. I really appreciated and enjoyed the time he spent with me.

I had two offers in Des Moines. One was from the then largest firm in Iowa, and the other from the one that was to become the largest firm in Iowa.

The largest firm offered more money, and my interviewers were impressive, as was the client list. The firm had a great reputation. The firm's leaders were active in politics and conducted my interview. One was a Democrat state party leader and the other a Republican state party leader. I had met them both while a law student. I found it odd that they made it clear that they expected their attorneys to work half days on Saturdays. I expected attorneys would work long hours, but I didn't think they would work on weekends except when necessary.

They also used a compensation system which put a premium on bringing in new clients. I didn't see myself as a rainmaker! The litigation area of their practice seemed based on insurance defense cases for existing insurance company clients and business litigation from existing business clients. I had made a lot of political contacts in the community, but I didn't view them as sources of "rain." I viewed myself as a stranger in town with a law degree and political contacts. I wasn't otherwise connected to community "movers and shakers."

My last interview was at Nyemaster, Goode, McLaughlin, Emery and O'Brien. I still recall walking to lunch with Roy Voigts and Jerry Williams, the senior trial lawyers. It happened to be a Friday. I asked Roy what he was doing the next day. He said he was going hunting. I asked if he usually worked Saturdays. He looked at me and asked, "Why would I do that unless I had to?" He then went on to say that was a reason he was a lawyer: personal freedom and interesting work. They also had a different compensation system. Clients were considered firm clients and there was no set formula. Compensation was subjective, recommended by a committee and subject to approval of the firm's partners.

I had met Ray Nyemaster while I was in high school. He sometimes flew into Fuller Airport in Milford. I serviced his plane. I learned that Jerry Williams was a former Air Force pilot. Jim West was a former Naval Aviator. Don Muyskens was a former Marine helicopter pilot. Frank Comfort was a private pilot and owned a light plane. Several other members of the firm had served (Craig Shives was then serving) in the military in various other capacities. Two had been FBI Agents, Jack Goode and John McLaughlin.

I had decided that I wanted to be a litigator. I thought it made a lot of sense to practice in Iowa where I was born, raised, and educated in an Iowa law school. Most of my classmates would be practicing in Iowa. Some would be in politics and some would become judges. They would eventually constitute a statewide network of contacts. Also, I had made a lot of political contacts in Iowa. Governor Ray was a very successful lawyer before becoming governor. He thought, correctly as it turned out, that Des Moines had a great legal community. The lawyers were very professional and civil in their dealing with each other. He encouraged me to stay in Iowa and think about running for office. I had been approached about running for the Iowa House of Representatives. My State Representative was getting ready to retire. She would have urged her supporters to support me and I would probably have been elected. But I also knew that I couldn't afford to take the time away from my family and my new law practice. I remain engaged in politics, but only as a volunteer and unpaid advisor.

I set a personal deadline for my decision. I ultimately decided Des Moines offered the best opportunity. The decision then was between the two downtown Des Moines law firms. I accepted the offer from the Nyemaster Firm (Nyemaster, Goode, McLaughlin, Emery & O'Brien) and became its 16th member. I felt very comfortable with everyone I met there. I didn't have the Old Des Moines social connections prominent in both firms. There was not an expectation that I would be a rainmaker at Nyemaster. Their clients were firm clients, not the clients of the lawyers that happened to bring them in. Of course, new clients often became regular clients because of the lawyer selected to handle their initial matter. The firm policy was to ensure that clients were served by the member of the firm most qualified to handle their matters. I felt at home there. There was a real aviation and military tie. It had the feeling of comradery I so appreciated among officers and pilots in Air Force squadrons. They seemed to genuinely care about each other and considered the whole greater than their individual part. That law school classmate and good friend Jerry Newbrough would be joining the firm following his graduation in May sealed the deal. It felt like an ideal fit for me. I was also pleased that my friends in the other firm graciously accepted my decision and sincerely (as years of professional and social contacts verified) wished me the best.

Jack Goode was one of the greatest people I have met and honored to be associated with. A former FBI Agent, he was imbued with a wonderfully wise intellect. He was the firm peacemaker, able to keep it on course as a team enterprise where the whole really was considered more important than any single part. We had our standouts, of course. They also recognized the importance of each member of the team. It was bad form to toot your own horn too loudly.

Another stellar member was my contemporary, Don Brittan. Unfortunately, he died in the prime of his distinguished career. As a young partner he won a case for a client resulting in a huge recovery. The client had wanted the case handled on a contingent fee basis. Don shared that fee with all of us. He didn't try to keep it for himself or seek special compensation as the attorney who had generated it. It was a great windfall shared by all.

I made a good choice. The firm grew to become the largest firm in Iowa. It expanded geographically with new offices in Ames and Cedar Rapids. I went from the bottom of the attorney seniority list on the letterhead in 1973, to the top when I retired at the end of 2012. It not only was the largest (83 attorneys and growing when I retired) law firm in Iowa, but in my unbiased opinion, the best. Several years before, it had been decided to allow the firm name to evolve as the named partners retired. Prior to my retirement the firm name evolution was complete and remains Nyemaster Goode.

# 2

# The Oldest Young
# Lawyer in Town

AFTER PASSING THE bar examination in January and retiling the
main bathroom in our house in West Des Moines, Patti and I took a
vacation to Florida. We had a great time and made it all the way to Key
West. We then reversed course and headed back to Des Moines and the
start of my new career. I was to report to work in early February. The
trip home was notable for the blizzard we encountered—in Florida. We
first noticed snow beginning to fall in northern Florida. By the time we
made it to Macon, Georgia, it was a raging blizzard. The traffic was a
mess, and the local people had no idea how to drive on the ice and
snow. The governor closed the interstate, and we ended up spending
the night in a Macon motel. We found a place to eat nearby. I recall
helping some Georgia State Troopers install chains on their cars. They
recognized they were ill-prepared to deal with the driving conditions. I
gave them a little welcomed coaching.

The following morning, we used the motel room beverage tray
as a snow shovel to get the car cleared enough to attempt the short
drive to the interstate. We managed to continue our journey amid
the devastation caused by the snowstorm. The interstate was littered
with stranded vehicles almost all the way to Atlanta.

I was a day late reporting for duty, but report I did. I was at the office early in the morning, and no one really knew for sure what to do with me. After some others arrived it became clear that I did, indeed, have a small office with a desk and chairs—but no window! I have never been claustrophobic. I was able to handle the NASA re-entry simulator without problem. It was a very cramped capsule, and re-entry is very rough and noisy! The small punishment boxes at the Air Force POW SERE school were not a problem for me either. However, that office sure seemed to shrink as time went on! I was a pilot who had loved the open sky. I was also used to a varied schedule. Now I was an attorney with no view of the sky and a gut feeling that at least an eight-hour day was expected. At first, I had nothing to do except wander around and introduce myself to the attorneys and the staff I had not previously met.

John McLaughlin appeared in my office the next day with my first assignment: assist in preparing corporate debenture and indenture financing documents. I had no idea what he was talking about! I knew he was involved in banking and investment law. I knew our helicopter pilot, Don Muyskens, worked with him. Don was a couple of years older than me and I got help from him. I spent the rest of the day cutting and pasting from a copy of some documents Don had drafted for another client.

This went on for a couple of days before the trial department found something for me to work on. What a relief! I did research projects in our library—which had windows! It was eventually recognized that I should have an office with windows. I don't recall how long it took, but I was moved into an office with plenty of room and windows. That was a glorious day!

Not too long after I started, I was accompanying Roy and Jerry as they tried cases. They were great mentors. Every trial lawyer develops their own style and technique, and I was fortunate to learn from two of the best. It wasn't too long before I was trying small claims cases, representing people insured by our client insurance companies. A long winning streak developed. Those cases provided great learning experiences for new attorneys, even old new attorneys.

I should remember my first solo jury trial, but I don't! I participated in several with Roy and Jerry. They gradually gave me roles involving the selection of jury panels, the questioning of witnesses, arguing motions, and presenting arguments to juries. I became acquainted with the attorneys in Des Moines who handled most of the significant civil litigation. I began to appreciate the shared bonds of trial lawyers, and the need for civility and professional courtesy. I also became more at ease with the judges before whom I appeared. They expected that proceedings be handled in a professional and honest manner in their courtrooms. It was soon obvious to me that my mentors were held in highest regard. I benefitted greatly from that fact.

When I started practice, Des Moines was known to be a great place to litigate. There were a very few trial lawyers who had not earned the trust of their colleagues and the judges. They suffered the consequences! But for the vast majority their word truly was their bond. You could rely on their answers to discovery and scheduling questions. You could count on their understanding when a problem occurred with a client, or there was a scheduling issue.

On more than one occasion I took over a case set for trial for a partner who had become ill. The opposing attorneys would invite me to their offices and go through the case with me to help me get up to speed. It was a great legal and professional environment. Lots of cases were tried. The process was simpler then. In packing up my office upon retirement, I was surprised how many cases I had tried. It occurred to me that I probably had tried more cases than most of our current trial lawyers, and I hadn't tried a case in 20 years.

Now there are a lot fewer opportunities for young lawyers to develop their trial practices. The cost of litigation has exploded and given rise to what is known as alternative dispute resolution (ADR) processes which include arbitration and mediation. Plaintiffs and defendants have found that for many cases they are better off using

ADR. The fees and time invested in a case are usually significantly reduced.

The firm was also noted for its lobbying presence at the statehouse. When I joined the firm, there were two lobbyists: Kent Emery and Jim West. Kent had been an Army Cavalry Officer with real horses! He was getting close to retirement. Jim had been a Naval Aviator.

◆◆◆

## The City of Clive

Jim was also the City Attorney for the City of Clive, a Des Moines suburb. Lobbying is very demanding when the legislature is in session. Don Brittan assisted Jim by covering Clive when Jim couldn't be available. A trial lawyer, he also served as the Clive prosecutor. In those days Clive was a small community with a population of less than 1,200. The prosecutions were misdemeanor traffic offenses. Don's time was becoming limited too, and I fell heir to the position of Clive Prosecutor.

When I started that role, the cases were presented to a Justice of the Peace. That was soon changed when Iowa adopted a unified court system, with the lowest ranked court being the Magistrate Courts. Magistrate Court sessions were initially held at night. Clive was combined with three other suburban cities for night court.

I also began to fill in for Jim at City Council meetings. Eventually I became the City Attorney, a position appointed by the City Council. Representing Clive in both capacities was a very enjoyable and educational experience for me. Clive developed considerably while I was involved. It is now a prosperous city of about 17,000. While I enjoyed representing the city on zoning and development issues, the most enjoyable part of my job was working with the police officers. When I started, there were two officers and a dispatcher. In 2019 there were 25 officers and three full-time civilian employees and two part-time.

Night court was enjoyable in many respects. The stakes were usually low, the attorneys that represented defendants were friends.

It was not unusual for the Judge, defendants, cops, and attorneys to go out together for a beer after a court session. It was a small-town Iowa experience.

As the city and the police department began adding officers, they involved me in the hiring process. When a new officer was appointed, I would meet with them and explain how cases were processed through the court system. I would strongly emphasize that there was one thing that would result in immediate termination: lying under oath! I told them there would be cases where they would make a mistake costing us a conviction. Not to worry: there probably wasn't anyone on the force that hadn't experienced that. And there would never be anyone on the force who had perjured themselves.

I developed an ordinance establishing a police civil service and retirement system. Early in our process of implementing a formal civil service interview process for the hiring of future officers, there was an interview I will never forget. One of the newly established civil service commission members always asked interviewees if they had ever done anything for which they could be blackmailed. An applicant squirmed at that question, thought a minute, and then admitted that he had. His inquisitor asked what he had done. "Cheated on my wife, sir, but I'm not going to do that anymore!"

Inquisitor: "When did you last cheat on her, son?"

"On my way to this interview, sir!"

Our first appointed Magistrate was also a private pilot. In one of the first hearings, he indicated he was ready to dismiss a case because it was based on a radar speed readout. He wasn't sure he believed in radar speed measurements. I asked to meet with him in chambers where we could go over the equipment and its application. He agreed. He still expressed some skepticism. I reminded him that as a pilot he was dependent upon the same technology in a three-dimensional aerial environment. I asked if he didn't think it would be at least as accurate in a two-dimensional relatively low-speed ground environment. He got my point! So did the defense attorney.

◆◆◆

## Pope John Paul II Visits

Pope John Paul II visited Living History Farms in Urbandale, Iowa, on October 4, 1979. Living History Farms is located just north of Hickman Road and east of the Interstates 35/80 exit of that name. Hickman is the boundary between Clive and Urbandale. The Pope's visit was an historic event requiring significant preparation by both cities, as well as other metropolitan Des Moines area cities, Polk County, and the State of Iowa. The federal government was also involved, of course, as was Vatican security.

A huge crowd was anticipated. Crowd control, security, medical care, and the other amenities associated with serving large gatherings were all critical elements required of the entities involved. At least half of that crowd would be passing through Clive. The Pope was to say Mass in a large open field. He would arrive by helicopter.

My involvement was as the Clive City Attorney. I worked with the mayor, council, and city staff to draft city ordinance changes needed for the event. I also drafted emergency proclamations for execution by the mayor, if necessary, to invoke police powers to address unusual situations that could arise. A crowd control plan was enacted by ordinance, but not every contingency could be anticipated and addressed in that manner. Different crowd control procedures might become necessary in case of some medical emergencies, for example.

The Pope was scheduled to arrive at Living History Farms around 1:30 PM. The crowd control ordinances created a restricted zone in Clive and Urbandale that precluded entry before 5:00 AM (as I recall). There were entry security stations that the crowd would have to pass through. Obviously, we couldn't fence off the entire area. Clive Police, Urbandale Police, Sherriff's Deputies, State Troopers and Secret Service Agents patrolled the area. The mayor and I spent the entire night patrolling with the Clive Chief of Police.

I had my briefcase of draft Emergency Proclamations at the ready. It soon became apparent to us that the crowd was going to be huge! Early in the evening we realized there was no way we could enforce the perimeter restrictions. People were ignoring the checkpoints and working their way to the area where the altar was set up. The security priority was necessarily shifted to control of the crowd within the perimeter, rather than trying to keep it outside.

As dawn began to break, we were amazed at the people coming from all directions. They were walking significant distances as there was not adequate parking close to the site. A shuttle bus system for remote parking existed, but it didn't open soon enough to have significant impact. People were lugging lawn chairs and coolers. There were people in wheelchairs and kids in strollers. To my surprise, we were informed by security personnel that approximately 17 death threats to the Pope had been received.

Around noon it was gridlock! We lived about a mile south of the altar area, but it was at least a two-mile walk. I was dropped off at home about an hour before the Pope was to have arrived. He was about an hour late. Patti and I set off with Kathleen and Kristina. Kathleen was nine and Kristina was five. We had a stroller for Kristina. We made our way toward the altar area. We were not able to get close to the altar, but we probably had a better view from where we were on a little hill about 80 yards away.

The crowd was awed by the Pope's presence, and he seemed to be very enthused about his reception. The crowd estimates were in the 300,000 to 350,000 range. The Pope was on site about two and one-half hours. I must confess that I was relieved to see him safely depart from the Des Moines Airport a little after 6:00 PM. It was a cooler than normal fall day, no doubt a good thing. I was exhausted, having been up for thirty hours plus by the time we got back to our house. It was a wonderful experience. Thankfully there were no serious injuries to anyone, and the crowd was very well mannered.

◆◆◆

## Police Shooting

As the Clive City Prosecutor, I spent a lot of enjoyable time with the growing police department. The most serious incident during my time of representation involved a police shooting. An officer on patrol noticed a pickup parked late one night in the city's Greenbelt Park, in violation of the park curfew. He parked his squad car and approached the pickup, which was facing towards him. The driver's seat was occupied by a male. He approached the fellow and asked for identification. Suddenly another male and a female assaulted him from behind. The couple had been enjoying each other's company and the starlight from the bed of the pickup. A struggle ensued. The officer fired his weapon, wounding the attacking male. Luckily the injury was not life-threatening.

The officer was able to keep control of the situation until backup arrived to make the arrests of the two uninjured assailants, and secure ambulance service for the other. The dispatcher called the police chief and then called me, at the Chief's direction. We met at the scene along with two other officers. The chief and I established a secure perimeter and sent an officer to a nearby residential street to get a list of houses that had interior lights on. Then he was to conduct interviews of the occupants of those houses. At the time we were not sure where the bullet had gone, or if more than one shot was fired. Later in the morning the officers returned and obtained statements from other nearby residences.

The wounded man sued the city for a significant amount of money. The insurance company was very impressed with our investigation and took a hard stand in defense of the city. The case went to trial with the city very ably represented by one of my law school classmates, Harry Perkins. The jury decided in favor of the city.

◆ ◆ ◆

## Police and Fire Politics

The police chief and fire chief had become good friends. The police chief called me early one Monday morning to tell me he had to talk to me. I might have to prosecute him. I was shocked of course and asked what he had done.

He had a good relationship with the mayor, who was facing a tough election the next day. His challenger was going to shake up the city. The police chief and the volunteer fire chief, also my friend, had found a bit too much fire water the night before. They decided that it would be a good idea to make sure the incumbent won. Their jobs could be in jeopardy should the challenger win. They decided it would be a great idea to take down some of the challenger's signs. He caught them in the act.

The chief asked what he should do. I told him emphatically, "GET OUT THE VOTE!!!" They worked the phones, and the next day drove people to the polls when necessary. The incumbent won by a handful of votes. Best political advice I have ever given! Fortunately, the challenger turned out to be a good guy who also became a friend. He was elected to the council at the next election, two years later, and served with distinction. He never said anything to me about the sign thefts and apparently all was forgiven. Both chiefs continued to serve until they retired.

# 3

# The Big Computer Case

MY INTEREST IN aviation, amateur radio, and technology in general, led me to an early interest in, and appreciation for, the potential of computers. Roy Voigts, our lead litigator, came into my office to discuss a call he had received from the CEO of a California computer manufacturer being sued in federal court in Iowa. Roy had a national reputation and the CEO was interested in retaining our firm to defend the case. He had confessed his ignorance about computers, but indicated I was knowledgeable about them and would also work on the case. He discussed the case with me, and I agreed to rearrange my schedule to work with him. It sounded very interesting.

The plaintiff was a prominent privately-owned Iowa company with a national reputation. It was in transition from founding father to son. The defendant client had made a breakthrough in the development of a manufacturing processing computer system that they thought would also have value as a business management system with necessary software adaptations for that use. The son was interested in finding a computer that could be used to make the plaintiff company more efficient.

The son and our client were both extending their reach. The son did not have the business acumen or focus of his father. Although an advanced computer system, it was pioneering new capabilities.

Software and hardware problems occurred. Even today problems are encountered when taking a significant business into the computer age. In this instance, the son's management weaknesses coupled with computerization issues led to problems for the business. The new computer system was an easy scapegoat. So off to the courthouse we went!

We grossly underestimated the time and effort that would be expended on this case. We spent years on it, and depositions were taken weeks at a time in California, Iowa, New York and, I think, Florida. The plaintiff's attorneys sought thousands of pages of our client's documents, and each production of documents led to a new list of depositions. By the same token, our defense required large document productions and engagement of a forensic certified public accountant. The CPA picked by the client practiced in California and, coincidently, was someone I knew from my Air Force days.

The client's plant was located about an hour's commute from my Uncle Pat's home. He lived with a friend in a beautiful home near a mountaintop overlooking Laguna Beach. It had plenty of room and Pat told me we should use it as our California office. I spent several weeks there. It soon became obvious to me that the friend, Charles, was the love of Pat's life. Charles was a well-known physician. Uncle Pat was twenty years older than I, and Charles was a year younger than Pat. Nothing was said about their relationship and they maintained an appearance of being just friends.

The plaintiffs designated Adam Osborne as their expert witness. He was the developer of the first commercially offered portable computer. It was too big to be called a laptop, but it was an innovative predecessor. I arranged to meet with him to discuss his testimony. He lived in the San Francisco Bay Area. He recommended I stay in a nice hotel that had a large outdoor swimming pool. He was a member of the hotel's health club, and regularly swam there. We arranged to meet at the pool, swim a few laps, and then go to dinner. He was a few years older than I.

We had a nice dinner and he freely discussed his opinions on our client's system. I paid for dinner and we agreed to meet again the next day at his plant. He enjoyed showing me around and demonstrating his portable computer. He also autographed and gave me a couple of books he had written on computer technology. We had further discussions about the case. I left feeling comfortable with his opinions and his integrity. I decided I would not take his deposition as it would only serve to educate the plaintiff's attorneys.

Adam Osborne testified honestly during the trial. The plaintiff's attorney brought up the fact that we had met and talked in San Francisco, and I had taken him out to dinner. I cross examined him and elicited information helpful to our case. As I was wrapping up my cross examination of Mr. Osborne, I asked if he enjoyed our dinner. He stated that he did and smiled. He then asked me if I thought it was worth it. I returned the smile and said that I thought it was. The plaintiff's attorney objected, and the judge struck the question and my answer. The jury appeared amused.

In preparation for trial we spent considerable time at the plaintiff's facility in Iowa. There we used the company founder's large and beautifully decorated corner office for taking depositions, most of which he attended. He was a gentleman's gentleman of the old school. I will always remember him looking at his watch the first day we used his office and declaring the business day's end. He stated he had dinner reservations for all the attorneys and himself at a very nice local restaurant. But first we should have a drink. He walked over to a bookshelf, and at the push of a button it revolved, and a well-stocked bar appeared. He got our drink requests and served us. He was a most gracious host while we attorneys battled it out in his office. He insisted on paying for dinner. He did this several times.

The plaintiff demanded settlement in the amount of $10,000,000. We countered at about $100,000 as I recall. We went to trial and the judge was urging that both parties try to settle the case. Our client upped their offer to around $300,000 and the plaintiff dropped their demand to about $6,000,000. It went to the jury after a couple of thousand exhibits and weeks of testimony. I recall that the jury awarded the plaintiff about $250,000. The judge refused to grant the plaintiff court costs because he deemed them the losers despite their recovery of the $250,000. Our client was very pleased with the outcome.

It was an early computer litigation case, and the most significant of my career. It had national coverage in the computer press.

# 4

# Uncle Pat and Charles

THE TIME SPENT in California with Uncle Pat and Charles while working on the computer case was most enjoyable. I became closer to both and enjoyed their company. We had many meals together, and I met several of their friends. Some were celebrities, but they had a common touch and easy grace that led to the conclusion they did not expect special treatment.

Pat was very successful with his clothing business, which had a celebrity customer base. But he had a problem: he needed managers in an area where housing was tremendously expensive. He would make a deal to prospective managers: I will take you and your wife house hunting, you find a house you like, and I will buy it for you to live in. If after ten years you are still working for me, I will deed the house to you and your wife. None worked the full ten years for him. One died in an accident. I understand the widow was well cared for. Another was given a house in Pat's will. Pat's buying of these homes generated very significant gains as real estate was rapidly appreciating in the area.

I saw Pat and Charles occasionally over the years when they would visit Iowa. In addition to a home in Laguna Beach, Pat had a home in Palm Springs. When Patti and I married he had homes in Corona del Mar and Balboa Island, which he offered to us for our honeymoon. We chose Corona del Mar. It was a short walk to a better beach.

Later, Pat acquired a summer home on a lake near Toronto, Canada, that he kept asking us to visit. I wasn't particularly interested in visiting it, nor was my brother or our wives, whom he also invited. Finding the time was a problem for us. My sister and her husband had visited it and urged that we accept Pat's invitation. Dean and I agreed that we ought to make the visit. We arranged to visit in the fall.

Pat and Charles picked us up at the Toronto airport. We drove to a very nice resort near the house, where we were treated to an excellent dinner. When we got to the house, Dean and I were directed to our bedrooms to unpack. I finished and went to Dean's room, and asked if he noticed anything different about Pat. He said that he did: Pat didn't seem his usual entertaining self. He seemed troubled, almost. We both expressed our hope that he was well. But we feared that he might be seriously ill and that was the reason he was so eager to have us visit.

After Dean and I got settled, we gathered in the TV room to watch a televised boxing match. Pat had been an amateur boxer and still loved the sport. Charles soon indicated he was tired and was going to bed. Dean and I watched TV with Pat. He seemed even more preoccupied. I finally said I was tired, thanked him again for a fine dinner, and said I hoped he didn't mind if I went to bed. He turned off the TV and told me I couldn't go to bed, that he had something important he had to talk to us about. Dean and I looked at each other, fearing the worst.

Pat noted Charles had gone to bed, then stated, "Charles went to bed because I am 'outing' him tonight." I asked what he meant by that. He replied, "Perhaps you guys may have suspected, but I am formally announcing that Charles and I are gay and we love each other."

I said, "Of course! We know that!"

"How long have you known?" he asked.

I replied, "It isn't that at some specific point in time we were told by someone or made a sudden discovery. We just grew up gaining in realization of the significance of what we observed. It was not a matter of concern to us. It was just the way we came to appreciate the way things were between you and Charles." He seemed to appreciate that we accepted the fact. We enjoyed the good feeling of having relieved Pat of an unnecessary worry.

I stood up and said, "Pat, it has been a long day and I am very tired and ready for bed. Please excuse me."

Pat said, "I understand, but please stay up anyway. There is more I want to talk about. I want to discuss what it was like to grow up gay." There followed a about three more hours of wonderful conversation. He started from when he first thought he might be "different." "At about five years old I began to think I was somehow different than my older brothers. I tried to be like them, but it did not come naturally to me. I was a good hunter and I could box. But, still I just felt I was somehow 'different.'

"I really suffered from this feeling of 'differentness' as I reached puberty. This pain was noticed by the parish priest, who spent time counseling and helping me. I really think I would have killed myself had it not been for Father Meyers. Father Meyers counseled that God loved us all and recognized the value in all of us, even those who thought themselves 'different.' He emphatically told me I was not to doubt God's love for me because I am 'different.'

"When I entered my late teen years I tried to adapt. I dated girls and was popular with them. If I say so myself, I was very handsome and had a very outgoing personality. In fact, I thought I found a girl I might make a life with. I thought I loved her. But then the war came along. I volunteered to serve as a medic."

Medics were invaluable to troops in the field. They were supposedly protected by the Geneva Conventions on Warfare, but somehow the Nazis hadn't gotten the word. They were targets. Sometimes priority targets. His performance under fire earned him two Silver Stars, three steps below the Medal of Honor. During his Army service he kept in contact with the special girlfriend left behind in Milford. She also happened to be the best friend of one of his sisters.

He told about coming home to Milford after the war ended. He was in turmoil, as most are who have been in heavy combat. They try to reenter the world they left behind, only to discover they really don't fit in like they did before. After WWII, returning soldiers tended to band together in service clubs like the American Legion where they could open up to other men who shared like experiences and were equally burdened.

"With time, most of us adapted. At least we appeared to fit in where we left off before the war. But in my case, I knew I was different even before going to the war. I had begun to understand the significance of that fact. By the time I returned I knew I would never be able to give my girlfriend the love and family she deserved. I fretted about it. I finally faced up to it and managed to explain my feelings to her and for her. We had no future beyond maintaining our friendship. There were lots of tears as we worked through my revelation. Eventually reality set in for both of us. We have remained friends and will the rest of our lives. I am sure you know her and that she eventually married and had a nice family. Her husband is a good man and has become a friend as well."

He spoke of moving to California where being "different" really wasn't so different. I don't think he went to California only for that reason. It was a fact he discovered while living and working there. He went there with the dream of starting his own business. He sought the advice of career counselors there who assessed his farm background and lack of a college education. They recommended he return to Iowa and farm. Instead he went to work for a large business. He saved his money to start his men's clothing store.

I interjected to tell about my first visit to a Pat Marley's Men's Store in Montebello, California, when I was in about the eighth grade. My brother was too young to remember. It was a tiny store in an arcade in the Los Angeles area. Even at that age I was worried that Uncle Pat didn't have much merchandise to sell. A couple of years later more space became available in the arcade. He leased it and expanded. The next time we visited, a few years later, he owned the arcade.

He discussed being friends with several people who were successful in Hollywood and professional sports. He went to their parties, played golf with them, and sold them upscale clothing. Some were famous actors and actresses. Some were sports heroes. Some of each were also gay. Many came from backgrounds like his. He fit in. They were filling the beach communities and urged him to open a store in the Newport Beach area. He established a very successful store there and enjoyed a very interesting and successful clientele that appreciated upscale clothing.

Pat went on to tell how he met the love of his life in that store when Doctor Charles Brubaker stopped in shopping for a suit. Charles was not looking for a partner. He was married to a doctor and they had two children. But there was a mutual attraction and things got very complicated. Eventually Charles got a divorce and moved in with Pat.

It was a very moving evening that extended well into the wee hours of the morning. Uncle Pat seemed relieved of a burden that we didn't realize existed. Dean and I appreciated hearing about his youth and experiences as a gay person.

In the morning I was awakened by the noise of someone getting breakfast in the kitchen. That was Charles' role. I got up and walked into the kitchen. We were the only ones awake. I looked at him, and said, "Charles, I want you to know that to my brother Dean and me, you have always been family." We hugged, and he thanked me. It was a very emotional moment for both of us.

Uncle Pat passed away about a year after Kristina and Aaron's wedding in 2005. He was able to attend the wedding, but in a wheelchair. I still miss him!

Uncle Pat did not live to read the Iowa Supreme Court opinion deciding Varnum v. Brien, 763 N.W.2nd 862 (Iowa 2009). In this historic decision the Iowa Supreme Court addressed the issue of whether gay couples are entitled to the same legal recognition of a marriage as accorded non-gay couples' marriages pursuant to the equal protection provisions of the Iowa Constitution.

The Court did not "vote in gay marriage" as some assert. This was not an activist court exercise. The decision resulted from a conscientious consideration and application of existing constitutional principles which led the justices to the unanimous opinion that the application of established and cherished Iowa rights of equal treatment under the law applied to and required legal recognition of gay marriages. The Court made it very clear that the decision had no application to religious marriages and that churches were free to not recognize or perform gay marriages. I recommend reading the Varnum decision itself. It is a very thoughtful analysis and application of rights created by the Iowa Constitution masterfully written by Justice Mark Cady and subsequently cited with approval by many other courts. For a thorough analysis of the impact of this decision *See* Allen W. Vestal, *Vindication: Varnum v. Brien at Ten Years,* 67 Drake L. Rev. 2, 463 (2019).

Iowa has a retention system that requires judges be periodically subject to a vote of the public upon whether they should be retained in their positions. In the fall following the issuance of this opinion, the three supreme court justices up for retention that year were denied by similar margins of about six percent. Long-time friend Chief Justice Marsha Ternus was one of those justices removed from office by the voters as were Justices David Baker and Michael Streit. I was very active in the unsuccessful fight for their retention.

Tom Witosky and Mark Hansen have written an excellent book concerning this decision and the aftermath: "Equal Before the Law (How Iowa Led Americans to Marriage Equality)." It is published by University of Iowa Press and available through Amazon. I presented a copy to Charles for Christmas autographed by former Chief Justice Ternus and her successor, Chief Justice Mark Cady. They took the time to write thoughtful inscriptions as well. I now especially treasure my similarly inscribed and autographed copy.

While working on the final draft of this book I was shocked to receive notice of the sudden death by heart attack of 66-year-old Chief Justice Mark Cady on November 15, 2019. It is with a heavy heart that I add these last three sentences.

Charles is doing fine at age 96 as I write in 2019. We are in contact, and I consider him my last surviving uncle. Though he and Pat were never able to marry, they had a great love that lasted more than thirty years. Charles is mentally alert and is in good physical shape. A year or so ago he told me about attending his 99-year-old brother's birthday party at a ski resort near Salt Lake City. He said the altitude was beginning to wear on him, but he still had a good time. But this time he left the skiing to his brother. I laughed and said he called to mind an old joke. "Me: 'So, how old was your dad when he died?' You: 'What, you called to tell me my dad has died!!'" Charles had a good laugh.

# 5

# Other Memorable Litigation Cases

NOT LONG AFTER I started practice, one of the senior partners (John McLaughlin) asked if I would handle an aviation plaintiff's case for the widow of one of his clients. I readily agreed. I was aware of the small plane accident in bad weather that had taken the lives of the pilot and his three passengers. John's client was one of the passengers and left a wife and, as I recall, three children. I investigated the case and determined the accident resulted from clear negligence. The pilot was not wealthy, but he had insurance coverage. I contacted the insurance company and demanded settlement of the widow's claim in the amount of the policy limit. They quibbled and offered 90%. Not going to happen! I sent them my analysis to share with their expert. Shortly thereafter, I got a call that they would pay 100%.

There were two other widows represented by other attorneys. One was a very highly regarded trial lawyer. The other had a good reputation too. I told them of my settlement and sent them my analysis for their use. They too got their clients their full 100% with very little effort.

John asked what I thought we ought to charge the widow. He had agreed to represent her for a contingent fee of 33% of the recovery. I told him that I thought the case was one of obvious liability. It did not come close to justifying a 33% fee. He asked my suggestion. I only had about 25 hours or so in it and suggested we bill her about $2,500 as I recall—she and her family needed the money a lot more than we did. John agreed and seemed pleased that I saw it that way. I later was told the highly regarded plaintiff's lawyer took 40% of his client's settlement. I think the other lawyer also took a reduced percentage, but I don't know for sure.

There are good reasons that support the contingent fee system, but it is easily subject to abuse. Based on this early experience in my career, I have always been skeptical. I tried cases on a contingent fee basis, but I was always careful not to take advantage and always discussed and offered other options to my clients.

The most unusual situation I encountered in the trial practice involved a friend from law school who represented an elderly widow whose more elderly husband was killed in an all-night restaurant parking lot. The restaurant was a part of a national chain. I was defending this deep-pocketed establishment against a poor widow's claim for damages arising from the wrongful death of her husband in their parking lot at 3:00 AM.

The soon-to-be-deceased and his friend ended up at the restaurant after leaving a bar at closing time. A group of four motorcyclists left their biker-bar and were seated at the same restaurant shortly after the deceased and his friend. The place was very busy, and service was a little slow. There occurred some kind of hostile interaction between the two groups. The widow and her husband and his friend were African Americans, and there may have been a racial remark spoken by one of the bikers.

Whatever occurred, things settled down and all were served. While the wait staff was busy bringing out orders, a tray was dropped. The waitress did a quick clean-up leaving more to do for later.

The two groups left at about the same time and another spat occurred at the register. The two gentlemen left and were followed out by the bikers. The deceased turned around and made a provocative remark to one of the bikers, who reacted by decking him. Unfortunately, he fell and hit the back of his head on a curb stop. The impact killed him!

The decedent was elderly and there was little evidence of economic loss that could be presented by my friend at trial. There was no income that was lost, and there were no prospects for future prosperity had he not died. My friend played upon the sympathy of the jury as much as he could. Since the decedent died instantly, there wasn't even pain and suffering to argue. Despite my objections to such arguments and testimony, the case presented was mainly sympathy appeals to the jury about the poor widow, her loss of companionship, and insinuations about deep pockets of the defendant that prevailed. Recipe for disaster! I recall the settlement demand was around $150,000. I think we offered about $40,000.

Corporate counsel from San Francisco sat with me during the trial as the defendant's corporate representative. He was a very nice fellow and complimented me on my handling of the defense. He returned to San Francisco as the jury started its deliberations.

My friend, the plaintiff's attorney, was a notorious lady's man. He was a real charmer! He regaled me with his exploits several times while the trial was in recess. He was "taking care of" a young woman whose live-in boyfriend worked a night shift. I told him he led an exciting life—but a very reckless one! I warned him that one of these days a boyfriend or husband was going to come home unexpectedly and shoot him.

I think the trial probably lasted around three days. The jury deliberations consumed the rest of the week. Late that Friday I got the call that a verdict had been entered. I think it was for about $200,000!

I called the attorney in San Francisco and reported the result. He asked if that was a record for that kind of case in Des Moines. I said it wasn't a record, but it was way out-of-line based on the evidence. He chuckled and said he thought I had done a great job, and that the company held records in some states. They were what is called in the profession a "target defendant"—a company viewed as having deep pockets that could afford to compensate a downtrodden plaintiff. He said I should proceed with the usual post-trial motions seeking reduction of the award. Failing that, I should take an appeal to the Supreme Court of Iowa.

There then began a series of meetings and offers and counteroffers between me and my friend. To my shock, I picked up my newspaper one morning and there was a headline about an attorney having been a victim of a double murder and suicide. You got it! The boyfriend had come home early. Another attorney, a mutual friend of the murdered lawyer and myself, took over representation of the widow. He didn't know much about the case of course. I invited him to my office and opened my files to him and helped him get up to speed.

One of the post-trial efforts involved interviewing the jurors. Why did they find liability and how did they come up with such a large verdict? I learned the finding of liability was not predicated on anything the restaurant was responsible for in its parking lot. It was based on the "negligence" of the waitress for not doing a thorough job of cleaning up the spilled tray. Some admitted they just felt the poor widow needed the money and our corporate client wouldn't miss it.

We had strong grounds for appeal. There were several legal errors during the trial that could be urged in support of a new trial. This was acknowledged by my late colleague and recognized by the new attorney. We eventually settled the case for what I recall was $50,000. Of course, I was keeping the attorney in San Francisco informed of all developments in the case. He couldn't believe the murder of the plaintiff's attorney. In Clive, Iowa! San Francisco yes, but Clive, Iowa! He had grown to like him. I don't think the murdered attorney's estate made any claim for fees. The new attorney was also generous with the widow as I recall. She was a nice lady, and I think she was able to keep most of the settlement amount.

# 6

# Just What the World Needed—Another Lobbyist

I FIRST REGISTERED as a lobbyist in 1972 while in law school and clerking for the law firm in West Des Moines. We represented motorcycle dealers who opposed the mandatory helmet bill. We lost the battle but eventually won the war. The legislature passed the helmet bill, and promptly repealed it the following session. Neither my mentor nor I was very effective. We really didn't understand the intricacies of the legislative process. Both of us knew some legislators, though. He was a very active Democrat and I was very active in the Republican Party. We both had friends in the other's party too. I found it an interesting experience. We made clear our limitations to our client, and he was happy with our effort despite the initial outcome.

I re-ignited my lobbying career in 1981. This launch was much more successful. I lobbied every year thereafter, until my retirement in December 2012.

I had always been interested in the firm's lobbying practice and in politics. I continued to be involved politically and closely followed the issues. I enjoyed engaging in the political discussions that occurred at firm luncheons. In 1980 lobbyist Kent Emery retired and Jim West, the firm's other lobbyist partner, got swamped during the legislative session and asked if I would help him. I didn't have a trial scheduled for the near future and agreed.

Jim, a Republican, was a great teacher. He was highly regarded as a legal scholar, draftsman, and lobbyist by legislators and staff of both parties. He had a great reputation for skill and integrity. I benefited from his reputation, as I did from Jerry's and Roy's in the trial practice. I wasn't working at the Capitol very long before I had a client of my own.

For the first few years I maintained my trial practice, as well as serving as a lobbyist. As my lobbying practice grew, it was more difficult to do both. I eventually decided to forgo the trial work and concentrate on lobbying. I enjoyed working with prominent clients on the major issues of the day.

Jim and I were a great team. We had a good solid client base that developed during the firm's then sixty-year lobbying history. All clients had important issues of concern to them. Some of those issues were of general interest. Clients' interests varied from year to year. I will mercifully limit my discussion to issues of general interest that have had an impact on the citizens of Iowa. Those issues were significant, challenging, and quite interesting.

Each Iowa General Assembly operates with a constitutionally set term of two years. The constitution requires they meet in regular session once each year. Senators serve four-year terms and Representatives serve two-year terms. Issues are carried over from first sessions to second sessions. Each session has its own personality, as does each General Assembly.

Ten year required reapportionments or redistricting is done by color-blind and politically unaware computers under the control of the non-partisan legislative services agency. This process has served Iowa well for several decades and is a model increasingly attractive to other states.

Political control of the legislative bodies and executive branch offices is subject to change. Iowa is a very politically competitive state. For example, Iowa had both a Democrat and Republican United States

Senator for several years (Chuck Grassley and Tom Harken). It has not been unusual to have split control of the legislative chambers. US Representative Berkley Bedell, a Democrat businessman, represented my home district in Iowa from 1975 to 1987. Part of that time, if not all of it, our County Republican Chairman was his brother, Jack, an attorney! Most of us Iowans know how to disagree without being disagreeable. But not all, unfortunately.

There is always a change in Membership of the General Assembly due to health, shift in political success, change in employment, and retirement. I am surprised how many new faces there are following an election.

I am invited every two years to participate in a Joint Session of the Iowa General Assembly held every first annual session to honor members of the Pioneer Lawmakers Association. I became a proud honorary member of that Association by Resolution of the 79th General Assembly in 2001.

It has been most rewarding to have enjoyed the opportunity to participate in shaping the issues of the day. Helping bridge gaps between politicians and clients to forge better public policy was very challenging and interesting. I feel that Iowans benefited from my having been involved. I don't recall ever working on an issue that produced harm to the citizens of Iowa. I will discuss several that greatly benefitted Iowans.

◆ ◆ ◆

*Skeptics Abound*

The above discussion reminds me: daughters Kathleen and Kristina turned 11 and 7 when I began my lobbying practice in 1981. Legislative sessions usually run from early January until late April or early May. They are intense and demanding physically and mentally. Long hours are required every day the legislature is in session, and weekends are spent reviewing new legislation, drafting legislation and amendments to pending legislation, and reporting to clients. It is hard on family life!

Not long after my first session finally ended in late May as I recall, I noticed a certain attitude on the part of the girls. They weren't treating dear old Dad like dear old Dad was used to being treated. After an activity together one day, we ended up sitting on the front porch after lunch. I asked them if there was something wrong. Kathleen responded that there was, they didn't like what I was doing. I was trying to think what I had done recently that would have angered them. I couldn't think of anything.

I asked Kathleen what she meant. She said they didn't like my new job, lobbying. I asked her why and what she thought lobbyists did. I will always recall her reply: "You pay people to break the law!" I was shocked! I thought for a minute and then suggested we go for a ride in the car.

I took them to our beautiful state capitol and told them that was where I spent most of my lobbying time. We went inside. I showed them the legislative chambers and the very impressive law library. I was hoping to find some legislative leaders I could introduce them to for a discussion of the roll of lobbyists. I found Lt. Governor Bob Anderson (D) in his office behind the Iowa Senate. Bob was a friend and welcomed us into his office. He explained what lobbyists did: informed legislators on issues of interest, presented their clients' opinions and legislative proposals, and suggested changes to pending legislation. He told them lobbyists had to be very honest or the legislators would not listen to them. He told them their dad was highly regarded for his honesty and knowledge. They brightened up!

Now that dear old Dad's reputation was restored, we began leaving the statehouse when I got the idea of showing them the Iowa Supreme Court chambers, which at that time were in the state capitol building. I had argued cases before the Court and knew several Justices personally. I occasionally had breakfast with Chief Justice Ward Reynoldson. I decided to stop by his office to see if he was available to talk to us. His secretary checked with him and came back to tell us he would be out shortly.

He was wonderful with the girls. He showed them through the

court's chambers, and I saw rooms I had never seen before. He explained the court's functions and duties. He explained how important it was that the legislature enact good, understandable, and practical laws for them to interpret and apply. He told them lobbyists played an important role in that process. He really laid it on thick about the high regard legislators and supreme court justices had for their dad. The girls were really impressed now!

Two happy girls and their restored father had a great time at the statehouse! A few days later I ran into the Chief Justice and thanked him profusely for helping me out. He said, "Well, I could see right away that it was a case of a dad in trouble!" He was like that! A great man, a great friend, and a great Chief Justice.

◆ ◆ ◆

### *The Lobbyist Stock in Trade—Credibility*

Informing clients on legislative procedures and the political realities of an issue is an important duty. I have turned down potential clients because what they sought was not achievable. I have also turned down some who wanted to advance terrible ideas, creation of a referenda system for example. A lobbyist gathers and provides information to decision makers. That may take the form of informal discussion, formal written research papers, testimony of experts, or the rendering of a well-grounded statement of opinion on an issue.

Lobbyists do not have to be lawyers, but legal skills are valuable to lobbyists who work with legislators and staff to draft legislation that addresses clients' concerns. Skillful drafting of legislation can solve many client problems. It is an art to affirmatively address client's issues without arousing opposition from others. Sometimes battles are unavoidable as interest groups are put in direct conflict.

Often lobbyists operate in a defensive role. A well-drafted curative amendment to a bill otherwise harmful to a client's interest that does not impair the original legislative goal, is usually welcomed. Legislators like to please people, not alienate them. Legislating often depends upon the ability to forge compromises. A successful lobbyist must be knowledgeable about his or her issues and have a reputation for honesty and reliability. Like any other profession, there are varying degrees of perceived honesty and reliability! They are, however, critical ingredients of credibility and success.

Lobbying in Iowa is regulated. Transparency is the basic goal of that regulation. By "transparency," I mean registration and reporting subject to public review. Lobbyists are required to register clients, and to make reports indicating which legislative bills they are working on and for which clients. A general statement of position on each bill is required that indicates whether the client is for, against, or monitoring a bill.

Clients are also required to report what they pay lobbyists, and any other expenses they incur relating to lobbying. Lobbyists and their clients cannot give gifts to legislators and executive branch officers exceeding $3.00 per day in value. They may not make campaign contributions when the legislature is in session. Campaign contributions and the financing of campaigns are sources of concern, as they can lead to corruption of public officials. Once again, transparency is the remedy in use. Campaigns are required to report in detail contributions received and expenditures made.

The Supreme Court of the United States has generally refused strict regulation of campaign finance due to concerns about infringing upon rights guaranteed by the First Amendment. Transparency and public opinion are regarded as practical restraints.

In 2010 the Supreme Court of the United States ruled that political spending is a constitutionally protected form of speech, and government may not prohibit corporations or unions from spending money to support or denounce candidates for public office, or advocate on issues. The ruling did include a statement allowing reconsideration of that position should it result in corruption of the political system. The power of big money and special-interest groups was bad enough in 2010. In my opinion, the situation has gotten much worse since the Court rendered this decision. How much worse must it get before the Court will be willing to reconsider? We won't know until the Court is presented with and accepts a case that creates that opportunity.

# 7

# Governor Friends

*Governor Ray*

WHEN I BEGAN lobbying with Jim West, Governor Robert D. Ray, a friend from my days as a law student and POW advocate, was Governor. He decided not to run for another term in 1983, having been Governor since January 1969. My law school friend, Lt. Governor Terry Branstad immediately announced his successful candidacy. I have been fortunate to have been friends of all of Iowa's governors since returning to Iowa in 1970. While none agreed with me on everything, all were willing to listen to me.

***

*Governor Branstad*

I remember being at the governor's mansion when the Branstads were packing up in late 1998. The Governor and I were sitting on the main floor steps having a beer, while First Lady Chris and my wife Patti were elsewhere. I asked him if he had any firm plans yet. He said he was still considering a couple of options. I asked if, God forbid, one of our US Senators were to die, would he accept an appointment to the vacancy. He said he would not. I asked about an appointment to a cabinet office. Not interested. He said he had promised Chris he was not going to hold public office ever again. He did not want to do anything else in government. He told me, "Once you have been a governor, there is no other public office worth having!"

◆◆◆

## Governor Vilsack

Democrat State Senator Tom Vilsack came from way behind and upset Congressman Jim Ross Lightfoot, to become governor in 1998. Tom had been propelled into politics when the mayor of the City of Mount Pleasant, where he lived and practiced law, was shot to death by an irate citizen during a city council meeting. He was asked to fill the position, which he did ably, under very difficult circumstances. He was soon elected to the state senate. His background was as an excellent plaintiff's attorney. We knew each other professionally but had never spent significant personal time together.

While he was in the Iowa Senate, we had some heated arguments over my tort reform lobbying. I represented physicians and insurance interests seeking tort reform while he was in the senate. We did, however, eventually manage to work well together on other issues and formed a friendship. Governor Vilsack is viewed as a popular and successful governor. He was re-elected in 2002 but chose not to run for a third term in 2006. He became Secretary of Agriculture in the Obama Administration in 2009, serving nearly eight years (a record) in that capacity. In 2012 I was pleased to recommend employment of his son, Jess, as a member of the Nyemaster Law Firm where I had been a shareholder.

◆◆◆

## Governor Culver

Democrat Iowa Secretary of State Chet Culver was elected governor in 2006. His father, John, had been a US Senator. After college Chet lobbied at the Iowa Statehouse. In 1998 he was elected Iowa Secretary of State at the age of 32. Although he is much younger, we became good friends during our lobbying years, even though we were sometimes placed in conflict by the differing interests of our clients. We remain good friends.

Popular Republican Governor Ray passed away at age 89 in 2018. I had not seen Chet for quite some time when we met in July 2018 at a memorial service for Governor Ray. The last time before that was a coincidental meeting late one night a few years before in Washington D.C. I was there on firm business and Chet was there for a birthday party for his father, a former US Senator and Senator Ted Kennedy's college roommate.

Chet and I had a chance to catch up following Governor Ray's service. At one point he observed that Governor Ray had been a great leader and wonderful person. Chet had the misfortune of being elected to serve as governor in what turned out to be a period of very bad economic times. The state's budget was under great stress. Eventually he had to order a ten percent across-the-board cut of the state's budget, a move that was not well received by the electorate.

◆ ◆ ◆

*Governor Reynolds*

Lieutenant Governor Kim Reynolds became the first woman to serve as Governor of Iowa upon Governor Branstad's resignation. She ran for governor in 2018 and became the first woman elected governor on November 6th. She won with 50.3% of the vote and carried 88 of the 99 counties. I first met her when she was a county officer. We became good friends over the years. Patti and I were strong supporters when she ran for governor against another friend, Democrat Businessman Fred Hubbell, who won 47.5% of the vote.

# 8

# Iowa's First Woman Member of Congress, Senator Joni Ernst

IOWA REPUBLICANS WERE looking for a United States Senate candidate in 2014. Long serving Democrat Senator Tom Harken was retiring, creating an open seat. It was my expressed opinion that only two Iowa Republicans had a chance to defeat the Democrat candidate, US Representative Bruce Braley: State Senator Joni Ernst and Lt. Governor Kim Reynolds. Iowa had never sent a woman to Congress. I spoke to both individually (they are good friends) and urged them to discuss it together and decide which of them would run. I don't know the details of how the decision was made, but the citizens of Iowa were given the opportunity to elect Joni Ernst to the United States Senate in 2014. Joni won the Republican nomination in a hotly contested primary. She went on to defeat Representative Braley in the general election 52.2% to 43.7%.

# 9

# Branstad Again: Longest Serving Governor in American History

IN EARLY 2009 Terry called and asked what I thought about him running for governor against Governor Culver. I was surprised and exclaimed, "Are you crazy?! You have a great job as President of Des Moines University. The alumni, faculty and students love you! And Chris is happy!! What are you thinking!"

He laughed and asked if I was backing anyone else. I said I had talked to some people about running and they were not interested. It turned out we had talked to some of the same people. We agreed we would make some final passes and compare notes. We did, with no positive results. We talked again. He said, "I think I might have to run to get the state back on a firm footing."

I told him, "I still think you are crazy."

He laughed and replied, "That's what all my real friends are telling me!"

I asked him what Chris thought about it. He admitted he hadn't yet discussed it with many people, Chris included.

As luck would have it, the Des Moines Register published a story one morning in early May about Branstad possibly running again. We were attending the same small function in Des Moines that evening. At that time the Branstads lived in a very nice log home in a rural area near the small town of Luther, Iowa. I remember when he called to tell me about purchasing that home. I laughed when he described his "log cabin!" "You have done things backwards! If you had started out in a log cabin, you would have ended up President of the United States of America instead of Des Moines University." He just laughed!

Terry drove to the dinner from the University and Chris drove from home. Chris arrived first and was talking to Patti. I joined the conversation and asked if she had seen the paper. She had. I asked her what she thought—she replied, "He's a dead man!!!"

Terry arrived. I met him at the door. I commented about the news story and told him what his biggest fan had said. He laughed and said that he had some work to do with Chris, and that he hoped Patti would help, which she did.

During the summer of 2009 there were more conversations. I recall one in which Terry reported there had been a family meeting, and the kids thought he should run. He said a vote was taken which was something like 8 to 2. He explained that oldest grandchild Mackenzie always voted with Grandma!

In January of 2010 Terry officially announced his candidacy. He ran a great campaign, and defeated Governor Culver. During the campaign I remember getting a call from Terry while I was in a meeting at Iowa State University. I excused myself and took the call in a hallway. He was laughing and said he had just come from a meeting during which he was chewed out for being too liberal. He said he thought of me and just had to call. We both observed that times had really changed. Now he was viewed as being too moderate! Wonder what that makes me?!

Terry Branstad defeated incumbent Governor Culver by a margin of 55%/45% in the 2010 election. His running mate and newly elected Lt. Governor was my friend, State Senator Kim Reynolds.

In 2014 Governor Branstad won re-election as Governor against

State Senator Jack Hatch by a margin of 61%/39%. His running mate, again, was Lt. Governor Kim Reynolds.

On December 14, 2015, Terry Branstad became the longest-serving governor in the history of the United States. A grand celebration was had at the state fairgrounds.

# 10

# Ambassador Branstad: Okay, One Last Branstad Chapter

IN 2010 WHEN Governor Branstad was considering running again after a 12-year hiatus, we recognized and discussed the need to develop new young leaders in Iowa. He chose State Senator Kim Reynolds to be his Lt. Governor running mate. His unannounced plan was to serve two more terms and hopefully be replaced by Iowa's first woman governor, Kim Reynolds. There were rumors (when aren't there in politics!) after the election that Governor Branstad would resign during his second term making Kim Reynolds Iowa's first woman governor. If there was any such plan, I am unaware of it. These rumors were in circulation long before there was any thought, other than my own, that Governor Branstad would resign to become Ambassador to China. Were it not for the ambassadorship, I believe Governor Branstad would have served two complete four-year terms.

Early in 2016 I suggested to Governor Branstad that if a Republican were to be elected president that fall, he would be receiving a call to serve as ambassador to China. I advised he start thinking about it and discussing it with his wife, Chris. He told me he had no interest in the position and was happy serving as governor. He didn't think he would get such a call despite the well-known fact that he and the incoming president of China, Xi Jinping, had established a good personal relationship.

Their friendship began with Xi Jinping's visit to Iowa more than thirty years before. They had stayed in touch. There were several visits back and forth in the years that followed. President Xi made a state visit to Washington not long after becoming President of China in 2013. On his way back to China, he made a visit to Des Moines. One of the first foreign politicians invited to visit President Xi in China was Governor Branstad.

I mentioned the ambassadorship possibility several times and always got the "not interested" answer. In one of our conversations, I observed that he would be put in a position of telling the President of the United States that he did not want to serve his country and his state as Ambassador to China. We kidded about it, but there was also developing a seriousness about our discussions. It wasn't long before others were beginning to talk about the possibility. He told me that Chris was not opposed to the idea and he began to appear interested in it. They had family meetings about it. His children wanted him to accept the position if offered.

I was certainly not thinking it would be Donald Trump who would be making that appointment! To my surprise he became the GOP nominee, was elected president, and the one who made that appointment.

Eventually the call came, and he agreed to serve. Chris and the family were in full support. He and Chris met with President-elect Trump in the Trump Tower in New York City. Trump came into the room. After some preliminary chitchat, he looked at Chris and asked, "Chris, are you on board?"

"Yes, Sir!" she replied.

He banged the table, looked at Terry, and proclaimed, "Done deal then."

Hopefully Terry will remain Ambassador to China until I finish this book, I am tired of writing Branstad Chapters! And the country needs him there!

# PART V
# TRIAL LAWYER
# TO LOBBYIST

# 1

# First Breaks: My New Firm Clients

## Iowa Society of Certified Public Accountants

WHILE HELPING JIM West, I benefitted from exposure to other lobbyists, their clients, and many legislators. I enjoyed working with Jim and we made a good team. He was very good at introducing me around the Statehouse. I had help from many of Jim's friends, and I can't begin to name them all. Two stand out: Senator Dick Drake of Muscatine and Attorney Lobbyist George Wilson III. Senator Drake and I had something in common: we were both service academy graduates. I was especially nice to Senator Drake—I felt sorry for him, he was an Annapolis Grad. We enjoyed a lot of banter over that fact. George was the son of George Wilson who had served Iowa as Governor and US Senator. George had served as a tank commander in World War II. We had respect for each other's combat experience. George and Jim did a lot together and included me in all but their Canadian fishing trips. I think they figured out that I wasn't interested in fishing trips. For a while I lived in fear of being invited!

After my fist General Assembly Session, I began to attract clients. Jim and I always worked as a team and had familiarity with each

250

other's clients and their issues so we could back each other up when necessary. Though the firm considered clients to be firm clients as opposed to clients of firm members, firm members assumed responsibility for clients when providing their specialized services.

I was fortunate to have a long run with "my" first client, the Iowa Society of CPAs. They remain a firm client today. Stan Bonta, CEO, and Judy Chaplin were great to work with and retired shortly before I did. CPA Cindy Adams is the current CEO. The staff, and Society members and member leaders (Cindy was one) were also great to work with! I made many new friends and learned CPAs know how to have a good time.

The representation was not at all what I expected. Accounting can be very interesting! A lot of the issues involving accounting involve the licensing and policing of the accounting profession. There are national standards of practice that are promulgated and adopted by the states. While there are variations in what individual states adopt, uniformity is the desired goal. As with the rest of society, advances in access to information and ease of communications has led to demand for standards that can be applied across state and international borders. With those demands came need for streamlined regulation and modes for control of cross-border practices. Many changes in financial and accounting practices and procedures became necessary during my tenure.

The ISCPA staff and member leadership were a pleasure to work with. Governor Branstad was asked to serve on the board of the national association, AICPA (American Institute of Certified Public Accountants) after he retired as Governor. He also enjoyed his experience. He regretted having to resign that position when he became governor again. The ISCPA continued, for several years after my retirement in 2012, to invite us both and our wives to their annual holiday party which we enjoyed very much.

One of the most intense legislative battles I was involved in arose from a dispute with the State Auditor involving the performance of local government audits. Those audits are submitted to that office for review and filing. A rather undiplomatic advisory was issued to local government entities required to obtain and submit those audits. Many hire private practice CPAs rather than relying on the State Auditor's office staff, which is an available resource that some use. But the office does not have the capacity to do all the audits the law requires. The advisory found fault with some aspects of the performance of some of the private practice CPA auditors. The advisory contained some requirements for audits that were not thought to be required by law, which would increase costs and delay reports. A copy of the advisory was provided for my review. I read it and concluded it must have been issued by someone lower in the hierarchy of the Auditor's office.

I thought it would be beneficial to meet with the State Auditor and resolve the issues inherent in the advisory in a low key, non-confrontational manner. It turned out the advisory was issued by the State Auditor himself who had strong feelings about a couple of disputed points. He was going to insist on his interpretation. It became clear the ISCPA could either agree with the Auditor or fight for legislative clarification. We successfully advocated for passage of legislation during the next legislative session which clarified the governing statute to resolve the disagreement in our favor. It was a hard-fought battle. But with the passage of time, wounds suffered on all sides healed, friendships were restored, and life went on.

◆ ◆ ◆

## Iowa Propane Gas Association

Next came the Iowa Propane Gas Association. Again, I had great people to work for and made many life-long friends. Lori Squires was the Executive Director. She was replaced by Deb Grooms when she moved to the Association of Builders and Contractors. That move gave Lori the chance to hire me again—which she did. The Propane Gas Association continued with me, and Deb was great to work with. I represented the association for several years until my retirement. Usually their issues were not very controversial. The association's membership is mostly small businesses that supply LPG throughout Iowa and their suppliers. It is an essential product in rural Iowa necessary to farming (crop drying) as well as a widespread use as heating fuel.

The political strength of the association is attributable to the grassroots activities of these many businesses. At the time the price for LPG was increasing dramatically, and it was especially concerning to Governor Culver (D) and legislators who had people in their districts dependent upon LPG, many of whom were in LIHEAP (Low Income Heating Energy Assistance Program). LIHEAP provides for supply of propane and other heating energies to people unable to afford it during the winter. LPG is a commodity that is extremely subject to market volatility.

We were alerted to the issue in late 2007. I was requested to meet with Governor Culver's Chief of Staff, an attorney. The meeting did not go well. I couldn't seem to make him understand we had no ability to influence market prices of our product. The Chief of Staff suggested a state government takeover of the industry. Thankfully Governor Culver (D) apparently understood LPG dealers had no control over price and the issue died. The governor never mentioned it to me personally despite several opportunities.

In 2008, we became embroiled in a session-long fight-to-the-bitter-end. Newly elected State Senator Steve Sodders took up the cause of the LIHEAP population. He proposed legislation that would essentially put the state in control of pricing and distribution of LPG. The dealer's association had no choice but to fight for survival.

It was a harsh battle waged until the last 15 minutes of the session which occurred well after everyone with any sense was sound asleep. Brad Epperly, experienced member of Nyemaster Goode, joined me on the hill that session. Thank God! He is an extremely fast learner and was as determined and tenacious as the senator. It was an exhausting battle and I don't know what I would have done had Brad not been there to man the front lines every day. The senator involved was not happy with the result.

◆◆◆

## Associated Builders & Contractors (ABC)

I had the privilege of representing the Iowa Chapter of ABC for several years. Lori Squires was the first Executive Director I worked for at ABC. She was followed by Greg Spenner, a former legislator. I considered both to be good friends before they worked for this association. ABC is a national organization. The Iowa chapter was initiated in 1972 and formally incorporated in 1974 due to the efforts of two prominent independent contractors, Larry Meisner (Meisner Electric Inc.) and Bill Yeager (Yeager Mechanical). They shared a common problem: finding qualified workers. Larry discovered ABC and, with Bill, started the Iowa chapter. Its first office was in a room located under a motel. ABC national dealt with many issues, but the emphasis was on worker training through establishment of apprenticeship programs. The local ABC chapter made that their primary focus. I was retained to represent them several years after they had become established.

When they started, there was an apprenticeship program run by Meisner Electric that was turned over to ABC by Larry Meisner. I was hired to represent them in 1996. My first mission was to work on state legislation regarding apprenticeship programs. ABC was incorrectly viewed as a group of non-union contractors at that time. The issue of support for apprenticeship programs involved union and non-union contractors.

When I was hired, Bill Dotzler, a Waterloo Democrat, was first elected to the Iowa House of Representatives. Bill was a union member and John Deere employee. He was very interested in apprenticeship programs. Apprenticeship legislation was the first thing he and I worked on together. Fortunately, it was the beginning of a great working relationship. We worked together on several issues in the years to follow.

It quickly became apparent to both of us that union and non-union apprenticeship programs benefited Iowa generally. There was no reason to differentiate in the legislation. I also benefited from working with union lobbyists in this effort. We forged good relationships that led to solving other problems we encountered over the years.

Those programs have been of great benefit, especially to young men and women who have participated in them. Contractors hire apprentices-in-training. They earn as they learn. The tuition is $640 per year (2019). These programs are key to the efforts of Governor Reynolds, Economic Development Authority Director Debi Durham, and Workforce Development Director Beth Townsend to revitalize rural Iowa.

ABC is now located in Grimes, Iowa, with an 8,000 square foot hands-on training lab with six classrooms. They are in the process of adding four more classrooms and doubling the size of the lab facility. There are established training centers in Hiawatha and Davenport, as well as 19 remote sites located throughout Iowa. A record 1,400 apprentices were enrolled last year. In July of 2018, 257 apprentices graduated from six different trade apprenticeships.

As ABC grew, their need for an in-house, full-time governmental affairs person became apparent. That person is also involved in local government issues, a service we could not provide. I was pleased to assist in that transition and am proud to have had the opportunity to represent ABC.

◆ ◆ ◆

## Monsanto

I had very enjoyable and educational experiences representing Monsanto for many years. It was a great client, and the firm continues to represent them. It was a company made great by the people it employed. I was initially hired in the mid-eighties. I warned them that I did not have a farm background and had not worked on agricultural issues. That was not a problem for them as I had a science education and a good reputation. They were very concerned about the fast-developing issue of ground water contamination from agricultural chemicals. It was an issue being driven by a group of four very idealistic liberal young Democrats with whom I had good friendships. I was interviewed in Des Moines along with other lobbyists by a very impressive woman from the St. Louis headquarters, Vivian L. Eveloff. She had a great personality and a style that enhanced it.

Shortly after the interview, she called to tell me that they wanted to hire me. We agreed on a contract amount. I was asked to come to the St. Louis headquarters to learn about the company, its issues, and participate in a new government affairs employee class.

I was introduced to government affairs department leaders, the General Counsel and staff attorneys, executive personnel, and scientists. I was drinking out of the firehose and enjoying it. In the new employee classroom, I was seated next to a very attractive and personable young African American woman, Gwen Wesley, who had been a computer system's analyst at McDonnell-Douglas where she met her husband, Ben, an Aeronautical Engineer. She worked several years in a similar capacity at Monsanto before being promoted to Government and Regulatory Affairs. On weekends she sang with an R&B band called Bittersweet. She eventually left the band and joined the St. Louis Symphony In Unison Chorus in which she remains active. After a few days of classes together we had become friends. At the conclusion, we said our goodbyes thinking we would probably never meet again. Wrong!

◆◆◆

## The Groundwater Bill

When the legislature started the following January, my four friends immediately went to work on the ground water issue. Anything involving farming and groundwater is a big deal in Iowa! They were breaking new ground and they generated a lot of fear in the process. Farmers were concerned of course. The big, bad ag chemical industry was very concerned! Monsanto was part of a group of those companies and other interested parties. It soon became apparent that the industry group believed in a scorched earth attack strategy. That was not my style! I consulted with Monsanto on strategy and advised against participating in the group's approach on this issue. There were other issues the group worked on that Monsanto could support, but it should not support the group's attack strategy on the groundwater issue.

I suggested pursuing the issue on a friendly basis with the four main legislative proponents. It wasn't long before those four were working with us and taking our advice and suggestions into consideration in the development of their legislation. They appreciated the scientific information we provided and our recognition of the need to responsibly address the issue. That made me a traitor in the eyes of several others in the group.

Legislation relating to a complex and controversial issue is a very anguishing process in many respects. Time is always a scarce commodity in a legislative session, and it is difficult, if not flat unadvisable, to rush when deciding complex issues. My legislator friends drafted versions of ground water legislation and I would often react in horror. Monsanto was not opposed to reasonable scientifically based legislation addressing groundwater contamination. I would point out the flaws from that standpoint to my legislator friends. It got to be a process of them drafting and filing something and me drafting amendments to their drafts. As they were running out of time, they asked me to help them develop a draft acceptable to Monsanto.

The legislative committee chairman had been a leader in the Iowa ACLU. It just so happened that Vivian Eveloff, the woman who hired and directed me, was then President of the Missouri ACLU. The chairman was in a state of shock when Vivian appeared to work with us on the final draft. He had no idea ACLU Vivian and Monsanto Vivian were one and the same! How could she be working for Monsanto?! Good legislation was produced, and in large measure is intact and serving the Iowa environment today. Vivian left Monsanto and had her own consulting firm. She has been the director of the Institute for Women in Public Life at the University of Missouri-St. Louis since its inception in 1996.

As an aside, I often used mathematical analysis when working on scientific or engineering-based issues at the legislature. I did so on the ground water issue. The argument in large part was based on the finding of contaminants in the water. The science of detection had evolved to the point that it was possible to detect ever smaller amounts of a substance.

I don't recall the ground water contaminant detection levels that concerned the legislators, but recently in Iowa there was a newspaper crusade about the presence of lead in drinking water. The resulting alarm created reached the point of the ridiculous. I did some calculations. Lead contamination of drinking water is undeniably a significant health issue. The EPA deserved criticism for its failure to produce a health-hazard standard for lead contamination of drinking water. In the meantime, some perspective is needed. The 15 part per billion existing "action level" can be visualized as 15 gallons of contaminate contained in a square mile pool of water 4.8 feet deep. You would have to drink 733 gallons of the water from that pool to ingest just one drop of the contaminate.

The CEO of Monsanto at this time was from Iowa and was a high school classmate of an Iowa legislator, Delores Mertz (D). I was contacted and asked to organize and moderate a panel discussion of groundwater issues that he wanted held in Des Moines in front of his executive staff. It was to include a social hour and dinner afterwards. It was highly successful and both sides were heard and mingled with each other both before and after the panel discussion.

A few years later I got a call from my Monsanto training school classmate, Gwen Wesley. She asked if I remembered her, which I did. She asked how I would feel about her being my company legislative liaison and supervisor. I said that would be great. She expressed concerns about how she might be received by Iowa legislators. I assured her that she would love working with them and they with her. This was indeed the case and we worked as an effective team for several years.

After one grueling legislative session, Gwen called and asked if I could come to St. Louis the following week for a meeting. She organized a great day for me. We had our meeting and then did a tour of St. Louis which included the zoo and a visit to the Arch. We topped it off with a St. Louis Cardinals game followed by dinner with her husband Ben. I enjoyed meeting Ben and discussing aeronautical engineering.

Gwen went up the ladder at Monsanto and I lost contact with her. Recently I learned she was president of a civic organization in St. Louis and I emailed her. She responded with a phone call and we got caught up. Gwen has retired and music remains a critical part of her life. She sent a copy of an enjoyable CD which she had just completed. She also serves on three significant boards dealing with philanthropy, college education, and social justice.

◆◆◆

## The Genetically Modified Organisms Uproar

Over the years I represented Monsanto on many issues. One of the most interesting involved the fuss over the development and use of genetically modified organisms (GMOs). Monsanto was at the forefront of the effort to modify plants by genetic engineering. Monsanto developed and marketed Roundup, a glyphosate based nonselective herbicide. Unless a green plant has an immunity to glyphosate it will be susceptible to it. Monsanto also discovered a gene that could be inserted into a plant that would create that immunity. This herbicide was tremendously effective when applied to crops that were genetically modified to include the immunity gene. Monsanto also devised a GMO crop modified to contain Vitamin A that would greatly reduce occurrences of blindness in children with a deficiency of that vitamin in southern areas of Africa.

Before any GMO crop can be planted, clearance is required following testing as to the fitness for human consumption of that crop in the food chain. Several testing agencies in the United States and abroad with expertise in these matters found no evidence of harmful effects. But opponents soon surfaced and worked against issuance of permits.

They succeeded in delaying use of GMO crops. Eventually

GMO crops achieved widespread international acceptance. But to my knowledge vitamin A infused GMO crops have not yet been accepted in parts of Africa. It is depressing to think of the many children whose blindness could have been prevented had Vitamin A GMO crops been available in their countries.

While fighting the GMO battle, I was introduced to Dr. Ted Crosbie, PhD, of Monsanto. I had been working on the issue with Dave Tierney, another outstanding Monsanto representative. We decided it was time to bring to the legislature a highly-qualified scientific expert to help us address the issue and provide scientifically based answers to the many questions being asked. Ted was that company supplied expert. He was a leading seed scientist and lived on his farm in the Des Moines area. He earned his BS at Iowa State University in Agricultural Education in 1973. His Master's Degree (1976) and PhD (1978) were also earned at Iowa State in Plant Breeding and Cytogenetics. He grew up on a farm in Northwest Iowa (Paulina). He had served on the faculty at Iowa State.

He began his career at Monsanto in 1996 where he was Vice President of Global Plant Breeding for 16 years. He then served as integrated Farming Systems Lead and was recognized as a Monsanto Distinguished Fellow of Science. When we met, I recall that he was responsible for fifteen or so research and development facilities in eleven countries scattered around the world. He traveled a lot and wasn't always aware of time zone relationships when calling. If I got a call in the middle of the night, I assumed it was Ted, not a family emergency!

As you might expect, Ted was used to dealing in facts and scientifically proven theories from the vantage point of one whose opinion was internationally respected. Nobel Prize winner Norman Borlaug was his friend. It was through Ted that I had the privilege of meeting Dr. Borlaug and members of his family. My wife also got to meet the family while she was serving the World Food Prize as a volunteer interpreter.

Monsanto supplied me with the best they had to offer! Ted was an expert's expert on GMO matters, but not so much a politician. He tried to train me in biotechnology, and I tried to train him in politics. Patience is not natural to me and that was certainly true of Ted. The legislative process drove him crazy at times (me too, for that matter)! But we had lots of fun together and we learned a lot from each other.

We became a great team and were successful in our efforts to persuade legislators they should not get involved with national GMO regulatory issues. It helped that before I met Ted, he had met and worked with Governor Branstad on agricultural issues. Ted was a Democrat, but that was fine with the Republican Governor. They had a mutual respect and the relationship that developed was very beneficial to the State of Iowa. While making his appearances at the capitol to help me, Ted developed a deeper interest in politics and recognized the value of being involved. With each appearance before different groups of legislators, Ted was developing a bi-partisan group of legislators who valued his opinion on matters relating to agricultural science and creation of a state biotechnology economic development base.

◆ ◆ ◆

### *Dr. Ted Crosbie, PhD*

Ted Crosbie was to become a valued friend. We ended up working together on several matters not always directly involving or benefitting Monsanto. But we had Monsanto's encouragement and support. Governor Branstad was very interested in the economic development potential biotechnology afforded Iowa. He held Ted in high regard. Ethanol plants were being developed which gave farmers a new market for their corn. The governor was very supportive of that effort as was Monsanto. Ted was interested in ethanol too, but he saw beyond that. He felt that the bi-products produced in the production of ethanol would become a resource base for other products. It would be another opportunity for Iowa farmers. He was correct, as usual.

In November of 1998 Democrat State Senator Tom Vilsack, a

noted plaintiff's attorney, was elected Governor of Iowa. There was great concern in November of 1998 about how Governor Vilsack would address agricultural and biotechnology issues. I advised Monsanto that Senator Vilsack was a policy wonk and would read anything they wanted to give him concerning issues. He had impressed me with his work ethic in the Senate and his openness to new ideas and technology.

Governor Vilsack was an excellent trial lawyer skilled at drilling into an issue. He was an expert at sorting the wheat from the chaff. I told Monsanto to assume he would give thoughtful study to their issues and that they should have little concern about him making a rash judgment. Monsanto worked with him on agricultural and biotechnology issues. Governor Vilsack became a knowledgeable politician who recognized the value of biotechnology and its importance to Iowa and the United States.

Soon after his election, Monsanto asked me if I thought he would cut the ribbon for the grand opening of their remodeled facility in Ankeny, just north of Des Moines. I pointed out that Governor-elect Vilsack had to be exhausted from the campaign and consumed by the effort required to put an administration together. They requested that I ask him anyway. To my surprise, he seemed happy to do it. He appeared at the ribbon-cutting event looking very tired and fighting a cold. He gave a great speech and enjoyed mingling with the crowd of guests. Afterwards, he and I used an office to discuss the transition.

Ted was also very interested in technologically based start-up companies. He urged creation of a state entity that would encourage those enterprises. Monsanto approved of my spending time assisting Ted in this endeavor even though it was not likely to result in any direct benefit to Monsanto. In 2004, he co-founded the Bio Alliance of Iowa and served as its chair until 2010.

In 2005 the legislature created the state office of Chief Technology Officer (CTO). Governor Vilsack appointed Ted to that position. Governor Vilsack had quickly grasped the need for pursuit of responsible biotechnology projects necessary to meet the world's growing need for a sustainable food supply. He was a very powerful influence in advancing biotechnology for the benefit of mankind during his sixteen years of combined service as Governor of Iowa and US Secretary of Agriculture. He remains actively involved with those issues today in his capacity as President and CEO of the US Dairy Export Council.

Governor Culver continued Ted's service as CTO. Early in the governor's first year in office (2007) I was asked by his staff if Ted and I could help in developing a new economic development plan grounded in biotechnology and targeted manufacturing. Ted agreed, and we began to quietly work with the governor's staff.

We were walking out of the statehouse after a meeting on the project when we were approached by some Democrat legislators who were also working on a similar program. They asked if we could assist them. We agreed to help. A week or so later, the same occurred with a group of Republican legislators. Again, we agreed. We discussed in the parking lot what would happen if any of the three working groups knew we were helping the other two groups. They would certainly find out when all three plans matured into draft documents ready for circulation. We decided in the meantime we should keep an especially low profile. We would eventually become involved in reconciling the approaches into a consensus bill. Thankfully, the efforts resulted in very successful bi-partisan legislation. Ted and I were thanked by all concerned for our help.

In 2010 the Iowa Innovation Council was created resulting from the effort begun in 2007. The 2010 statute designated the CTO chair of the Council. A primary purpose was to address the need to nurture start-up technology companies. Incentives and assistance programs resulted. A funding mechanism was created for assisting those companies through what became known as the "valley of death," the point when additional capital is usually required to enable start-ups to mature into functioning companies. Investors needed to be found and favorable tax incentives created to compensate for the significant financial risk involved. Ted was very engaged in this effort and in the effort to convert academic research into commercial applications, also a part of the plan.

In the 2010 gubernatorial campaign, economic development was a campaign issue. Governor Branstad campaigned on the idea of enacting a public/private partnership to replace the existing Department of Economic Development (DED). He wanted to draw on the expertise of private entities with experience and ideas for the use of technology in the state's economic development efforts. I recall asking just prior to the election what exactly he had in mind for this new approach. He replied that he hoped Ted and I would help him devise a working plan for the establishment of what became the Economic Development Authority (EDA). Ted was again re-appointed CTO.

After many long hours and lots of bipartisan input (Republican Governor, Democrat Senate, Republican House) and cooperation, the new concept was enacted during the 2011 session of the Iowa General Assembly. Ted and I were very involved with the governor's staff and the DED staff who were looking forward to morphing into the new entity.

In 2013, Governor Branstad presented Ted with the Lifetime Achievement Award of the Iowa Innovation Corporation for his efforts in support of innovation and job creation.

By now Ted and I had become good friends and enjoyed the opportunities we had to work on Iowa biotechnology and economic development issues. I got to know Ted's wife, Rowena (Ro), when soon after meeting Ted, he asked me to take her with me to a political fundraiser that he could not attend. She appeared to enjoy the experience and demonstrated a real talent for meeting people and being conversant in a variety of subjects. Ted was always interesting, and I looked forward to the times we would get together, both professionally and socially. Patti and I shared some great times with Ted and Ro.

There was never a dull moment where Ted was concerned. I

recall driving to the office one spring morning soon after the legislature had gone home for the year. Ted called. "Keith, I need help—fast!" He seemed unusually agitated.

"What's wrong, Ted? Can it wait until I get in my office in about ten minutes?"

"No!" he shouted. "I'm in real trouble!"

Now he had me worried! "What kind of trouble?"

"I thought I had bought a boat."

"What do you mean, 'you thought?!'"

He began to explain that he bought a boat from a dealer and it appeared the dealer went under water (I learned financially failing boat dealers go under water, they don't go belly-up).

I inquired further and found he had bought and paid for a very big, very expensive boat on the Internet. It was to be inspected and prepared for delivery on the east coast. Now he understood "some bank" somewhere on the east coast had it. By then I was pulling into my parking spot and had heard enough!

He urgently needed a lawyer experienced in banking transactions. I told him I had a partner who would be great in dealing with the problem and hopefully he was in the office. I told Ted I would call him back ASAP. Fortunately, my partner was in and agreed to free up the day to help Ted unravel his situation. A successful result was obtained, and Ted got his boat.

Governor Branstad, Dave Tierney of Monsanto's Ankeny facility, and I were at Monsanto Headquarters in St. Louis as part of an economic development trip. We met with high level Monsanto executives and discussed a proposed program with them. Ted was not available to attend. After a period of presentation and discussion, it was receiving a favorable reaction. Ted's name came up as someone who should be involved. One of the executives asked another what he thought Ted's role should be. The reply was, "Whatever the hell Ted wants it to be! We all know he'll do what he wants anyway!" Everyone had a big laugh—we all knew Ted well!

I retired from the law firm and representation of Monsanto in

December of 2012. But, thankfully, my connection with Ted continued. He retired from Monsanto in 2014. He and his wife, Ro, and his son Jonathon, a physician, started a tradition of hosting a Kentucky Derby Day Party at their farm every first Saturday in May which my wife Patti and I looked forward to every year. Ted and Ro owned horses and enjoyed fox hunting. My wife, a Kentuckian from Louisville, especially enjoyed these parties. She is also a great Mint Julip-connoisseur and coach.

We attended the May 2016 party and had our usual good time. The governor and his wife also attended. We were all looking forward to a fun summer. Ted and Ro were going to be spending more time at their home at the Lake of the Ozarks. They were on top of the world! Ted talked about giving us a ride on that great boat!

We were shocked a few weeks after the Derby Party to get a call from a mutual friend who advised that Ted had suddenly taken very ill and was hospitalized in Kansas City. He fought a heroic battle of several weeks but succumbed to a rare heart/lung affliction on July 23, 2016. He was a very young 65-year-old. I miss him very much! He was a treasured friend and one of the brightest people I have had the pleasure to know. Together we accomplished things that will benefit Monsanto (Bayer) and the people of Iowa well into the future.

Ro and Jonathon have continued the Derby Party tradition. This year we have had an unusually rainy spring, but the sun shone on the Crosbie farm on Kentucky Derby Day. We attribute that to Ted. We, like Ro, think he continues to have influence in high places!

◆ ◆ ◆

## Iowa Association of Electric Cooperatives

I also was retained to represent the Iowa Association of Electric Cooperatives (RECs) for several years. Many rural areas are served by RECs. They are the result of an early federal effort to bring electricity to rural areas. Over the years many mergers have occurred, and economies of scale attained. Some RECs are wholesalers of electrical power and some are distributors of power.

◆ ◆ ◆

*Net Metering*

Regulatory issues were of primary concern during my representation. One issue of interest concerns pricing of electricity produced by customers. As wind energy developed in Iowa, it became increasingly popular for some utility customers to erect their own windmill powered generators. The law was shaped to allow them to connect those windmills to the general power grid that delivered power to customers. Keep in mind the cost to the power purchasing customer includes administrative costs, the cost of the power delivered, and the cost of providing and maintaining a delivery service line to serve the customer.

Some wind power promotors and their customers who generated their own power advocated what came to be called "net metering." When the wind produced more power than needed, the owners of wind generators wanted to be able to sell the excess to the utility that served them. They wanted to be paid the full retail price for the wind power they generated and put on the grid. Power distribution utility companies agreed to buy the excess power, but at a price less than retail in order to cover the overhead costs attributable to distribution of a customer's generated power. To do otherwise would result in non-generating customers paying all the overhead costs necessary for the delivery of power to them plus the costs of distributing their wind power producing neighbor's electricity. The self-generators wanted to be able to use the power grid to distribute their product at no cost. Ultimately it was determined that the utility companies would pay the customer-generator a wholesale price for his or her power. This issue surfaced again in the 2019 session. Some small solar power generators have been allowed use of the grid for distribution of their electricity at no cost.

I began my representation of the RECs when their in-house lobbyist left one fall and they needed to get someone hired before the next session started. Their executive director, Wes Ehrecke, asked if I could represent them. I had no conflicts of interest and I had a minor in electrical engineering.

During that discussion of my engagement, he asked if I had any recommendations for a person who could take over the following year as their in-house lobbyist. I told him he should talk to Dawn Vance who lobbied for a state agency at the time. She did an excellent job for her agency. She was married and had two small children.

Wes hired Dawn and we worked together for several years. My role was reduced, but there were issues on the horizon that warranted keeping me involved. Dawn and I became close friends and had only one area of friendly disagreement. She smoked, and I had quit. I nagged her about it occasionally over the years. After working together for several sessions, I noticed she was coughing a lot. I suggested she see a physician. She kept putting it off and the cough seemed to be getting worse.

Dawn liked to take me out to lunch a few days after the legislature adjourned for the year. The lunch I will always remember was the one that followed her doctor's appointment for the cough. She was late to the restaurant and I could tell by her expression as she walked toward me that she had bad news. She had been given an appointment with a surgeon for evaluation of her suspected lung cancer. She died about two and a half years after a long, hard-fought battle. Julie Smith, an attorney and lobbyist with whom I was always doing battle, was also a close friend of Dawn's. Julie and I were friends despite our annual battles. We teamed up to spend time with Dawn as her health declined. Dawn showed great courage. Her loss was a real tragedy.

◆ ◆ ◆

Rolling the Dice with Bill Harrah & Friends

My lobbying partner, Jim West, and I had decided we did not want to represent gambling interests. Riverboat gaming became an issue in Iowa and ultimately legislation was adopted that permitted it. Jim and I watched from the sidelines. The riverboat gaming became casino and racetrack gambling and we were off and running in Iowa, which I am told now has more legal forms of gambling than Nevada.

After riverboat gaming was authorized and as gaming expanded to racing and casinos in Iowa, the issue of taxation became a center of controversy. Iowa state government was becoming more and more dependent upon gaming revenue. Harrah's, a Nevada casino company, entered Iowa with a riverboat on the Missouri River in Council Bluffs. As the tax issue got more complicated, we were approached by casino groups to represent them on that issue. Litigation was underway and the United States Supreme Court essentially ruled that Iowa's different tax rates applicable to different gaming settings did not violate the US Constitution. But ultimately the Iowa Supreme Court found that it did violate the Iowa Constitution.

Legislation was consequently needed to develop a workable tax system and rate structure. We needed to decide if we wanted to become involved in that issue. I told Jim that I had met Bill Harrah, the founder of Harrah's Club. While Bill was no longer involved, he had a reputation for honesty which appeared to have been instilled in the culture of Harrah's Club. We were contacted by Harrah's and interviewed with them. I think I was the only one in the room who had known Bill Harrah. We eventually agreed to represent Harrah's in the upcoming tax battle. Harrah's had an outstanding public affairs executive that we worked with, Richard Klemp. He became a great friend and truly was inculcated with Bill Harrah's values of honesty and integrity.

The battle drug on for that entire session and was not settled until near the end. The Speaker of the House became the spokesman for the legislature and a bill was brought out and put on the calendar for debate. We all knew it was not the bill that would pass, but it established the framework for negotiation. It came down to the issue of tax rates (surprise). The Speaker announced the bill would be debated on a certain day regardless of whether there was agreement. The day before that deadline, negotiations became intense. The affected gaming companies and the Speaker didn't reach an agreement until well after midnight. Our clients had gotten the bill they wanted with a satisfactory tax rate. There was one minor point that Richard conceded that sealed the deal.

The bill passed the House later that day and we were off to celebrate. But one of the Harrah's executives was unhappy with Richard for agreeing to the small side issue without getting company approval. This despite the fact the deal was reached in the middle of the night and there was not time to get approval. The bill in its entirety was very favorable to Harrah's. The word got around that someone at Harrah's was not happy with Richard. Legislators from both parties came to me concerned about Richard. They asked if they could pass something that would take him off the hook. Richard appreciated the support, but declined the offer.

Later we represented another gaming company, Isle of Capri. They had three or four locations in Iowa. They were concerned about the regulatory climate and expansion of their operations. They were based in St. Louis. They also had great people to work with. I enjoyed my meetings with Don Mitchell. It was also a pleasure working for them. The law firm also did other business with them.

◆◆◆

## John Deere

The law firm has a long history of representing John Deere, a truly great company noted for manufacture of farm implements, especially tractors. The "Green Machines" are everywhere! They also, by the way, manufacture lots of other agricultural machinery and machinery for other purposes, such as forestry and construction. Our lobbying team was invited to company headquarters in Moline, Illinois, to discuss representation of Deere before the Iowa General Assembly and the Executive Branch. Deere had always had its own in-house lobbyists in Iowa. We had a good working relationship with the people who were in these positions. They were not always able to be present, and we then informally served without charge as their eyes and ears.

John Deere is a very impressive company with a headquarters befitting it. It was a pleasure just to get the tour! It was a real honor to win a contract to represent Deere. Our period of representation was moderately peaceful. Deere is a member of the state's business leadership groups and is a company very highly regarded by political leaders of both parties. I was privileged to meet and work with some truly outstanding individuals who were part of a great corporate leadership team. Thom Iles had lobbied in Iowa several years and eventually represented Deere as a company employee. We had a good relationship with Thom from his prior representations. We met and enjoyed working with Deere's Jason Francque and his supervisor, Charlie Stamp.

◆ ◆ ◆

## Johnson & Johnson

I also was privileged to represent another great American company, Johnson & Johnson. We didn't have the close ties with J & J at the start that we had with Deere. The issues were not as high profile, but the people I worked with were highly qualified, as I had come to expect of companies with great reputations. It was a pleasure to work with them. They were very reasonable in their approach to legislation.

◆ ◆ ◆

## Iowa Economic Development Authority (IEDA)

As is true with most good politicians, the senator who fought against us on the LIHEAP issue (Propane issue discussed above) pulled it together and worked with me on the major piece of legislation that created the Iowa Economic Development Authority (IEDA). Republican Governor Branstad had defeated Democrat Governor Culver in the fall of 2010. Also, the House of Representatives had fallen to the Republicans. The Democrats remained in control of the Senate. For this major change in approach to economic development proposed by Governor Branstad during the campaign to pass, bipartisan support was needed.

271

The LIHEAP senator, Senator Steve Sodders, called me after the 2010 election to tell me that he was going to be chairing the subcommittee assigned to handle the IEDA Bill. He suggested we meet over a beer and get to know each other from a different perspective! We had our beer summit and found we liked each other and shared a goal of passing economic development legislation that would benefit all Iowans. He did an outstanding job getting that bill through the Iowa Senate. Were it not for Democrat Senators Sodders and Bill Dotzler, the IEDA Bill probably would have died on the vine. Also, Tim Whipple from the DED staff was very helpful. He had worked for the Legislative Services Agency as a bill drafter. Debi Durham, the new DED Director slated to become the IEDA Director also played a key role. They were instrumental in crafting the final product, which the Republican House accepted with only minor changes.

The bill was running up against the deadline for Senate action, and we were working intensely to address Senate Democrat Caucus concerns. It came down to one final issue: the term of the IEDA Director. The governor, from the beginning, told me he wanted the director to have a six-year term so that there would be continuity from one administration to another.

While we were working on this project, another issue had surfaced. Customarily when there is a change in governors, especially governors of a different party, department heads tender their resignations. Most are eventually replaced with directors who are members of the party in power. It is usual for a new governor to ask some of these department heads to delay their departures. Those involved are motivated to serve the public, and typically agree to extend their service as they are needed. And not every resignation is accepted. I can name one Democrat department head who remained in his position for serval years in Republican administrations until his recent retirement.

One department head did not tender his resignation. The governor invited him to his office, and they had a good discussion. The governor thought the fellow understood that it was nothing personal, but he wanted to make a change. He assumed he would be getting a resignation. Didn't happen. Eventually the issue ended up in court.

While this sideshow was underway, the IEDA Bill was ready for Senate debate, but the Senate Majority Leader, Mike Gronstal, advised the Democratic Caucus was adamant that the term of the Director be four years, not six. Mike was and is a friend and we trusted each other. I met with the governor the day before the bill was to be debated. I went over several issues that had been resolved by changes which he approved. I said there remained one obstacle: the length of the term. He said he insisted that it be six years.

Good personal friends from law school days, we are not hesitant to speak our minds or needle each other. I looked at him and said something like, "I can understand why you are so adamant about this issue, it has worked so well with X, the department head who refuses to resign!"

He looked at me for a few seconds and we both burst out laughing as he said something like, "Okay, okay, I get the point! Four years it is!"

I informed Senator Gronstal the governor appreciated his caucuses work on the bill, and he would accept their desired four-year term. The bill passed the Senate the next day. There was some back and forth between the House and Senate, and some adjustments were made in that process. The bill became law with the four-year term.

My primary clients in the IEDA Bill effort were the Iowa Chamber Alliance (ICA), an organization of the largest chambers of commerce organizations in the state, including, my client, the Des Moines Partnership (DMP). The DMP was the Des Moines organization of the chambers of commerce located in the Des Moines area. It was an honor to serve these groups.

# 2

# Changing the Landscape: Vision Iowa

THE MOST HISTORICALLY significant lobbying project I worked on was on behalf of the Des Moines Partnership and Polk County (where the State Capitol is located) in an effort supported by business and professional groups interested in building a new arena befitting a state capitol city. I also represented the supportive Iowa Chamber Alliance, made up of chambers of commerce of the fifteen largest Iowa cities, including Cedar Rapids and Des Moines. This project is memorable because of its scope, the coalition-building required, its impact on the rest of the state, and the degree of difficulty in developing and enacting enabling legislation requiring a complex financing mechanism. I feel a great sense of pride when driving by the great edifice in Des Moines known as the Wells Fargo Arena.

Putting it together was a multi-year project which began for me in 1996. The goal was creation of a financing mechanism for the development of a new arena in Des Moines while simultaneously enabling several smaller projects throughout Iowa. It was recognized that we needed to create a benefit for smaller communities as well as the capitol city to gain their necessary support for the legislation being developed.

274

Jim and I recognized that this project would consume a significant amount of time. We recognized earlier that we needed to bring in another attorney as a lobbyist. We had a few who helped on occasion, but they did not want to make lobbying their primary work. In 1994 the firm hired a bright young man, Andre Merrett, who had graduated from the University of Iowa Law School. He was from Des Moines and a well-regarded family. He also happened to be the first African American attorney who applied to and was hired by the firm. Jim and I asked him to consider lobbying. He was interested and joined us in 1996. I believe he was also the first African American professional lobbyist on the hill. He was a great choice, but it wasn't long before he was hired away by an out-of-state company. He now is in private practice in Phoenix.

From the beginning we knew we needed bipartisan support in the General Assembly. The Senate was controlled by Democrats and the House by Republicans in 1995 and '96. In the fall of '96 the Republicans gained control of the Senate and retained control of the House. After the November come-from-behind election of Governor Vilsack (D) in 1998 to replace retiring Governor Branstad (R), it became a priority to gain his support. Governor Branstad had been supportive. We had also been working preliminarily with the State Treasurer, a Democrat, and the State Auditor, a Republican.

Simultaneously, public relations experts and interested groups began the process of building support at the local level throughout the state. Wrestling is a major sport in Iowa, and the state wrestling tournament draws huge crowds to Des Moines. There were many complaints about the lack of capacity in the existing auditorium in Des Moines. High school wrestling fans throughout Iowa immediately signed on! They went to work promoting the plan to their local legislators.

Legislation began to be drafted for the arena project in 1997. What evolved to become known as the Vision Iowa Bill began to take shape in 1998. One of its features included a special program for projects in smaller communities, which has turned out to be very popular. Its inclusion gathered some key votes needed for passage of the entire program.

It should be noted that the cooperation of the City of Cedar Rapids was very significant. The Speaker of the Iowa House of Representatives, Republican Ron Corbett, represented a district in Cedar Rapids. The Cedar Rapids Chamber of Commerce and local elected officials supported the project. The project had potential for the development of a proposed indoor rainforest project in the Cedar Rapids area. Other larger cities also ended up supporting the legislation, even though there was no big project in the works for their cities.

After the 1999 session of the Iowa General Assembly, Speaker Corbett announced he would not be a candidate for reelection. Former Democrat Congressman Michael Blouin was the President and CEO of the Cedar Rapids Area Chamber of Commerce, and announced he was taking a similar position in Des Moines. Ron Corbett applied for Mike's position and was hired. Michael Blouin became the director of the Des Moines Partnership, and played a key role in this project from that position. Ron was valuable in his new role, as he ensured the members of his Chamber understood the value to the state of the Vision Iowa proposal.

Ron Corbett was succeeded as Speaker by Republican Representative Brent Siegrist. He represented a district in Council Bluffs. From 1998 until 2000, Republican Senator Mary Kraemer from West Des Moines was President of the Iowa Senate. Both were key players and supporters of the proposal.

Majority Leaders of both chambers are key players in the legislative process as they have control over the agenda of their chamber. Republican Senator Stewart Iverson from Dows was the Senate Majority Leader, and Republican Representative Brent Siegrist was the House Majority Leader until becoming Speaker. He was succeeded by Republican Representative Christopher Rants of Sioux City, another supporter.

The Senate Minority Leader was Democrat Senator Mike Gronstal of Council Bluffs. The House Minority Leader was

Democrat Representative David Schrader from Monroe. Senator Gronstal was supportive, and Representative Schrader was initially opposed but became a supporter.

In the beginning several lobbyists and legislators told me I was taking on an impossible task. But some of those lobbyists had clients who became supporters of the project. Those clients enlisted their lobbyists in the cause. Those lobbyists and their clients were invaluable in helping forge the coalitions that enabled the ultimately successful result. Interest and support started to build.

The lobbying support by the Polk County Board of Supervisors and the Des Moines Partnership was fantastic. We were making favorable contacts and attracting interest. Support was building, and coalitions were forming. Lobbyist Brian Johnson was engaged to assist in coordinating efforts of lobbyists who had clients who supported the effort. City of Des Moines lobbyist Jerry Fitzgerald helped as did lobbyist Kent Sovern. Greg Edwards, President and CEO of the Greater Des Moines Convention and Visitors Bureau, rallied support. Public relations professionals were engaged and rendered great assistance with the grass roots efforts. Planning consultants rendered essential services.

◆◆◆

*Avoid Personalizing Issues—Today's Foe Could be Tomorrow's Friend*

State Senator Tom Vilsack was the upset winner of the governor's race that occurred while this project was starting in 1998. Governor Vilsack and I had known each other for several years before he ran for the state senate. He was a plaintiff's attorney and I was a defense attorney. That resulted in a certain amount of natural tension from the beginning. His campaign office was near mine. Often when I walked by, he would smile, wave, and give me the thumps-up signal. We had established a friendship despite often finding ourselves in opposition on legislative issues.

Years before becoming governor he had served as a public

member on a legislative interim study committee addressing medical malpractice issues. I was representing the Iowa Medical Society and pushing hard for caps on non-economic damages, such as pain and suffering, in medical malpractice cases. There was a physician from Cedar Rapids also appointed to the committee. They formed a productive friendship despite their disagreements on tort reform. They arranged to share rides to and from Des Moines for the meetings.

The day before the final committee meeting where votes are taken on proposed findings, I arranged to meet with a Democrat member, Senator Bill Palmer, who I thought could be convinced to go with a cap. His son was a physician. We met for lunch and after four hours of visiting he said, "You didn't ask me to lunch to hear my life's story, did you?! What do you want?"

I replied, "Senator, all I want is your vote on the cap issue tomorrow. You know the issue and you ought to be with me on this."

He looked at me for a few seconds, smiled and said, "Okay, I can do that. But don't tell anyone. I want it to be a surprise!" Was it ever!

No legislation resulted from this study committee with its Democrat majority. But a search of statehouse records will show a Democrat interim committee recommendation for a cap on non-economic damages in medical malpractice cases. All these years later, that still has not been achieved.

Then Senator Vilsack was not pleased with the maneuver on the cap issue. Months later we had a harsh discussion of tort reform just prior to the debate on a comparative fault tort reform bill I also lobbied for that passed over his opposition. It was out of character for both of us, was brief, and never happened again. Not long afterward he asked if I would meet him in the law library to help with drafting a piece of legislation he was working on. It did not involve an issue I was working, so I was happy to help. We worked on the problem together that evening and produced a good result. Governor Vilsack and I did have a history of working together when he was a Senator, exemplifying the lawyer's art of engaging in vehement disagreement not to be taken personally. I don't recall any specific examples, but I am sure that he supported most of my client's positions on their legislation. Most of my clients were non-partisan, if not all. All had officers, directors, employees, and members or shareholders of both political parties. Partisanship was to be avoided.

◆◆◆

## Coming Together to Build a Bipartisan Bill

Jeff Lamberti, an attorney from Polk County, and his good friend, Russ Teig, a farmer from rural Jewell in Hamilton County, were both Republican members of the Iowa House of Representatives when the project started. Both became key leaders of this effort. By the time the bill was ready for enactment, Jeff had been elected to the state senate, and floor managed the bill there. Russ was the floor manager in the House.

Without the inside work of these two legislators, this bill would not have succeeded. Both had great credibility with their colleagues of both parties, both were able to deal with complex issues, and both had the work ethic required to accomplish great things. They both dedicated significant time to the effort during the interim periods when the General Assembly was not in session. Meetings were held with other legislators of both parties, and work on the legislation occurred throughout the years the issue was pending. This work intensified in the fall of 1999.

In early 1999, I met with Governor Vilsack about the proposal. He was very popular and carried a very high approval rating going into his first legislative session as governor. He had been a mayor involved in economic development. He had become aware of the Vision Iowa proposal while a member of the senate and was supportive.

I updated the governor on recent developments and asked him to consider spending some of the political capital he had accrued on this project. His active endorsement of the legislation was necessary to its bipartisan passage. And, of course, his signature on the bill was the essential final step. He responded that he wanted to think about it and would get back to me. Shortly thereafter he called to tell me that he was on board and would be putting his staff on notice that they were to help the effort.

The governor's active support was very important. We were striving to enact a very significant, non-partisan piece of legislation that would be supported state-wide, rural and urban. We were building momentum, and the Democrat governor's support ensured Democrat cooperation in development of that legislation in a Republican legislature.

I initially planned to discuss the individual roles the many other key players had in this success. As I looked through my big box of files, I realized how many there were, and how diverse their roles. There are too many to name. Also, there are many, whose names remain unknown to me, who made tremendous contributions to the effort at the local grassroots level. While unaware of the identity of many, I am very aware of their contributions because of the great results they produced.

The bill has a bonding provision that was of key interest to Republican State Auditor Richard Johnson, and Democrat State Treasurer Michael Fitzgerald. They and their staffs were most helpful on the technical issues of preparing the bonding parts of the legislation. It truly was a bipartisan effort. Towards the end of the drafting phase, I met with Dick on a technical issue relating to the financing provisions. He said he thought he was satisfied with it, but he wanted to discuss it with Mike.

I then stopped by to discuss it with Mike and ask him to check in with Dick. Mike seemed surprised that Dick, a more senior office holder, cared about including him in the resolution of that issue. I laughed and said he shouldn't be surprised. After all, "Dick is State Auditor and you are State Treasurer. Dick won't sign off unless you do too!" Mike chuckled. He later reported back to me that they had a productive meeting and felt the bond provisions were sound. And they developed a regard for each other that benefitted the state they served when encountering other issues of interest to their offices.

The final bill required the input of highly competent bound attorneys. The Ahlers Law Firm is recognized as having an excellent staff of government bond attorneys which they made available to provide valuable assistance in the drafting of the bonding provisions. Also, economic development experts were consulted on aspects of the programs in the bill as they pertained to both rural and urban settings. Public relations experts advised how to appeal to rural and urban constituencies. Urban and rural legislators of both parties became supporters and spread the gospel among their colleagues. Many became advocates of the program back home in their district meetings.

Eventually (after many drafts and meetings) Senate File 2447 (sponsored jointly by the majority and minority leaders of the Senate) passed the Senate by a vote of 40 to 9 on April 18, 2000. The House amended and passed the bill by a vote of 72 to 27 on April 19. The Senate concurred in the House amendment and passed the bill as amended by a vote of 40 to 8 on April 20. At the time of passage, the Senate was divided 30/20 and the House 56/44, with Republican majorities in both chambers. Governor Vilsack signed the bill on May 9, 2000. He gave me a pen he used to sign it. It was a great day!

There were hundreds of people, lobbyists, private businesses and local government entities who contributed to this success. I can't begin to individually thank them all. Without them there would be no Vision Iowa!

◆◆◆

*The Successful Aftermath*

The bill contained more than just the Vision Iowa Program, which was limited to vertical infrastructure projects which extended benefits to persons residing outside the county where the project was located, and with a value exceeding twenty million dollars. Project applicants were required to demonstrate local public and private financial support equal to at least half the cost of the project. The bill provided bonding authority as the state funding mechanism.

The bill also created the Community Attraction and Tourism (CAT) Program to assist communities in the development and creation of multiple-purpose attractions, or tourism facilities, consisting primarily of vertical infrastructure. Eligibility was limited based on the applicant entity's population. The grants could be based on a repayment requirement. What became popularly known as the CAT Fund provided support to numerous projects throughout the state, with rural locations deriving the most benefit. Continued funding for this program is provided by annual legislative appropriation.

A School Infrastructure Program was created under the control of the Department of Education. The State Treasurer is empowered to establish reserve funds to secure limited bonds issued pursuant to the program. The bonds are supported by available revenue streams, and do not constitute debts of the state or any of its political subdivisions.

The Wells Fargo Arena was built. There was, however, a hurdle that was a little higher than we had wanted. Significant private funding had to be found, and a plan presented to a committee created by the bill to scrutinize and approve applications for funds. In retrospect, I think that committee chaired by Pulitzer Prize winner Michael Gartner did an outstanding job and made a significant contribution to the success of the programs contemplated by the bill. Available funding was wisely leveraged and administered, resulting in an enlarged fiscal impact. Susan Judkins, Iowa Department of Economic Development Vision Iowa Program Coordinator also deserves recognition for making Vision Iowa work.

A plan illustrating how the arena project would positively impact other aspects of downtown Des Moines needed to be presented. It was by no means a "done deal."

I recall meeting Polk County Board of Supervisors Chair, Democrat Angela Connolly, late one evening at a Court Avenue bar, where we sketched out our plan for Des Moines. Angela was a major force who through her leadership made the Vision Iowa dream a reality. We both wish we had kept the napkin we used! It called for the re-relocation of a proposed new Science Center building, a new

Library, turning the existing library building into a totally refurbished building housing the World Food Prize, placement of the Arena, and location of a future supporting hotel. As I write in 2019, all these objectives have been achieved.

Downtown Des Moines largely reflects the plan put together that night. Of course, we had been working together on the project for years and the ideas in our plan were not original with us. But we worked to bring several existing ideas into a cohesive plan for downtown Des Moines. Without the combined and coordinated support of City of Des Moines elected officials and staff, Polk County Board of Supervisors Chair Connolly, members of the Board and their staff, Red Brannan (former supervisor and Democrat operative) and Michael Blouin (CEO Great Des Moines Partnership) with the support of his members and the Iowa Chamber Alliance we could not have been successful. The Board of Supervisors also made its Public Information Coordinator, Phil Roeder and Sue Elliott, available to the effort. They were the driving force for the establishment of the Coalition for Brighter Communities, which helped generate support throughout the state.

Working on this project, the stress I felt personally continued to build. Towards the end of the process there were lots of details that had to be addressed and resolved. They involved various legislative and executive branch players with different political and constituent perspectives. I recall attending a meeting of a group working on the bill at the Hotel Fort Des Moines, just a block from the building that had housed the firm. We had moved into a new building several years before this meeting. I was thinking about the bill as I walked out of the hotel late that night. I was trying to come up with a wrap-up plan that would bring everybody and everything together. I entered my old office building and pushed the elevator button. Only when the elevator doors opened did I realize I was in the wrong elevator in the wrong building!

In concluding discussion of the Iowa Events Center Project, which led to building what is now known as the Wells Fargo Arena, I include three letters. A letter was addressed to me on April 28,

2000, from the Chairperson of the Polk County Board of Supervisors, Angela Connolly:

*On behalf of the Polk County Board of Supervisors, I want to personally thank you for your outstanding efforts in securing passage of the Vision Iowa Program. We had a great team of people lobbying for this legislation and your leadership of the lobbyist group was instrumental in our success.*

*The Vision Iowa Program is a monumental achievement for the State of Iowa. It also is an essential element to making our Iowa Events Center project a reality. County officials will now be able to proceed with the Project and make our community a better place.*

A letter was addressed to me on April 21, 2000, from Attorney Tom Whitney, a Democrat leader in Polk County:

*Just a note to say again congratulations and how much respect I have for your efforts in making the arena legislation happen. It is said that hard work creates success. In my mind, you are the absolute definition of that statement. I look forward to another day in which my office can hang on to your coattails. Great job!*

That Christmas Tom brought a gift-wrapped package to my office. Jim West came in and said hello to Tom. Jim jokingly asked, "What's the present, a hand grenade?" We laughed, I opened the package, and it was indeed a hand grenade with an inscription on the handle ("VISION IOWA 2000"). I still display it.

We also had good support from our local newspaper and other

news media outlets around the state. I wrote this letter which was published in the Des Moines Register on April 25, 2000.

*Having worked on the Vision Iowa Plan legislation, your editorial support has been appreciated. The two work horses were the bill's floor managers, Senator Jeff Lamberti and Representative Russ Teig. These two legislators spent countless hours before and during this session to craft the legislation that would ultimately receive enthusiastic bipartisan support. The list of others deserving thanks for their efforts on this legislation is too long to publish. But Representative Teig has also earned the special recognition accorded Senator Lamberti in your editorial of April 21.*

*The legislation is the product of unusual bipartisan, interagency and interbranch cooperation. There were meetings where the Democratic governor's staff, the Republican auditor's staff, the Democratic treasurer's staff and legislators of both parties and their staffs worked together in the exchange of ideas necessary to make the legislation successful. If that spirit of cooperation filters down to the local level, truly great projects benefitting all Iowans should result.*

I believe that indeed has been the result, as communities around the state have made good use of the three programs the legislation created. I was honored to have had the opportunity to work on one of the most significant pieces of economic impact legislation passed in Iowa. And my thanks again to all who rendered support without which Vision Iowa would never have come into being.

# PART VI
# OTHER MEMORABLE OPPORTUNITIES PROVIDED

# 1

# Iowa Broadcasters Association and the Iowa Newspaper Association

I WAS FORTUNATE to represent several great clients that Jim West had acquired who were involved in issues that afforded an opportunity to address legislative issues that benefited all Iowans. Those clients, and their issues that provided a public benefit, made lobbying a very rewarding experience.

The concerns of our Iowa Broadcasters Association (IBA) and the Iowa Newspaper Association (INA) clients often affected all Iowans. Transparency in government and the free speech rights enshrined in the First Amendment to the Constitution of the United States of America are important to all Americans. In high school I wrote a paper expressing my still-held view that the First Amendment is the most important provision in our constitution.

I was very pleased to have the opportunity to fight the legislative battles of these two groups, though fierce competitors for advertising revenue, who worked together to constitute a strong force for the defense of First Amendment rights and privileges. The IBA and the INA share a common interest, along with the public, in the free flow of information relating to activities of our national, state, and local governments. Access to correct information and its dissemination is essential to meaningful citizen participation in the processes of government. It was an honor and privilege to have served the IBA and INA.

◆◆◆

## The First Amendment

I had the opportunity, through my military service, to spend time in several countries in five continents. I found that people the world over share many of the same goals and ideals. Their governments, and the relationships that exist between the people and those governments, vary greatly. I have been honored to formally address delegations of government officials from the Kyrgyz Republic, a small country in Southwest Asia and formerly a part of the Soviet Union. The members of those delegations have the rare opportunity to re-shape their country's system of government and work towards building a democracy. It occurred to me that they would be shaping their country's political and social culture in the process, an opportunity like that brilliantly seized upon by our forefathers.

In those presentations I expounded on my theory that America's success stems from a recognition of the importance of open government and a free press; the importance of citizen access to, and participation in, the processes of government; and, the importance of establishing a political culture that values integrity, dignity, and civility in the management of political disagreement and debate.

It is my observation that there is one fundamental difference between the United States and other countries. It isn't that the people are different—our citizens are very diverse whose ancestors arrived from all over the world. I think the difference is due, in large part, to the efforts of our founders. They were in rebellion against a colonial power, England. They were fiercely independent men who debated at length how best to protect citizens from their government. They did so at great personal risk. They gave voice to the concept that a government ought to serve its citizens, not the other way around. They strove to create a system of government based on citizen participation.

I read a translation of the Kyrgyz Republic's constitution, and it was apparent its drafters recognized the value of a free and open exchange of ideas and citizen participation in the affairs of government. I hope their judicial system supports and gives life to those values as does ours. We have been very fortunate in having a judiciary that has embraced those values and enforced the rights granted in the years since adoption of our constitution. The protections afforded by the Courts have led to freer and more effective citizen participation in government. A fortunate consequence is our country's great economic freedom and the success it has provided.

The First Amendment to the Constitution of the United States of America is the great distinguishing provision our founders authored. It has provided a very great and lasting benefit to the citizens of this country. It is worth quoting. It strongly, eloquently, and absolutely mandates as follows: "Congress shall make no law respecting an establishment of religion, or prohibiting the free exercise thereof; or abridging the freedom of speech, or of the press; or the right of the people peaceably to assemble, and to petition the Government for a redress of grievances."

Note that the "petition" provision in the First Amendment is the basis for the right of a citizen to employ a lobbyist. A lobbyist is a person who petitions the government on behalf of someone else. As you know, people lead busy lives and don't always have the time or opportunity to be in contact with their government. This right of petition and the practical inability to always personally exercise that right have created the need for a lobbying profession.

For citizens to participate in their government they need information about the issues and decisions of that government. Citizens also, of course, need another critical component: a sound education enabling them to evaluate information received. The more open and transparent the government, the more effective it is. That's because the more open and transparent, the more confidence citizens have in their government. Common goals are developed and respected, sometimes forged amidst great public controversy. When the ability of educated citizens to observe and participate in the debate is provided, confidence is built leading to peaceful acceptance of the result.

Open discussion of controversial issues is required. Citizens benefit from watching their leaders struggle with issues. It informs them about the complexities involved. They discover that solutions are not always easily found. The important role compromise plays gains recognition and appreciation. Our politicians are themselves well served by an open and transparent government. I have always advised office holders, beginning with my city attorney days, that the better course is to let the public see the struggle that accompanies a controversial decision. The public may disagree with the resulting decision; but when the process is open, they learn to appreciate the difficulties encountered during the struggle to reach a conclusion. Open and public struggle leads to better citizen understanding and acceptance of the result.

Despite the popular image of strife and conflict, our politicians of differing opinions often share a mutual respect and try to conduct their debates and address their disagreements civilly. Those are very important characteristics and are to be encouraged at every opportunity. The existing trend towards a toxic political climate is of great concern. That approach has been spectacularly unsuccessful at solving the nation's problems. Historically there have been even worse examples of the breakdown of political tolerance and civility. Even so, today's acceptance of, and even encouragement of, demagoguery should be of greatest concern. The idea that compromise is traitorous, and absolutism is patriotic is a dangerous articulation of ignorance.

It would greatly benefit our citizens and politicians if they would recognize that the grant of great privilege carries with it great responsibility. The current irresponsibility and abuse of First Amendment rights and privilege concerns me greatly. Careless and biased reporting of information and scandalous campaign advertisements and statements diminish the effectiveness of our democratic form of government. I am appalled at the triumph of immediacy over accuracy. Consider the damage sustained by the community of Ferguson, Missouri, due to the riots that arose out of the erroneous rush-to-judgment reporting on a police shooting. Unfortunately, that is not an isolated incident. Subsequent examples appear regularly.

The naïve grant of unearned credibility to "informants" and "bloggers" found on the Internet by otherwise supposedly responsible journalists is appalling.

Even more appalling is the apparent absence of an educated citizenry which creates an environment which allows, even embraces, false and misleading campaign advertising and incomplete and incorrect reporting of information which too often become the basis for decision making. Ignorance and lazy citizens are dangerous enemies of democracy. They empower the unscrupulous political demagogues and journalists.

Journalist friends who have established themselves through responsible reporting express their dismay at the direction their profession seems to be taking. Likewise, citizens who would make good political leaders refuse to subject themselves to the existing political climate. It is becoming increasingly difficult to govern responsibly.

We do not need more people voting. We do, however, need more people voting who have qualified themselves through education and effort. Such voters will not be so easily swayed by the demagoguery that serves for campaigns these days.

I fear expanded grounds for legal liability for such irresponsible and flagrant disregard for "truth" is a likely result. Such an approach will ultimately, though gradually, result in curtailment of the free exchange of ideas and weaken effective citizen participation in their governance. Failure to exercise self-restraint and compliance with accepted journalistic standards can be expected to eventually produce just such a result. Large damage claims against media organizations based on new legal theories are beginning to surface in response to harm caused by irresponsible journalism.

I hope we soon return to an attitude that has served as the exemplar that guided my lobbying career: my grandfather's respect for political opponents despite their many policy disagreements. Their relationships shaped my approach to lobbying and participation in the political process. I learned at an early age to respect members of both parties and recognize that there often is no "correct" answer to complex policy issues. If one party did have a monopoly on those answers, there would, by now, be no second party!

As you can see, I considered the broadcasters and newspapers a perfect match for me. Each had some business issues that required attention from time-to-time, but always priority was given First Amendment and Freedom of Information issues. Fortunately, there were many like-minded legislators of both parties who carried the flag into battle. And the four governors who held office while I was lobbying were also very supportive.

I am especially pleased to have been inducted into the Iowa Broadcasters Association Hall of Fame and to receive the Randy Brubaker Free Press Champion Award from the Iowa Center for Public Affairs Journalism, the Distinguished Service Award from the Iowa Newspaper Association, and the Harrison "Skip" Weber Friend of the First Amendment Award from the Iowa Freedom of Information Council.

◆ ◆ ◆

*Iowa Public Information Board*

One of my proudest achievements as a lobbyist was passage of legislation that established the Iowa Public Information Board. The IPIB enabling legislation was enacted in the 2012 session of the Iowa General Assembly, my last lobbying session. It was a six-year slog! In speeches about the IPIB, I give credit to the IBA and INA for their patience. There were two conclusions that could be drawn from the long time it took to obtain passage: that it was very difficult and unique legislation to pass, or they had an incompetent lobbyist. I am grateful to them for having reached the correct conclusion.

The bill was very difficult to pass because it affected every governmental entity in the state and citizen relationships with those entities. The premise was that while the state had good open meetings and open records statues, and politicians of both parties recognized the value of transparency in government, there was no real enforcement mechanism when there were violations. These statutes are complicated and sometimes difficult to apply. There were penalties for violations and enforcement rights in both statutes, but in many cases an aggrieved citizen would be required to engage a private attorney to enforce those rights.

Some states had created advisory bodies to assist citizens by providing advice and offering training in the application of transparency laws. But no state had created an entity that advised and educated citizens and government officials while also possessing legal enforcement powers.

The IPIB legislation broke new ground. It is empowered to initiate administrative actions and levy fines to enforce Iowa's transparency statutes. It has subpoena power. Its decisions are subject to review by the state's courts, as is the case with any other state administrative enforcement action. The IPIB is empowered to issue formal and informal advisory opinions. Public officials are granted immunity from liability if they comply with these opinions, even though an opinion might subsequently be determined to have been erroneous. The IPIB is also empowered to issue declaratory orders with the force of law.

Bill Monroe, then Executive Director of the Iowa Newspaper Association (INA), was the instigator of the effort that produced the IPIB. Bill was one of the finest association executive directors I had the pleasure of working with, as was his wife, Chris Mudge. When Bill retired, Chris was hired by the INA as Bill's successor. Her entire 34-year career was with the INA. When she retired in 2016, Chris and Bill moved to their lake home in Minnesota. Everyone who had worked with Chris mourned her passing from metastatic breast cancer on March 7, 2019. She was a great person missed by all who knew her.

Sue Toma Garvin, Director of the Iowa Broadcasters Association (IBA) garnered support of the state's broadcasters in the effort.

There were several legislators of both parties known as transparency supporters. When contacted in 2007, they expressed support for establishing an IPIB. Key legislators recognized the problems that had developed with the interpretation and enforcement of Iowa's open meetings and records statutes. Iowa Freedom of Information Council Executive (IFOIC) Secretary Kathleen Richardson made a very well received presentation to the state government committees of both houses during the 2007 session of the General Assembly. Rep. Pam Jochum (D), chair of the House State Government Committee and Senator Mike Connolly (D), the chair of the Senate State Government Committee supported creation of an interim study of the proposal. The committee began its work during the 2007 interim.

University of Iowa Law School Associate Dean Emeritus Arthur Bonfield, the drafting consultant for the original open meetings and records statutes, was asked to serve as a consultant to the study committee. With the help of law students, copious research was conducted, issues identified, and recommendations developed. The interim study committee produced a masterful report, which included a recommended bill for consideration by the general assembly when convened in 2008.

But the bill was very complicated and vehemently opposed by lobbyists and public officials from all sorts of public body groups. Many I didn't even know existed! The bill started in the Senate. In this instance, there were lots of subcommittee meetings and lobbying contacts made. There were many meetings where the room would be packed by opponent groups. All this activity generated lots of issues and amendments to address those issues.

I recall one meeting attended by Professor Bonfield where we disagreed on a point. The senators told the professor and me to go into a room and stay there until we had worked out an acceptable resolution. It took a while, but we produced an amendment that improved the bill.

Although we were often in contention over various points affecting open meetings and records, I am pleased that after several years of working on these issues we formed a great friendship. His input was invaluable. One of the great moments in my legal career occurred a few years later when he looked at me in his office one day and said, "Keith, you are a really great lawyer!"

There are lots of ways to kill a bill. One of the primary ways is to cause delay by filing amendments and conjuring up fearsome specters. In Iowa there are deadlines which must be met to keep a bill "alive."

In 2008, the bill was passed by the Senate, but too late to receive consideration by the House. House supporters made a valiant effort to get the bill to the House floor for debate before the expiration of the deadline. Despite best efforts, they were not successful. The effort needed to begin anew in 2009.

Senator Connolly, the Senate floor manager of the bill retired from the Senate in 2008, and Representative Jochum was elected to the Senate as his replacement.

As they had from the beginning, government opponents continued to express fears to legislators during the 2008 interim, an election year. They feared prosecutions would abound. It was, however, admitted that there was confusion and misapplication of the law that required education and guidance. We gave assurances that prosecutions would not be a priority. We repeatedly stated our belief that most public officials want to obey the governing statutes, but sometimes the statutes lack clarity and compliance isn't always easy. We stated many problems could be eliminated by developing uniform training standards and materials for the use of public body organizations, by making presentations to their memberships and being available to provide authoritative solutions to problems they encountered with these statutes. I told legislators that my clients felt, as did I, that prosecutions would be an indication of failure of our primary missions: solving problems for citizens and their officials and providing education and authoritative guidance that could be relied upon by public officials and citizens alike.

In December of 2008 we met with the legislative leadership. The principal leaders favored enactment of the IPIB bill in 2009. However, the idea surfaced of considering locating an enforcement activity within an existing agency due to financial constraints. Senator Jochum indicated a willingness to consider that option, provided it included strong enforcement powers.

The 2009 session saw the introduction of three bills: Senator Jochum's Senate File 161 (the Bonfield-based version we favored), Senate Study Bill 1231, filed by the Senate State Government Chair, Senator Appel (D), and an identical bill, House Study Bill 234, filed by the House State Government Chair, Representative Mascher (D). SF 161 and SSB 1231 were both assigned to a subcommittee of Senators Jochum (chair), Danielson (D) and Behn (R). HSB 234 was assigned to a subcommittee of Lensing (D)(chair), Mascher (D), Isenhart (D), Koester (R) and Pettengill (R).

The study bills proposed an open meetings, public records, and privacy advisory committee (hereinafter referred to as "advisory committee") to serve as a resource for public access to government information. The advisory committee consisted of 16 members with no enforcement powers. The makeup of the committee and lack of enforcement powers, coupled with the charge to balance openness against privacy concerns, ensured a result that would produce little more than a debating society. Also, the membership was stacked against transparency advocates. We expressed our concerns with legislative leaders and the chairs of the State Government Committees. At the beginning of the session we were told that the legislation would begin in the House.

Representative Lensing extended an invitation to members of the Senate subcommittee and they began holding joint House/Senate subcommittee meetings to develop a consensus bill. Several meetings were held, and many of the issues from the prior year were rehashed. We worked against the debating society approach in favor of the Bonfield approach with its manageable board with enforcement powers.

While further discussions with the House were being conducted, the Senate State Government subcommittee and committee approved the senate study bill as submitted. The subcommittee chair, Senator Jochum, noted that it was a work in progress and that they had every intention of addressing the issue in a very meaningful way. She stated her belief that transparency in government and the public's right-to-know were critically important to make sure that government functioned properly. The bill, renumbered as SF 282, favored the Bonfield approach.

It soon became apparent that the House subcommittee would be hard pressed to meet the first legislative bill deadline. We were very pleased when the bill came up at the last minute and the Bonfield provisions of SF 161 were inserted into the House study bill by amendment. The resulting new bill was HF 777. However, Representative Lensing stated during the committee discussion that after the bill was to be sent to the House Calendar to meet the House deadline, it would then be returned to the state government committee and subcommittee for further work.

That work commenced on March 16. Representative Lensing asked for comments on the bill. The attorney general's office and the ombudsman's office reported at this meeting that three recent cases cited by the INA as examples of egregious violation of law had been acted upon satisfactorily. No enforcement legislation was needed because the existing law was succeeding.

On March 25 the House State Government subcommittee did a complete reversal and returned to the debating society approach. Subcommittee chair Lensing indicated that with the current budget problems there simply wasn't funding available to create a strong enforcement agency. Coupled with our disappointment over the enforcement mechanism were unfavorable transparency policy changes to existing law that the subcommittee amendment also proposed.

The consensus following that meeting by openness advocates was that to do nothing would be better than advancing HF 777 with the adoption of the proposed debating society amendment.

However, all was not lost. Grassroots and onsite lobbying yielded favorable results at the next meeting. While the House subcommittee again stated it could not afford a good enforcement mechanism, it recognized the need to put balance into the advisory committee and change some of the policy provisions. Members also indicated a desire to codify the current arrangement between the ombudsman's office and the attorney general's office. That idea was not well received by those entities.

Following that meeting we met with House Majority Leader Kevin McCarthy (D). He had consistently been an openness supporter throughout his legislative career and was encouraging the subcommittee to move in our direction. We then met with Representative Lensing who characterized the advisory committee approach as an interim step to a full-fledged enforcement agency when it became affordable.

Ultimately the House State Government Committee passed an amendment to HF 777 which was adopted by the full House when it passed the bill. In committee, Representative Lensing characterized the new amendment and the bill as a work in progress.

We continued to have discussions with the Senate subcommittee chair, Senator Jochum. Following the House action, she expressed her disappointment and indicated that the Senate would not be taking up the bill. Senator Appel expressed her dismay as well and indicated her desire to "just start over." Both senators indicated their intent to work over the summer to craft an improved bill.

In 2010, the Senate took up consideration of HF 777. Senator Jochum proposed an amendment that was adopted by the full Senate State Government Committee to completely strike the text of HF

777 and replace it with a bill substantially similar to her bill, SF 161, creating an enforcement agency. That amendment was adopted by the full Senate and the amended HF 777 passed the Senate on a 35-13 vote on March 10, 2010, just before the deadline.

When the bill came back to the House, its fate was uncertain. Lobbyists for local government entities continued to fight hard against creation of an enforcement agency. The House seemed unsure of what to do with HF 777 as amended by the Senate. Lobbyists for local governments (and elected officials in legislators' districts) kept up their opposition. The House never debated the Senate amendment. The issue would go through another election cycle and into a new general assembly in 2011.

In 2011 Senator Jochum filed a Bonfield-based bill which eventually was approved by its Senate State Government Subcommittee of Jochum (D-Chair), Danielson (D), and Sorenson (R) with a recommendation for passage. It was then approved for passage by the full Senate State Government Committee and designated SF 430, on March 7, 2011. The amended bill passed the Senate by a vote of 49-0 on March 14.

It was assigned to House State Government subcommittee of Koester (R-Chair), Lensing (D), and Raecker (R). The Republicans had taken control of the House in 2010 while the Senate remained under Democrat control. Former Governor Terry Branstad, a transparency advocate, was elected governor. He made known his support for the bill. The House State Government Subcommittee recommended committee approval of the bill on April 1. It was then rereferred to the House Appropriations Committee. But it was not assigned to a subcommittee before the House adjourned for the year.

On February 7, 2012 the bill was rereferred to the House State Government Committee and assigned to a subcommittee of Rogers (R-Chair), Cownie (R), Koester (R), Lensing (D), and T. Taylor (D). The full committee approved the bill with a positive amendment on March 15. It was then referred to the House Appropriations Committee and assigned to a subcommittee of Rogers (R-Chair),

Hagenow (R), and Gaskill (D). The House Appropriations Committee approved the subcommittee recommendation for passage on March 20. On March 21 the bill was rereferred to the House Ways and Means Committee which approved the bill on March 21. The House debated and amended the bill on April 17. It passed the House by a vote of 92 to 7. The Senate concurred in the House amendment and passed the bill for the final time on April 23 by a vote of 49 to 0. Governor Branstad signed the bill on May 3, 2012.

Representative Walt Rogers was assigned floor manager of this very controversial bill as a freshman legislator. I confess to having had serious misgivings. It was going to be a very hard-fought battle. It was indeed and he did a truly outstanding job handling it. There were many attacks on the bill from opposing factions which he fought off. He handled the amendment fights successfully and improved the bill in the process. One of the adopted amendments removed the filing fee provision from the bill thus allowing citizens to file complaints with the board without incurring cost.

This bill was very contentious. There were many times when opposing factions were surely as exasperated as I was. My recollection is that all the legions of opposition lobbyists conducted themselves in a civil manner. I counsel new lobbyists that one of the first and most important things to learn to be a successful lobbyist is to not take things personally. As their practice grows, they will find they are contending against many different colleagues with whom they will have become friends. Lobbyists don't last long if every battle results in personal animosity. I also emphasize the importance of keeping their word. It hurts lobbyists and their clients if the lobbyist's word can't be relied upon. The lobbyist will soon lose the respect, trust, and friendship of colleagues and legislators. Respect of colleagues and legislators is essential to a successful lobbyist.

A sad epilogue: Larry Pope, a Drake Law School Professor, former Republican House Majority Leader and a lobbyist when the bill was proposed, vehemently opposed it. He and his partner, Julie Smith (D), both good friends, lobbied for the Iowa League of

Municipalities. Larry had a good legal mind and was a tenacious advocate. For some reason, he just despised this bill. His maneuvering greatly contributed to stringing this battle out an extra couple of years!

A few months after the bill's passage, Julie called to advised me that Larry had been stricken with cancer and the prognosis was not good. The last time I visited Larry was not too long before he passed away. We had a lot of laughs recalling legislative battles we had been involved in. Some we were on the same side. As we were wrapping up, we talked about the legislative session underway that spring. We had some more good laughs about some of the issues. As I was leaving, he remarked, "You know Keith, the environment on the hill is perfect for introduction and passage of the 'Larry Pope Memorial Bill.'"

I laughed and asked, "And just what would that be, Larry?"

He replied, "Repeal of that damned IPIB bill you got passed last year!"

We parted for the last time enjoying our last good laugh together!

# 2

# Iowa Medical Society

I ALWAYS HAD an interest in medicine and had briefly considered medical school. But it takes a long time to become a board-certified physician—and a lot of dollars! Patti also had an interest in medicine. I think she would have pursued that had the necessary resources been available. We had many physician friends.

Jim West had represented the Iowa Medical Society (IMS) before I joined him on the hill. He brought me into that representation, which I enjoyed and appreciated, even though I soon became convinced doctors were the most challenging group to represent. I came aboard at the right time, as the medical malpractice issue was increasingly of concern.

Again, I had great people to work with. Eldon Houston was the nationally recognized executive director of the IMS. He was succeeded by Mike Abrams. On legislative issues I worked at various times with Tim Gibson, Meridith Olson, Amy Bishop, Paul Bishop (Amy & Paul are not related), Jennifer Harbison, Karla McHenry, and Becky Roorda. Drs. Clarence Denser and Kevin Cunningham were chairs of the IMS Committee on Legislation during my representation of the IMS. I know I am leaving some out—please accept my apologies!

I had the litigation experience that Jim lacked, and he had the insurance law experience that I lacked. We made a good team for the doctors.

◆ ◆ ◆
*Death with Dignity—the Living Will*

The Iowa Medical Society's legislative concerns were not limited to medical malpractice. I had the opportunity, through my representation of the IMS, to work on other leading-edge issues affecting Iowans. The "death with dignity" issue surfaced, and some very poor legislative efforts to address it were made. These efforts focused on creation of legal instruments now known by names such as "Living Wills" and "Health Care Powers of Attorney." They attempted to address the concerns arising out of scientific advances that enabled extension of the dying process to a point well beyond patient benefit. These early legislative proposals were successfully opposed by the IMS. The IMS recognized the problem, but the proposed solutions were thought to create additional problems.

After two or three years in opposition, I was bluntly told by a couple of legislative leaders (one being Senator Jo Ann Zimmerman, a nurse, who was to become the state's first female Lt. Governor in 1987) that the legislature was going to pass legislation the next session. They were friendly about it and asked that I tell the IMS they should have me draft a bill which the IMS could support. I so advised the IMS, and they authorized the project. I spent a great deal of time that summer with many interested groups. Those groups included religious organizations (Catholic, Jewish and Protestant), pro-choice and pro-life groups, hospital groups, and other health care providers. They all had their points of view. Fortunately for me, they had provided responsible representatives and reasonable positions. Disagreements were discussed calmly and reasonably. We found it was possible to accommodate significant concerns raised by changing our working draft, or through increasing mutual understanding by thorough discussion.

When working on the final draft, I became convinced that properly stated reasonable statutory provisions and requirements should be applicable in every case, regardless of whether a Living

Will existed. The goal was to avoid over-treatment that the patient in a terminal condition would not want if able to express his or her opinion. After considering input from several sources, it became apparent that this practical benefit was more important than the legal benefit. The existence of a legal procedure for advanced decision-making would foster family discussions before the onset of a need for application of that decision. The resulting statute (Life-sustaining Procedures Act; Iowa Code Chapter 144A) adopted in 1985 created a legal living will document (called a "Declaration" in the statute) providing for a statement of patient intent respecting withdrawal of life-sustaining procedures when death is imminent. The legislation also contains a process for addressing withdrawal of life-sustaining procedures for patients who have not executed a living will. The criteria and procedures are essentially the same except as noted below.

Legislation is always somewhat risky. You never know when a legislator might come up with a concern or idea at the last minute that has the potential to upset months of work to produce a bill that represents a compromise of well analyzed and stated positions. It was thought there was total agreement on the Life-sustaining Procedures Act when it was set for debate by the Iowa Senate. When I came into the Senate Lounge the morning of the debate, I was approached by a senator who was very concerned about the fact that the bill did not require confirmation of a patient's terminal condition by a physician other than the patient's attending physician. He showed me a draft amendment he was filing that added this requirement. I told him the concept had been thoroughly considered when the bill was being developed, and a consensus formed that such a requirement merely added expense without corresponding benefit. He was not to be deterred. He told me he would be filing his amendment and that he thought he would have the votes for its adoption. I thanked him for telling me.

In legislation perfection is too often the enemy of the good! I gathered the representatives of the many involved groups who were present and advised them of the problem. They asked my recommendation. I said we would be wise to accept the senator's amendment, and get the bill passed and over to the House as time was running out. After some discussion, everyone agreed. I advised the floor manager of the bill. I pointed out that the senator's amendment only went to the Declaration portion of the legislation and did not apply to a person in a terminal condition who did not have a Declaration.

The senator's amendment was adopted, and the bill moved to the House, which accepted it as passed and sent it to Governor Branstad who signed it into law on March 5, 1985. The statute has been revised over the years since, but the requirement for a second opinion by a non-attending physician of a patient's terminal condition before allowing the withdrawal of life sustaining procedures still exists. But it still only applies to patients who have signed a Declaration. No such requirement exists in the statute regarding withdrawal of life-sustaining procedures for a patient in a terminal condition without a Declaration! Despite this quirk, a Declaration is very helpful, especially to family members, when the time comes. See Iowa Code Sections 144A.5 and 144A.7.

I am grateful to the IMS for having provided me the opportunity to work on this issue that has benefited numerous Iowans and their families when facing life's final days.

◆◆◆

*Human Immunodeficiency Virus—AIDS*

I was given another great opportunity in 1999. Human immunodeficiency virus (HIV) had become a public health concern that generated an increasingly hysterical reaction requiring a political response. The virus produced the then almost always fatal acquired immune deficiency syndrome (AIDS). In 1999 there was no known medical defense to this syndrome.

Initially it was thought that AIDS was a homosexual affliction. Panic reactions began to set in when it became apparent that anyone could be infected through contact with the bodily fluids of a person infected with HIV. Adding to the horror was the fact that people with HIV almost never became aware of it before much delayed symptoms of AIDS appeared, or it was discovered through testing. AIDS became a matter of huge concern! It was viewed as an unstoppable superbug from which there was no sanctuary. Athletes and first responders became very concerned about exposure to anyone's blood.

The IMS was much involved with the issue. As HIV/AIDS became a political as well as a health care issue, IMS worked to develop logical and beneficial legislation addressing it. There were terrible examples of harmful legislative responses from some of the first states that enacted HIV/AIDS legislation. The IMS and Iowa politicians from both parties recognized that there was need for development and adoption of responsible legislation enabling a sound public health response.

It was my privilege to work with IMS personnel, public health officials, and a bi-partisan group of legislators. With gubernatorial support we developed a model legislative response. Iowa Code Chapter 141A, ACQUIRED IMMUNE DEFICIENCY SYNDROME (AIDS), is the result of a huge coordinated effort to develop an effective response to this public health emergency. While there have been amendments since its enactment, Chapter 141A remains a national model response to a significant public health emergency.

Chapter 141A designated the Iowa Department of Public Health as the lead agency for implementation of the comprehensive HIV plan enacted. It calls for testing and education concerning HIV/AIDS and established a program for notification and testing of persons exposed to HIV. Reporting criteria were established for treatment providers. Regard for the privacy of afflicted people was a high priority and is provided for in Chapter 141A. Confidentiality procedures are backed up with the creation of a right to legal redress in case of violation. And immunities are provided for persons making reports concerning possible exposures to HIV. Health care providers are relieved of any liability to warn third persons they know to have been exposed by their patients in order to protect their patient's privacy and encourage their patient's willingness to cooperate in tracing exposures.

Chapter 141A was enacted by Senate File 248, a bill floor managed by an IMS member and Sioux City physician, Senator John Redwine (R). It passed the Senate by a vote of 48 to 0 on March 2, 1999. A leading role was also played by Senator Johnie Hammond (D) who was able to garner bipartisan support. The bill was floor managed in the Iowa House of Representatives by Representative Gary Blodgett (R), a dentist from Clear Lake. It was amended and passed by the House on April 6 by a unanimous vote of 100 to 0. The House amendment added more detailed counseling requirements thought to be too specific by the Senate which rejected the House amendment on April 20. The House considered the bill again and receded from its amendment and sent the bill to the governor by a vote of 91 to 1 on April 22. The bill was signed by Governor Vilsack on May 26, 1999.

I am very proud of having subsequently received the coveted John F. Stanford Award from the Iowa Medical Society "in recognition of dedicated and tireless efforts to improve the quality of health care in Iowa."

◆◆◆

*Medical Malpractice*

Medical malpractice issues persist and continue to appear before the legislature relating to non-economic damages. Medical malpractice is especially concerning to physicians. In my opinion, shared by some physician friends, the concern is an especially significant issue because of the emotional impact. For example, when a lawyer commits legal malpractice the client can most often be restored by an award of monetary damages. Not so with medical malpractice. These dedicated professional health care providers live with the emotional consequences resulting when a patient sustains a bad outcome, especially one that cannot be reversed. In many cases the patient suffers problems that money cannot solve and for which there is no economic measure.

We all make mistakes, but for the physicians the consequences of their mistakes have the potential to be devastating and uncorrectable. A medical error can impact the well-being of a patient for the rest of that person's life or even prematurely end their life. Physicians are severely impacted by an allegation of malpractice, which can ruin their professional reputation regardless of the validity of the allegation. We had many hard-fought battles with the plaintiff's lawyers' groups over medical malpractice issues. We won some and lost some, but we never achieved the holy grail: a limitation on non-economic damages. The law continues to try to compensate for loss of one's most precious asset, good health, with mere money with no succinct standard by which to determine the proper amount. This issue is not limited to medical malpractice cases. It is relevant to all cases where "non-economic" damages are sought.

◆ ◆ ◆

## Scope of Practice

There also were acrimonious turf battles with other health care providers. There are many groups who are licensed health care providers, with limited scopes of permitted practice as befits their limited training. They are sincere in their belief that they are qualified to "do more" for their patients. Most of them, at one time or another, have waged legislative and regulatory battles to expand their scopes of practice. The IMS often opposed such efforts based on these practitioners' limited training and lack of credible oversight. We were not always successful. More people want to help others than can go to medical school and become doctors.

# 3

# Iowa Automobile
# Dealers Association

MY PARTNER, JIM West, did a great job representing the Iowa Automobile Dealers Association (IADA). When I started lobbying, the association executive had held his position for many years and was about to retire. The IADA hired Gary Thomas as its new executive director. I had known Gary from his days as a member of Lt. Governor Art Neu's staff. Jim got ahold of us both about the same time. He was our mentor, and Gary and I learned a lot together. I also learned a lot about associations in the process. Jim handled the heavy lifting for the association. I worked on several projects for the IADA under his direction. My wife and I got to know many auto dealers and their wives and association staff. Patti and I were included with Jim and his wife in the Association's meetings and social functions. We have some great memories and friends from those occasions.

Gary had a very successful career. I have had the privilege of working with some outstanding association executives, but Gary was truly exceptional. He was recognized nationally as such. He became President of the Automotive Trade Association Executives, a national organization. In that capacity he also served on key operating committees of the National Automobile Dealers Association (NADA).

Gary was in the right place at the right time. He had been involved in the Bush campaign. When the economic crisis of 2008 hit, Gary was consulted along with the incoming Chairman of the NADA, an Iowa dealer and close friend of Gary, John McEleney. John and Gary spent a lot of time in Washington in 2008-09. The auto industry and the country benefited from their input.

I met and worked with many great people employed by our clients and who were leaders of client associations that I might not otherwise have ever had the privilege of meeting and working with. There are so many whose outstanding work and support were key to my success. Several, but not all, have been discussed above involving issues especially relevant to my story. I regret space does not allow me to name and thank them all. I assure those not mentioned that I treasure the opportunities you and/or your entities provided that allowed me to be of service.

# PART VII
# MOVING ON

# 1

# Retirement 1: Leaving the World's Greatest Law Firm

THERE IS NO more important decision made by a new lawyer than the selection of a firm in which to practice, other than the selection of a spouse! It is a great boost to one's life, if after the honeymoons are over, you still love them both! I haven't earned the nickname "Lucky" for nothing! And Dolly Parton was able to put together a career without my help. I made the right choices.

I retired from the law firm on December 31, 2012, just short of 40 years of practice. I was a tired 71. I was ready for that beach Patti liked at Puerto Vallarta, Mexico. My solar batteries got recharged in style! Patti said I had promised her three months in Mexico. I told her I must have been very drunk! We settled on three weeks. It was a great time. Des Moines Federal District Court Judge Hal Vietor and his wife Dalia were winter regulars there. Dalia and Patti worked together as interpreters at Mercy Hospital in Des Moines. The four of us had great times together. We also had other friends from Des Moines who coincidentally visited Puerto Vallarta for a few days. We enjoyed spending time with them also. And there was a former litigation client and his wife who happened to be staying in the same beachfront high-rise condo we were in.

Our next-door neighbors were Canadians. We were introduced to their friends and had a great time with them too. Thanks to our Canadian friends, I did have a strange encounter. They were friends with a club owner whose property was in the foothills. When we arrived in Puerto Vallarta, I did a little quick checking on personal safety issues. I was told there was no problem in the beach area, as the cartels had so much invested there that they didn't permit any crime against tourists. But out in the foothills it was a different story.

The Canadians usually went to their friend's club in the foothills on Friday afternoons. They took the regular city bus. We were asked to go with them on one such visit. One of the group members was a fellow retired from the Cook County, Illinois, Sheriff's Office. He was a bodyguard for the Chicago Bear's Walter Payton. I decided we were probably going to be in good shape security-wise. At the appointed time the merry band proceeded to the foothills.

When we arrived, Patti and I were promptly introduced to the proprietor. He was a very nice and friendly fellow. He had a unique place. It was built on a stream which had a sand beach. He had a dining area near the beach and a bar near the dining area. All were open air, of course.

We settled on the beach and got our drinks and were having a great time. Nature called, and I headed off to find the restroom. I stopped by the bar for directions. It was a bit of a walk from the bar. It was in a little building with one of those light plastic corrugated-looking doors.

There was no one else there. I noted two toilet stalls as I walked in and proceeded to the two urinals. While about my business I heard the outside door open. I did not then hear a stall door open. I went on alert! (Old habits don't die easily.) Suddenly, someone slammed their left hand on my left shoulder and squeezed it. I quickly looked down to my right to check whether the guy had a gun or knife in his right hand. I wasn't expecting a gun, as they are not as common down there. But I was very concerned he might have a knife. He had neither.

I was a little more at ease. I thought it would be ironic to get shot or stabbed to death in a Mexican restroom after all the danger I had survived. The fellow was yelling at me in Spanish. I was yelling back in English. I had turned enough to be able to look at him. He appeared 18 or 20, of slight build, and about five foot six. His eyes were watery, and he was swaying just a little. But he kept a strong grip on my left shoulder.

What to do?! I noticed a towel dispensing machine on the wall behind him. The wash basins were to his left at the back of the room with big mirrors on that wall. Yell as I might, nothing changed. I figured if I took him out and he was connected, I would be put away to rot in a Mexican jail or worse. I gestured my need to zip my shorts. He dropped his grip, but almost immediately slammed his right hand down on my right shoulder. Some progress. But I could now pivot to my left and head for the wash basins. I would be further from the door, but I would not have to slam him against the towel dispenser. And I could buy time at the wash basin while watching him in the mirrors.

He let me proceed further into the restroom towards the wash basins. I made a production out of washing up which gave me a chance to assess him. He was probably a little drunk and a little high. He gave me space and continued yelling. He did not appear to have a knife or gun in his pockets, as there wasn't a bulge in the tight pants he wore. As I watched, he started towards me. He started to almost stumble. I seized on the opportunity his unsteadiness created. I swung around and decked him. He was surprised, and I made for the door. He did not try to get up and follow me out.

I went to find my new friend, the proprietor, but was unsuccessful. When I got back to my friends, I reported what happened. I thought the proprietor needed to know about it so he could deal with my assailant. The bodyguard suggested we go see if we could spot the guy. I saw him at the bar. The bodyguard said he would take care of it.

A bit later the bodyguard returned to the beach. He said the problem was solved. The proprietor was located and, with the help of the club's bouncer (as if Walter's guy needed help), the fellow was picked up and bodily ejected onto the street and told never to return. I was shown iPhone pictures to prove it.

# 2

# First Executive Director, Iowa Public Information Board

WHEN I RETIRED from the law firm, I chose not to go to "of Counsel" status and withdrew from the firm instead. There was another interesting opportunity under consideration that precluded that option. It would require that I be independent of the firm and its media clients. They would be ably represented by my Nyemaster successors, Attorneys Scott Sundstrand and Brad Epperly.

Governor Branstad was seeking a person to serve as Executive Director of the Iowa Public Information Board (IPIB). He suggested that I would find retirement boring and would be ready for a job within a few months. He asked if I would apply to be the first Executive Director of the IPIB. I agreed.

I already flunked retirement. I served as the first Executive Director of the Iowa Public Information Board when it opened for business on July 8, 2013. Prior to that a nine-member board had to be appointed, governing rules had to be drafted, office space had to be located, and an administrative person and deputy director had to be hired. Once space was found, the new office had to be furnished and made operational. I worked without pay or official status until after I was appointed Executive Director.

The board had no budget for the fiscal 2013 year ending June 30, 2013. But it was authorized to form and organize with an anticipated opening for business in July of 2013, the start of fiscal year 2014. The fiscal 2014 budget contained operational funding available July 1, 2013. The governor asked me to help with board appointments (which were made in spring of 2012) and oversee getting the board organized. Larry Johnson, staff attorney for the Governor's Office, was very helpful getting us organized.

The Board held its first meeting in April 2012 to address organizational matters. Bill Monroe, retired Executive Director of the Iowa Newspaper Association (INA), was elected Board Chair. Other Board members: Attorney and Mayor of Urbandale Robert Andeweg (R) with whom I practiced law; Attorney and Drake Law Professor Tony Gaughan (R) of West Des Moines; Semi-retired newspaper publisher and past president of the INA Jo Martin (D) of Spirit Lake; Attorney and former legislator, city attorney and county supervisor Andy McKean (R) of Anamosa; Community college board member and city councilman Gary Mohr of Bettendorf (I) (subsequently elected to state legislature as a Republican); Attorney, Drake Journalism Professor (later Dean) and Executive Secretary of the Iowa Freedom of Information Council Kathleen Richardson (D) of Des Moines; Senior Managing Attorney for MidAmerican Energy Suzan Stewart (R) of Sioux City, and retiring Carroll County Treasurer Peggy Weitl (D) of Carroll. Two other original board members also served as Board Chair: Robert Andeweg followed by Suzan Stewart.

The board members were chosen based on their backgrounds. The statute provides for a balanced board representing three constituencies: general public, government bodies, and the media. It was the expectation that the board would have input from people with direct knowledge relating to the issues they would adjudicate and would also be able to coalesce and produce recommendations to the governor and legislature for statutory changes.

I served the Board as volunteer counsel until I was appointed Executive Director on April 18, 2013 at an organizational board meeting, with compensated employment to begin July 8, 2013. Over twenty people applied to be Executive Director. After I was appointed, I served as Executive Director without compensation until July 8. The demands on my time were well over forty hours per week from April through July 7$^{th}$. Bill and I had spent a lot of time prior to April as well.

I soon enlisted assistance from another friend, Democrat Attorney General Tom Miller. Deputy Attorneys General Julie Pottorff and Pam Griebel were assigned to assist in developing the necessary administrative rules under which the Board would operate. They were both highly qualified experts in Administrative Law. Pam was the legal advisor to the Accountancy Examining Board. We had worked together on projects relating to regulation of CPAs and accounting practices. We didn't always agree on issues initially, but we trusted one another and were usually able to come to agreement. Likewise, I had worked with Julie on Administrative Law issues and had a good working relationship with her.

Bill Monroe and I put in a lot of time and effort as we worked to make the IPIB a functioning entity. It was a great experience. Bill and I had worked together on INA issues for many years. Our efforts had bipartisan support. Our old foes we were working against on the legislation made speaking opportunities available to us. We assured their constituent members that we wanted to help public officials serve the public. We made the rounds! We emphasized our priorities were on providing training and guidance relating to their service to the public. We did not want any part of being a "gotcha" agency. Prosecutions would be a sign of our failure. We would make IPIB assistance available to anyone who needed it. Our goal would be same-day service whenever possible.

Old foes began to see that the IPIB was a potential asset, not a liability. It could become a model of bipartisan cooperation to achieve the goal of better serving the public. Oh, what this country can accomplish when blessed with public officials that put service before self!

I soon learned that I had lots of friends in state government who wanted to be helpful in establishing the IPIB. I got offers of office furniture, conference room furniture, copiers, printers, file cabinets, and work tables from various state offices that had surpluses. It was all used, but it all worked. I didn't have to break anything in.

The first major task was to find suitable office space. There were suggestions, but none panned out. I was shown space in the basement floor of the Wallace State Office Building. No windows. Me, a pilot underground with no windows! No way! It was nice space, but I couldn't imagine not being able to look out a window. How can one think great thoughts without a window to gaze from?

I was then shown empty space on the third floor. The Wallace Building is fraught with problems, many caused by the fact it is of modern design with glass walls on its south side enclosing an atrium. I envisioned my office located with a great view. I could gaze out my window while thinking great thoughts staring directly at the capitol dome, simultaneously ensuring no one was steeling the gold off the dome! We had found our home. A reception area, conference room, and two offices were constructed.

When we opened the doors for business on July 8, I looked around and it occurred to me that the only things we had spent money on were telephones and computers. Everything else was used equipment and furniture supplied by various other agencies. We got the first citizen complaint about 15 minutes after we opened, before my desk had been moved into my office. I sat on the floor and worked the call.

We opened with two staff members: me and an administrative assistant, Cindy Meyerdirk. I found out while interviewing her that she was from Spirit Lake, about nine miles from my hometown of Milford. Cindy was very good with people and really worked hard to get things up and running. I hired her away from the Department of Public Safety.

Hiring a Deputy Director was a time-consuming task. I was lucky once again. Board Chair Bill Monroe and I interviewed Margaret Johnson, Fremont County Attorney, at my home. I had gone through the 20 or so resumes we received and scored them different ways and she was always in the top three. Margaret was a great find! She had gone to law school after getting a journalism undergraduate degree from Iowa State. She got her law degree from William & Mary Law School. She began her legal career as an Army Judge Advocate General officer. She served in that capacity at Fort Carson, Colorado, just on the other side of Colorado Springs from my alma mater, the United States Air Force Academy.

After the interview, Bill and I both were disposed to try to hire Margaret. We decided to make the final decision the next day, which we did. But she could not be available until July 22nd. Bill and I agreed she was worth waiting for and we hired her.

When we opened the doors on July 8, we were immediately busy. As I was involved with setting things up, I had occasions to speak with the Attorney General Miller and with Iowa Ombudsman, Ruth Cooperrider. They both cautioned me about a handful of perpetual complainers who would see me as someone else to whom they could bring complaints. They both thought a couple of them required watchful concern. They began to appear almost immediately. I told Cindy about them and told her that I would work with my door open. If she had a concern, she should signal me. If I wasn't there, she should keep the outer office door closed and locked. I think it was the second day when I got back from lunch, she told me that one of the persons of concern had appeared. She did not feel threatened and the person was very easy to talk with. She had set up an appointment for me. My experience with that individual was the same as Cindy's.

Being a new agency, everything we did required development of a new form and method for proceeding. Things began to pile up. I spent most of my time on the phone taking complaints and following up on them with the affected public officials. I did not have time to develop a file system or arrange for meetings with groups regarding our website, training materials, or speaking schedules. Margaret Johnson reported for duty on July 22nd. Cindy and I were really glad to see her!

She went right to work handling calls and organizing the office. I soon discovered that she excelled at developing file systems and office procedures. I quickly learned to rely on her for those aspects of our office. She did most of the work on getting our website up and running. She was great at working with local government entities to establish uniform training materials and booking our speaking engagements. We worked well together as a team. We reviewed each other's work to the benefit of both of us.

Shortly after Margaret arrived, we read a story in the state's largest newspaper, The Des Moines Register. They reported about a case they had filed based on a denial of a records request they had made to the state's human services agency. We wondered where they had filed it! They must have mailed it. We assumed they intended to file it with us, but we had not received anything. We were finally called and asked when we would respond to their complaint. It was discovered they had served the governor's office where it languished. Everyone assumed the Register knew where our office was. The governor's staff assumed they were being given courtesy copies. It turned out the Register had "filed" three complaints soon after we opened. None were insignificant cases and they hit before we had a reasonable chance to get organized and operational.

Our enabling statute gave us extensive powers and processes to use to resolve disputes involving open meetings and open records issues. The main thrust was to encourage informal resolution without resort to the formal legal process under the state's Administrative Procedures Act. When necessary, we were granted enforcement powers pursuant to that Act.

I soon learned that most disputes could be resolved by a call to the local governmental official directly involved in the activity that had generated the citizen complaint. We never set out to be an agency eager to prosecute people. We had neither the necessary time nor funds for that approach. I always believed that a clear majority of public officials wanted to comply with the law. But the open meetings and records statutes were not the easiest to interpret and apply. I almost always had good cooperation with local governments and the attorneys who represented them. I think they saw us as an authoritative body they could rely upon which would give certainty to their decisions and provide protection from litigation. Our enabling legislation specifically provided protection to officials who followed our advice, even if it was later shown to be incorrect.

I had made it known from the start that while I had spent a career representing media interests, the law would dictate my actions. Our first board chair, Bill Monroe, the long-time newspaper association executive director was of like mind. He also understood the importance of adhering to the requirements of the law, not the tug of our hearts. I had warned him that our former media constituents might find it hard to understand our approach. There was a lot of anguish in the beginning when we found the law didn't take us where we would have preferred to go! I was really pleased to hear Judge Neil Gorsuch's statement to this point the evening he was introduced to the nation as a nominee for appointment to the Supreme Court of the United States: "A judge who likes every outcome he reaches is very likely a bad judge."

Most board decisions were usually unanimous, but there were times when there was disagreement. As a former litigator, I was used to strong disagreement with friends and colleagues as a part of my advocacy for a client's position. I had to work at it sometimes, but I came to learn and respect the art of disagreeing without being disagreeable. The board maintained its mutual respect for each other's opinions through some tough decisions. Disagreements were decorously handled, and collegial relationships maintained. I don't think it was something they had to strive for, it came naturally to them as a characteristic of their ethical, friendly and principled natures.

A very controversial case (one of the original three) involved a request by the Des Moines Register for a video recording made by a security camera at the Toledo Children's Home. The video was alleged to show abuse of a young woman held in confinement. Considerable time and effort were expended by all concerned, which included the Register, me and Margaret, the Attorney General, and the Department of Human Service (the agency responsible for operation of the Home). It was my conclusion (and Margaret's) that the statutes governing Human Service facilities made the videotape confidential. I advised the board of my reasoning and recommended the case be dismissed. After extensive hearings and confidential review of the video, the board accepted my recommendation. The Register appealed the case to the Iowa District Court for Polk County. The Court upheld the Board's decision.

The Iowa Open Meetings and Open Records Statutes are complex. Many of the issues they address are very controversial. Legitimate controversy often demands compromise when addressed by the Iowa General Assembly. Respected contending parties have established well-grounded opposing positions. Consequently, statutes enacted out of such controversies often become convoluted with less than crystal-clear articulations of the position of any of the contending parties. Subsequent court decisions polish the law and provide further guidance.

Board Chair Bill Monroe and I strove to establish the IPIB as an entity helpful to the public, the media, and the governmental bodies serving them. Before opening for business, we began a round of speaking engagements with any group that was interested. That practice continues to this day. The goal remains to provide educational resources and participate in training programs to facilitate compliance with the governing statutes. It has never been about prosecutions. Prosecutions could be indicative of a weakness in our outreach programs. The Board continues to believe that the great majority of public officials wanted to comply with the laws. When I retired, I was very pleased with the regard which media and government bodies had for the IPIB.

Our best customer group was the general public at around forty-five percent of cases, followed by government entities at about forty percent, and the media at about fifteen percent. Those shares have remained consistent. Our goal of establishing better understanding of the public's right to information and the governments obligations to supply that information was being met. Case volume was more than double what we expected and has re-doubled since.

At the end of November 2014, I retired as Executive Director of the IPIB. I was a salaried employee, so no overtime pay. I was worn out! I had put in lots of 60 to 75-hour weeks in getting the IPIB up and running. There were controversial issues to be resolved which required extensive research and writing. I tried one case before an Administrative Law Judge (ALJ). Margaret did the investigation of the case and prepared it for trial. Since Margaret was going to be a witness, I tried it and obtained a judgment against a County Attorney for failing to comply with the Open Records Statute.

I have stayed in contact with Professor Bonfield. Recently (October 28, 2019) I visited him at his residence. He remains an ardent advocate for openness in government. We started there but soon veered off that subject. We had a great time discussing a variety of issues, disagreeing on some and agreeing on others. Towards the end of my visit we specifically discussed the IPIB. He asked me how I thought it was doing. I replied that my only disappointment has been that while we have been able to forge agreements on legislative issues as a Board, we have not been able to garner legislative support from our constituencies. We have not been able to secure the legislative changes we feel are needed. I also told him I haven't liked some of the decisions I thought the law required to be rendered, but that I guessed that was a good thing. I expressed further disappointment that significant numbers of my constituency fail to appreciate my obligation to apply the law as it is, not as I would like it to be.

# 3

# Retirement 2: Part-time Attorney and Consultant

WHEN MY RETIREMENT from the IPIB was announced, I was contacted by friends Chris and John Stineman. I had worked with them while serving mutual clients. I served those clients as a lobbyist and legislative counsel while they served as public affairs consultants and advisors. While I was establishing the IPIB they were building their firm, Strategic Elements (SE). Both had great reputations. They wanted me to participate in their firm. We had discussions and I agreed to serve as a legal advisor and senior policy consultant. I started with them in February 2015.

Way to go, flunked retirement for the second time!

John and Chris were great to work with. Their firm was made up of many outstanding young people who were a joy to work with. I helped the firm with business organization and public policy issues. They had a staff attorney, Megan Peiffer, with whom I had worked while we were both lobbyists. She worked against establishment of the IPIB as a lobbyist for the Iowa League of Municipalities. She is another with whom I was able to disagree without either of us being disagreeable. She attended law school while lobbying and was a newly minted lawyer when hired by SE.

I enjoyed collaborating with her at SE. It was great to be on the same side for a change!

SE had a Washington office. The firm engaged in representing clients regarding various issues involving government relations, policy formulation, and special events planning. They did not get involved in individual candidate campaigns. Regardless, the demand for our services increased as the January 2016 Iowa Caucuses and the November 2016 elections approached. It was assumed Hillary Clinton would be the Democrat presidential candidate; but, along came Senator Bernie Sanders and the race was on! The Republican party ended up with seventeen candidates contending for the Republican nomination!

SE represented ONE, an organization created by the musician Bono to advocate for foreign aid to southern Africa. Support committees were organized for each state and I was asked to request participation of Republican Iowa politicians. I contacted our Governor, Lt. Governor, US Senator Ernst, my US Representative David Young, and other Iowa politicians, past and present. In addition to those named, several others agreed to accept appointment as committee members. The role was not an active one, but their participation was valued as an endorsement.

This effort culminated in a large event held at the World Food Prize in Des Moines, the weekend before the presidential caucuses. It was a success with lots of prominent state and national political personalities, some national TV people, and at least one movie actor and his wife in attendance. Our daughter, Kathleen, accompanied Patti and me to the event and got her picture taken with Fox News Star Greta Van Susteren. I was impressed with how friendly and gracious Greta was.

The worldwide focus on the Iowa Caucuses created an exciting political environment. Anyone with any political interest who was an Iowan surely met at least a couple of the candidates. I had met Senator Lindsey Graham through Senator John McCain during John's campaign for president four years before. Lindsey has a great sense of humor and I enjoyed the meetings I had with him.

Governor Jeb Bush was my first choice. I had met him a few years before and had a cup of coffee with him then. Patti and I went to an event for him during the 2016 campaign and he was again very friendly. We enjoyed visiting with him and left with our choices confirmed. I remain a huge fan of his father, President George H. W. Bush, and still marvel at the stupidity of my countrymen for denying him a second term because changing economic conditions and fiscal responsibility made it necessary to abandon his earlier pledge not to increase taxes. I also had great regard for Jeb's brother, President George W. Bush. I found all three Bushes to be very courteous and qualified.

Governor Chris Christie is an interesting politician with whom I got to visit several times. He was very engaging and enjoyable. I first met him when he helped Governor Branstad in his campaign to reclaim the Iowa Governor's Office. The more I saw of him, the more I grew to like him. By the time the campaign was ending, we were very comfortable with each other.

Earlier in the campaign I got to meet Carli Fiorina, a very interesting candidate. I liked her a lot personally and wished her success. But I did not think she would be able to win the nomination. She had a good Iowa campaign staff, but I didn't think she could break through. She told me she thought she was the only one who could take the battle to Hillary Clinton and defeat her.

Patti answered my cell phone once when I was in the shower. The caller identified herself as Carli Fiorina and Patti thought it was the usual robocall. It wasn't. She talked to Carli after alerting me to get out of the shower. Carli wanted my endorsement just prior to the caucuses. After a long conversation I turned her down. My position with SE would not allow for my endorsement. She understood. We talked about the issues and how I thought she could best position herself. It was my thinking that she had an opportunity to be on the ticket as our candidate for vice president. She didn't seem at all interested in that position. I like her a lot, she has great energy, is very intelligent, and has much to offer our country. I hope someday our paths cross again.

Dr. Ben Carson and his wife impressed me as genuinely nice people. They are a couple I would also enjoy seeing again. I can say the same about the Huckabees. I visited briefly with Governor Rick Perry and we shared our mutual experiences as C-130 pilots. Nice guy. I saw Mark Rubio and Rick Santorum several times. I liked them both and assume I haven't seen the last of them. I took my sister and brother-in-law, then Californians, to the Iowa State Fair before the 2016 campaign where we ran into Rick. I had just seen him at a gun show a few weeks before. He was very friendly and enjoyed meeting Michele and Dave. I met Governor Bobby Jindal during the campaign. He appeared to be a very nice person, but I could not buy into his economic theories. Later events in Louisiana validated my judgment.

A neighbor was a college roommate of Governor Kasich. I wanted to meet him, but never did. The neighbor thought he would make an excellent president as a moderate not afraid to consider ideas outside the limits of "true conservatism." I met Governor Walker briefly. Another nice guy, but with some ideas I didn't think were workable on a national basis. I have seen Senator Ted Cruz speak, but never met him. My apologies, but I found him just plain scary!

I have never met President Trump, but I have met some of his family who attended the World Food Prize event SE arranged in Des Moines. They impressed me as very nice young people of whom any father would be proud. But not for a minute did I think their father would ever hold public office, especially not the presidency!

I have a friend who was an important part of the Trump team almost from the beginning, Sam Clovis. Sam is a fellow Air Force Academy Graduate (Class of 1971). He was a pilot and retired as a Colonel after 25 years of distinguished service. Sam became an economics professor and Chair of Business Administration at Morningside College in Sioux City, Iowa. He was also a talk radio personality on local radio. He first came to my attention in that capacity.

Sam was the Republican candidate for State Treasurer in 2014. He lost to a long-time incumbent. I admired him for taking on the challenge! The first time I heard him speak we talked briefly beforehand. His speech was very populist in nature and I was disappointed. I thought he had a lot more to offer. It seemed to me he was pandering to his audience. When we got together afterwards, I expressed my disappointment that he did not seize an opportunity to educate and uplift. I continue to like him personally. I think he has a lot more to offer than the simplistic answers of a talk show host.

After his election loss, Sam became a part of the Trump team. We met a few times when he was in that role, but we didn't have an opportunity to really visit. He played an important role in the campaign and served on the White House transition staff of advisors to the president.

After President Trump won the Republican nomination, I attended a meeting where Sam spoke to a small, but dedicated, group of Republicans. It was not long after the convention. The expectation among the group was that Trump would "act more presidential" after having secured the nomination. Sam finished his speech and asked for questions.

I started it off. "Sam, when are you going to get the candidate under control?" That was a subject of conversation among several of us before Sam made his speech.

Sam asked, "Keith, have you ever been to a Trump rally?"

"No, Sam, I have not, but of course I have seen news coverage of them. I acknowledge his ability to rouse a crowd. I just don't think that ability is enough by itself to bring home a victory."

Sam then said, "You should think about what Trump would do as president and not pay so much attention to what he says."

I replied, "Sam, I have real trouble accepting as my president someone whose statements I can't rely upon."

The next questioner stated that he had been to a Trump Rally. "What I saw concerned me; it reminded me of 1934 Germany."

I was never able to make myself a Trump fan! I liked some of his ideas and his willingness to address issues that should have been addressed by previous presidents of both parties. But his mannerism made it inconceivable to me that he could ever succeed as President of the United States! Nothing personal, he just didn't appear to me to have the character and background for a successful presidency. I walked to the ballot box on November 8, 2016, still not sure who I would vote for. It wasn't going to be Hillary Clinton! I held her in even lower regard. It seemed she was the beneficiary of just too many coverups.

I had begun thinking of writing in someone I considered worthy of my vote. I was torn between Heather Wilson, President of the South Dakota School of Mines and Technology, and Senator Joni Ernst. Heather is a 1982 Air Force Academy graduate, a Rhodes Scholar, and served as a Congressperson from New Mexico from 1998 to 2009. She was to become President Trump's Secretary of the Air Force. I met her in her congressional office and was very impressed with her. I volunteered my assistance with the Iowa Caucuses when she decided to run for president. She laughingly thanked me for the offer.

Ballot in hand, I still hadn't decided what I was going to do. Since Heather was not well known in Iowa, I decided to write in Senator Joni Ernst. When I told Joni what I had done, she didn't believe me. I told her to check with the Iowa Secretary of State's Office. I said that if she ever runs for president, I will take credit for having launched her! She laughed! She does a great job for Iowa. I am not sure the rest of the country is worthy of her.

Following the Trump victory, Sam Clovis was eventually nominated to a high post in the Department of Agriculture after having served on the transition team. His nomination became controversial due to his lack of agricultural background and he withdrew. He then served as the White House liaison to the

Department of Agriculture until he eventually resigned to pursue other opportunities.

Eric Branstad, Governor and Chris Branstad's oldest child, also ended up working for the Trump campaign. He did a great job for him and he too had a White House transition team position. Some say that it was Eric's hard work in the upper Midwest that sealed the Trump victory. Eric subsequently became the White House representative to the Commerce Department in the Trump Administration.

Eric left to pursue an opportunity to build a political consulting business in Des Moines. He tired of commuting to be home with his family on weekends. I think he enjoys life in Des Moines. He takes after his father in that regard!

2016 was the year of the real estate mogul for sure! My legal practice for the year involved a condominium issue. I took the opportunity to put my experience with three condominium associations to good use. I was president of two of them, one at Okoboji and one which is our permanent townhome residence in Clive.

I agreed to help a friend who was having an issue with her homeowner's association (HOA). She owned a public affairs firm which provided staff assistance to one of my lobbying clients. We had worked together on that client's behalf. We maintained our friendship after I retired the first time. I learned she had moved to a condominium. While asking her about her unit, she mentioned she had discovered water had been leaking into her lower-level storage area.

I told her I assumed that the HOA would take care of that. She said that they had told her to get it fixed and then send them the bill. But when she sent them the bill, they told her that since the repair to the foundation was made from inside her unit, she was responsible. I told her I would write a letter (no charge) for her to send over her signature stating the reasons why she should be reimbursed. I asked her for copies of the condo documents for use in drafting the letter. When I got them, I was amazed! They were very poorly drafted and deficient in many areas. She sent the letter I drafted for her to the HOA.

I had no idea who was on the board, but it turned out I knew a couple board members. They found out I had drafted her letter. I got a call from one of them who acknowledged the deficiencies in their documentation. He then said the board wanted to pay for the foundation repair, but they were afraid they might be exceeding their authority. He said the board asked if I would agree to redo the documentation for the association. I told him I would if my friend with the foundation issue did not object. I talked to her and she was glad they wanted to hire me to get their documents redone. The HOA adopted new Declarations and Covenants, and a new set of By-Laws I drafted for them based on their directions. And my friend was reimbursed.

In 2016 I had the two paying clients: SE and the condominium association. In December I told Chris and John, the SE owners, that I was ready to hang it up. They asked if I would stay available to them. I told them I believed in them and their goals, but I did not want to be obligated to do anything except to provide friendly advice whenever needed.

I also served in a non-paying position as Governor Branstad's, and subsequently Governor Reynold's, Transparency Advisor. The first holder of that position was Bill Monroe.

I have never been paid anything for my advisory services, but Governor Branstad promised to double my transparency advisor pay in 2017. HECKUVADEAL! But then he bailed out on me and became Ambassador to China. I performed the same function for Governor Kim Reynolds until she got her own staff in place. She is also a longtime friend, but she failed to honor the Branstad promise.

# 4

# Member, Iowa Public
# Information Board

THE IPIB BOARD membership of course changed over time. Bill Monroe notified the governor that he and his wife Chris were moving to a lake home in Minnesota in 2016. The governor asked if I would take his place as one of the three media representatives. I told him I would consider it. I said that a major part of that consideration would be based upon consultations with the Executive Directors of my former clients: Sue Toma Garvin of the Iowa Broadcasters Association and Susan Patterson Plank of the Iowa Newspaper Association. I had represented both groups for approximately thirty years and received their highest awards of merit available to a non-member.

They were made aware of my "strict constructionist" philosophy of statutory interpretation. After consultation with their leadership, both stated their leadership had given approval. The governor made the appointment in June of 2016. The appointment was criticized by the Des Moines Register in a story that noted he had appointed a person without a journalism background. The reporter was relatively new and apparently wasn't aware of my years of service to the media and my role in the drafting and advocating passage of several statutes enhancing transparency and opportunities for news gathering.

As of May 2019, there have been several other changes to the board membership. E. J. Giovannetti, an attorney who had been Mayor of Urbandale and was a Polk County Supervisor, replaced Gary Mohr who was elected to the Iowa House of Representatives. Monica McHugh, a CPA, replaced Drake Law Professor Anthony Gaughan. Retired publisher Rick Morain replaced retired publisher Jo Martin. William Peard, the Mayor of Waukee, replaced Carroll County Treasurer Peggy Weitl. Julie Pottorff, a retired Deputy Attorney General who prepared the IPIB Administrative Rules, preplaced Attorney Andy McKean who was also elected to the Iowa House of Representatives. Renee Twedt, Story County Treasurer, replaced Urbandale Mayor Bob Andeweg an attorney and member of Nyemaster Goode. Mary Ungs-Sogaard, a publisher, replaced Drake Journalism Dean Kathleen Richardson. Three of these board members also served as Board Chair: Mary Ungs-Sogaard, Renee Twedt and Julie Pottorff.

I am enjoying serving as a board member. I believe the IPIB serves a very important function. We are, however, called upon to make decisions involving complicated issues. My old media friends have become frustrated with me when I am unwilling to bend the law to their ends. It is my hope, however, that most understand the need to adhere to the law as given to us. We are merely a board, not a legislative body. We have enforcement and interpretive powers, but from the beginning legislators made it quite clear that we were not imbued with any legislative powers.

Recently a reporter covering an issue didn't agree with our need to consult our attorney in a closed session before rendering a decision. Our closed meeting was conducted as authorized by the open meetings law. The statute gives deference to the exercise of the attorney client privilege. As an attorney, I consider that privilege an especially important privilege granted to citizens of the United States. Following the closed session, we went back into open session. No final decision had been made. The public was advised we would be continuing to work on the issue in accordance with the guidance to be given by our attorney.

The reporter filed a formal complaint against the board the following day claiming we had violated the law. He sought a public apology and demanded the board fine itself. I revere our First Amendment which operates to the benefit of all when it comes to freedom of speech and press. I sometimes feel victimized by the free press, but I wouldn't have it any other way. We of course could not adjudicate a complaint against ourselves.

Eventually the state's Ombudsman did entertain a complaint about that closed meeting with our attorney. The complaint was based on a misunderstanding of the law by the complainant. Our position was reinforced by the law professor who drafted the statute, Professor Bonfield. Nevertheless, the Ombudsman found we had violated the statute and recommended corrective action.

The IPIB Board rejected the Ombudsman report and responded with a legal analysis supporting our position. Our actions were taken in accordance with the law. In Iowa, Ombudsman reports are required to include the responses of targets when reports are released. Our legal analysis and the professor's support have been ignored in press attacks. My disappointment grew when a Pulitzer Prize winning acquaintance wrote a column castigating the board without any reference to the legal basis for our position. Perhaps he wasn't aware of our analysis; but as Paul Harvey would have known, there is indeed a "Rest of the Story!"

# PART VIII
## LAWYERS DON'T RETIRE
## THEY JUST LOSE
## THEIR APPEAL

# 1

# Working at Being
# a Retired Guy

I HAVE OFTEN told people in their fifties that retirement is not all it is cracked up to be! They should consider what they expect to do with their free time. Since January of 2017 I have discovered the main benefit of retirement: you are your own boss not subject to the beck and call of others—unless they happen to be the Governor of Iowa or the Iowa Public Information Board. I have really enjoyed my contacts with the governor, the lieutenant governor, and their staffs. It has not been very stressful, and I have gotten to know more outstanding young people I am sure will rise to leadership positions in Iowa. Governor Branstad was dedicated to creating leadership opportunities for following generations of potential leaders. Governor Reynolds is of like mind. I am grateful for the opportunity to have served both in a volunteer role.

I went to inactive status as an attorney beginning in July of 2018. That means I am no longer entitled to practice law. As a practical matter I wasn't practicing much for the prior year or so. But I was paying the fees to the bar associations and the Supreme Court as though I were. And I thought even though I had no real exposure to liability claims, it made good sense to continue legal malpractice insurance. Going inactive really hasn't been much of a change as I had gradually been trending that way with the idea in mind of reaching a point of officially going inactive a year before. It has been beneficial in that I can no longer give the free legal advice I used to give.

I play a lot of golf which I enjoy. There is an economic consideration there too. My cost per stroke is a lot less than it used to be, even though I am playing a lot more. I suppose age may have something to do with that.

And now I have time to work on a book. That has been much more enjoyable than I anticipated. Hopefully you have enjoyed this one to this point and will enjoy the next book more. I can't wait to start on the next one. I eagerly await the first manned Mars landing which I intend to feature.

You would think I would have a lot of free time, but it seems I don't. You will be amazed at how busy you can be when you are retired.

# 2

# Gold Star Museum

I HAVE CONTINUED to be actively involved with things relating to my military service. I am honored to serve on the board of the local chapter of the Air Force Association. I have become acquainted with the leadership of the Iowa National Guard and the Iowa Air National Guard since leaving the Air Force in 1970. I have provided advice and worked on issues for them over the years. I very much enjoy their camaraderie and friendship.

I especially enjoy being included in the very informal Combat Coffee group that retired Air Guard pilots have formed which meets monthly. I consider that a real honor. They are a great group!

I was engaged in the unsuccessful struggle to retain the F-16 fighter squadron in Des Moines. We probably came out ahead in that struggle as the Air Guard now remotely flies pilotless combat missions from Des Moines. The Iowa Air Guard also has developed and expanded important training and mission planning capabilities that are highly valued. Air Force-wide training missions are routinely conducted from Des Moines.

I miss the sound of those F-16s and their afterburners, but I have to admit I think Iowa will come out ahead economically. The training and planning roles the unit now has may prove more valuable to the nation's defense than did the flying role. Guard pilots around the country benefit from the training directed from Des Moines.

I am also a member of Quiet Birdmen, an "elite" national group of civilian and military pilots who have satisfied certain membership requirements.

The Iowa Gold Star Military Museum is Iowa's only sanctioned military museum. It is located at Camp Dodge in Johnston, a northwestern suburb of Des Moines. I was asked to make a video about my Vietnam service for the museum's use a few years ago. Videographer Sara Robinson Maniscalco made me look good. It is still used by the museum and can be found on YouTube. Those of you who have read this probably already considered me a museum piece. Well, now you know just how good and insightful your judgment is!

I was honored to be named to the Board of Directors of the museum in January 2018. I became a member of the board's executive committee in June 2018. I serve with a great group and enjoy being involved. The museum is easily accessible from Interstate 80/35 and I highly recommend a visit. Don't be intimidated by the military entrance. All you need is a driver's license. But don't try to bring in any drugs and leave your guns at home!

# 3

# Family

I AM A most fortunate man. My family has brought me great joy and happiness. We have encountered some health issues, as would any family, but those have all been resolved without major detriment to well-being. I have survived the vagaries of the Vietnam War and a few other wars you haven't even heard of. My children, Kathleen and Kristina, are a great source of pride as are their spouses and children. I have five brilliant grandchildren and one brilliant step-grandson.

Kathleen was a beautiful baby and I loved showing her off. I left the Air Force and started law school when she was about four months old.

I was six months into the practice of law when Kristina was born. She, too, was a real charmer.

Kathleen provided our first grandchild, Kaitlyn Boecker (September 1989), whose father was Kathleen's high school classmate, Ted Boecker. Kaitlyn was born while Kathleen and Ted were starting their second year of college. They lived together for a couple of years, but they eventually went their separate ways. Amazingly, they both graduated from the University of Iowa in 1992 after four years in college. Kathleen got her teaching degree while raising her infant daughter, Kaitlyn. She attained a higher than 3.9 grade point average while graduating Summa Cum Laude. Ted went on to get his law degree and has established a very successful law firm in Omaha.

Kathleen began her teaching career in elementary education in Omaha, Nebraska. She had wanted to be a teacher for as long as I can remember. She was always playing school as a child and gave lessons to her dolls and little sister. My sister, Michele, was her inspiration.

Kathleen married Joel Johnson, son of Mike and Annette Johnson, in Omaha in May 1993. They had two children, Sam (June 1995) and Ben (March 2000).

Mike and Annette (AJ) quickly became great friends. While they had lived in Omaha, they lived in Jacksonville, Florida, when Kathleen and Joel married. Mike was about four years younger than I. We had great fun together. Tragically he developed pancreatic cancer and died after twenty-two months of a gallant fight in 2004. It was an ordeal for the entire family. It was devastating to both Kathleen and Joel.

Unfortunately, Kathleen's marriage ended in 2005. With the help of Kaitlyn, Kathleen struggled through the pain that goes with divorce while adapting to the role of single mother.

She obtained a Master's Degree in Elementary and Early Childhood Education with a perfect GPA from the University of Nebraska at Omaha in 2012.

In June of 2019, Kathleen and Brent Goracke married. It is the second marriage for both. We gained a son-in-law and grandson, Brent's son Gavin. Brent played college football. Gavin is playing at Midland University in Nebraska while excelling in academics.

Brent also has a military background and performed special operations as a Navy Seal. He is an electrical engineer for Burlington Northern Railroad. He is a great fellow despite having served in the Navy. We were impressed with Brent and how he and Kathleen seemed a great match when we first saw them together.

In July of 2019, Kathleen was hired by OneSchool Global, an innovative private school with locations throughout the world. She was selected Teacher of the Month her first month on the job.

Kaitlyn graduated from Duchesne High School in Omaha in 2007 and obtained a scholarship to Pomona College in Claremont, California, from which she graduated in 2011. She is a certified whale trainer, having worked for the Vancouver Maritime Museum as a summer intern. She also served a summer internship in Uganda. After graduation, she obtained a position on Vice President Joe Biden's senate staff. She has become a successful lobbyist in Washington.

Sam Johnson graduated from Creighton Preparatory High School in 2013. He graduated from the University of Nebraska in 2017 where he pursued interests in science and economics.

After graduation he accepted a position with Bank of the West in Denver. He transferred to an Omaha branch in 2017. In 2018 he began working for a software firm in sales and is now in a sales management position.

Sam is very interested in politics and loves a good argument. He is mastering the art of disagreeing without being disagreeable. I enjoy our arguments!

Ben Johnson graduated with honors from Elkhorn South High School in 2018. He is now a sophomore at Marquette University where he is pursuing a nursing degree. He loves Marquette and is getting excellent grades.

While Kathleen always knew she wanted to teach, Kristina had no idea what she wanted to do. She has a real talent for languages, excelling in French in high school.

At the start of her senior year of high school I asked her why she had not shown an interest in colleges or a course of study. She kind of shrugged. We sat down on our front steps on a nice summer day and talked. I will never forget it. I said every kid has a dream and I wondered what hers was. Kathleen always wanted to teach, and I always wanted to fly. I told her she could tell me anything and I would respect her thoughts. She told me she wanted to be a bum. My immediate reaction: "What!! Are you kidding me! A dirty rotten bum! What the hell are you thinking!!??"

She replied, "Dad, you said you would respect my opinion!"

I calmed down and she went on to explain that she meant she wanted to bum around Europe and learn various languages and about the people that spoke them.

I told her that she had a great idea after getting her college degree!

She attended Creighton University in Omaha for two years. Ultimately, she decided to study French, Psychology, and Anthropology (Native American Culture). To complete her studies in those fields, she transferred to the University of Iowa, graduating two years later Magna Cum Laude.

The last semester she only needed eight hours to graduate. She added Spanish to her curriculum.

Her professors were really impressed with her language abilities. They recommended she go to a Spanish immersion school in Antiqua, Guatemala, and perfect her Spanish. It was a school used by the State Department, the CIA, and the military. I talked to Patti about it and she was concerned about her safety, as was I. I said I would check it out with old friends. They thought Guatemala, especially Antiqua, would be safe. For the first time, Kristi had expressed a real interest in something that could lead to a career.

Kristina loved Guatemala and Guatemala loved her! She was in Central America for about a year. She told me she could pass for a Guatemalan, a Columbian or a Cuban by adapting to the nuances of Spanish as spoken in those locales. I once observed her reading a Spanish novel. I asked if it was as easy as reading an English novel. She looked back at the book and told me she didn't even notice that it was in Spanish. She said it worked the same with speaking. She just responded in the language in use.

She was recruited by the Des Moines School District to work with junior high students who were Hispanic and struggling to acclimate to life in Iowa. She accepted the offer and returned to Iowa. She enjoyed her time back home and we enjoyed having her around.

After a year, though, she was ready to move on. She talked to me about San Francisco. I am not a fan of San Francisco. I told her she would do much better going to San Diego. After a few days in San Francisco she called to tell me I was right (for once). San Francisco was not for her and she was going to San Diego.

In San Diego she got a social worker position. She was very valuable as her Spanish was perfect and lots of Hispanic children needed assistance.

She took a contract staff position (for a non-profit agency) as a Juvenile Recovery Specialist, in an office located in the probation department. She worked with kids with drug and alcohol problems. She met and began dating a probation officer, Aaron Rhodes.

She pursued a Master's Degree in Social Work at San Diego State. After obtaining that degree Kristina obtained a probation officer position in the probation department working primarily with juvenile offenders for the first year. Since then she has been working only with adults. She did presentence investigation reports. The judges liked her reports and she eventually assumed a liaison position working full time with the court system.

We really liked Aaron when we first met him. He was an impressive young man with a good sense of humor and a dedication to a public service career in law enforcement. We were concerned about the risks inherent in his job, but he seemed very competent.

We quickly concluded Aaron had overcome the handicap of his upbringing as the son of a United States Naval Academy graduate, Class of '69. Captain Richard "Dusty" Rhoades had an outstanding career as a Naval Aviator and finished as a leader in the Naval Test Pilot program at Pawtuxet River Naval Air Station. His wife, Vicki, is also an extraordinary person. I first met them while in Washington D.C. on business in 2014.

We two couples didn't get a chance to get together until we met in California for the wedding. Patti was also very impressed with Dusty and Vicki, and we have great times when we are together. Unfortunately, that has not been often enough.

Aaron and Kristina married on October 1, 2005. Dusty and I had a great time spoofing the service academy rivalry at the reception.

Vicki and Dusty have a daughter, Shannon. Shannon is slightly older than Aaron and is married to Larry, a bio-scientist. They are a great couple as well. Shannon and her mother share a notable distinction. Each is a heart transplant recipient. Vicki is close to setting the record for longevity of a recipient. Shannon is following in her mother's footsteps.

Kristina and Aaron are blessed with two wonderful children: Maxwell born in April 2007 and Madeline born in August 2009. They are excelling in school. Max has been a great big brother to Maddie. She truly adores him. She often calls him "brother" instead of Max. It is fun to watch their interaction. Both go to the same Stephen Hawking Charter School in Chula Vista, CA. Both have been tested and found free of the problematic heart gene of their grandmother and aunt.

Max is the student body Vice-President and is exceptionally adept at public speaking. He and Sam have political potential! Maddie seems to me to be a budding entertainer—she has an uncanny ability as a mimic.

They continue the chain of truly remarkable grandchildren and step-grandson we have been blessed with!

# 4

# Adapting to Retirement...Maybe

THERE IS A lot to enjoy in retirement. There is more time to enjoy family. In our case that means traveling. I discovered enjoyment afforded by the freedom to travel by car, without a set schedule dictated by professional duties or the caprice of a greedy airline industry. I have taken up golf again and have enjoyed making new friends in the process. Very frustrating sport, golf! It is especially so when you enjoyed some success with the game, and then essentially start over in your mid-seventies and play with a beat-up old body. I have found a treatment that provides significant pain relief. But I still hobble around like a thousand-year-old man in the morning!

We also have more freedom to enjoy our condo at Lake Okoboji, Iowa. It is a very nice location, and the other seven units in the building have been owned by nice people who we likely would never have had the opportunity to know otherwise. But it is a three-hour plus drive and I sold my last airplane in 2015! We haven't used it as much as we thought. Maybe there is a closer lake that will suffice.

We have settled into a comfortable schedule of Christmas in Omaha with Kathleen and Brent and their children (none of whom are by any means children anymore), then on to San Diego to visit Kristina and her family for two or three weeks.

We have enjoyed the spur-of-the-moment opportunities travel by car provides. We have spent unplanned time with Air Force Academy friends, Jim and Betty Sears, in Arizona while we were traveling the west. We have also enjoyed spending time with Iowa friends who live nearby in Clive but winter in Arizona and Florida. We usually get back to Iowa in mid-to-late January.

Then it is off to Florida for a few weeks, some on our own and some with our friends, Carolyn Orshak and Jerry Newbrough. This year on our way to Florida we "found" Academy Classmate Bill Boggs and his wife, Beth, in Georgia. They didn't realize they were lost, but we had not been able to find them on prior trips. One of the highlights of the Florida trip is the Nyemaster party. Besides Carolyn and Jerry, we look forward to seeing Bev and Don Muyskens, Kathy and Craig Shives, Jan and Doug Smith, and Susan and Bob VanOrsdel at this reunion.

On one of our trips we went to the Atlantic side of Florida to visit friends Nancy and John Maxwell in Vero Beach. John was in law school with me and has established himself as a nationally recognized conservative political operative in Washington, D.C. He was aligned with Terry Branstad from the very beginning of Terry's political career. We had a great time with them. Nancy arranged a tour of the Piper Aircraft plant, where they are still making Archer IIs (my last airplane) the old-fashioned way. They are essentially handmade, except for the cockpit instrumentation and engine. To go to modern computer-process manufacturing, a new aircraft certification process would be required. Automobile reliability has greatly benefited from modern computer-assisted manufacturing, but not light airplanes. Sometimes help from the government isn't very helpful!

# 5

# Conclusory Confessions

IN WRITING THIS family history and biography, I learned some things about my family and myself. War really is hell! In thinking of my father's loss of his brother and future business partner in World War II, I began to see and understand the dramatic impact that loss had on him and his family. My grandparents became withdrawn. Grandma rarely left the house except to go to church. Grandpa loved music, but abandoned professional appearances and only performed at Midnight Christmas Mass. He was a gifted violinist and people looked forward to those performances. The rest of his life revolved around fishing. Fishing can be a solitary sport, and it often was with him. But he did have a best friend, with whom he owned a boat and fished. He also seemed to enjoy painting wildlife scenes, another solitary activity. He was a gifted artist. His paintings sold well.

My dad carried on as required. His joy was his family and his boat, but I think he had frequent bouts of depression, especially when a decision of consequence needed to be made. His business acumen diminished with time. He hated painting. We marveled at his ability to sleep at the drop of a hat. Now I wonder if that wasn't a manifestation of depression.

My mother had three brothers, all of whom served with distinction in World War II. Their father suffered from another loss, the devastating death of his wife at age 40 after 16 years of marriage. That loss put a burden on him and my mother, who was the oldest (at age 15) of the children. My grandfather remarried several years after his wife died. I attended the wedding. The marriage was a short-lived disaster soon ended by divorce.

My mother left school after eighth grade to care for the family when her mother died. She was very intelligent and a gifted artist. Neither her artistic talent nor her intellect reached their full potential. And her siblings seemed not to recognize what she saw as a sacrifice made on their and their father's behalf. Their father was a lost soul for a long time after his wife's death. My mother, in her later years, grew to resent the lack of appreciation shown by her siblings. I suspect there were enough mistakes made to go around. But in my mother's mind, they grew into issues that took much of the joy out of her final years.

All three of her brothers saw combat in World War II. All were decorated for their service. Until recently I thought they had made good adjustments upon their return from the war. They were welcomed home as the heroes they were. They reconnected with their many friends with whom they could share common experiences. They could handle the horrors of war in good company with fellow veterans. They joined organized veterans' groups. They never discussed their combat experiences outside those circles to my knowledge. Perhaps they did with their families, but those I have asked, say they did not. They seemed to adjust, however. They seemed to get on with life. Appearances, as we know upon reflection, can be deceiving.

As a boy I was in awe of them, and what they had done. Fact is, I still am. When I became a combat veteran, I began to see things through a different lens. I grew to appreciate the difficulty discussing combat with people who had not experienced it. I feel the raw emotions that can be summoned up by an unexpected reminder. I visit a wall festooned with the names of many friends. It always brings tears to my eyes. I suspect it always will. Thinking about it does even now, as I write.

Personally, I quickly grew to realize there is no joy in killing. I was especially good at that, and it is the essence of the sorrow of Vietnam: all that killing on both sides for what purpose? My victims all had families who loved them and mourned their loss. Could they inspire hatred? You bet they could, but so could I. It wasn't that my killing was always the result of calmly-executed professional skills. It many times sprung from anger, fear, terror, and hatred.

I visited my Uncle Earle not too long before he died. We talked about war and his feelings. Faded though his memories may have been, they were still there to trouble him. He was still coping with what I, until then, hoped and expected would fade away over the years.

Just recently I visited with Charles, the love of my Uncle Pat's life. I sensed that wartime experiences troubled Pat, and we avoided talking about them. Recently Charles, at age 96, and I had a long conversation over the phone. Charles spoke of his love for Pat and how he still grieved his loss. He spoke of how a memory of Pat startled and upset him. It was sparked by a recent museum view in Italy of a sarcophagus. It contains the remains of an Italian soldier who resembled Pat, and who was dressed in a uniform like one Charles had seen Pat wearing in a picture. He said he completely broke down in sobs. While practicing medicine, Charles scoffed at depression as a debilitating illness. But he suffered severe depression after Pat's death. His opinion has changed, and he now understands depression and the PTSD that Pat suffered.

I had never known that Pat had been diagnosed with PTSD! I never knew there was such a diagnosis until after Vietnam. I didn't see much of my Uncle Lee, and don't recall ever discussing anything about World War II or Vietnam with him.

It is funny what a lost tooth can precipitate! I have been entitled to Veterans Administration benefits since I left the Air Force. Initially they provided care to me for a dental issue immediately following my discharge. I had suffered a dental injury at the Academy which resulted in periodic problems with a front tooth. I also experienced residual effects of injuries from Vietnam. My hearing was permanently damaged as the result of a canopy-seal failure at very high altitude in a jet fighter. I have had a constant ringing in my ears since. The diagnosis is Tinnitus, which impairs hearing in addition to generating a constant noise.

Enough whining! I made it home! Eventually the long-ago-injured tooth failed, and an implant was required. Implants being expensive and requiring a long-drawn-out process, I sought VA coverage. They had told me as a cadet that the tooth would eventually fail, and I could expect help.

To my surprise, I was told I was not covered. I told them that it should be in their records as a notation from the related treatment I had received. It was service connected. I was referred to a person in the VA who is a benefits specialist.

I next encountered my worst and best VA experiences. I showed up at the appointed time and knocked on the open door of my designated expert, only to see her look up and growl out, "What do you want!" I told her. She harshly replied that I wasn't entitled to anything dental. I asked how she could tell that. She said I should leave her alone and go see the lady down the hall. It was almost like a Tim Conway skit! The lady looked to be about two days from retirement. The last thing she wanted to do was to help anyone.

I shuffled down the hall, suppressing the urge to just say "to hell with it." I knocked on the designated door which was closed. A pleasant-sounding young female voice called out, "Just a second, please." The door opened a crack and she said she had someone in her office, but she would be pleased to help me in about ten minutes. She said she would come to the waiting room and get me. What a difference forty feet and forty years can make! This lady was very friendly and seemed eager to take on my problem.

When she brought me to her office, she couldn't have been nicer. She listened attentively and brought up my computer-available records. She looked through them and observed the dental records weren't there. She also noted I hadn't had follow-up on some other issues. She immediately set about making appointments for me to get those addressed and updated. She said she would have to get my Air Force records, including my cadet medical records. She would do this and get back to me.

True to her word, she had me in for a follow-up appointment. She said she had gone through my complete file, and not found any entry that would support a claim for my implant. She said the record of my injury related to my mouth, but stated my tooth was okay. It was, at the time, but I was told that it would be a problem later in life. Unfortunately, the medical notes didn't contain that statement.

She then told me my other checks indicated a general update was in order. She then asked if I had ever been assessed for PTSD. I told her I had not. She looked at me with a puzzled expression and stated she was surprised, especially after what my records indicated I had gone through. She asked if I ever had any indication of PTSD. I said that I had, but I didn't want to jeopardize my pilot's medical qualification. I mentioned the unexpected loss of my friend Mike Adams and the difficulties that has presented over the years. And my inability to feel up to making it to my sister's college graduation not long after my Vietnam tour had ended. By then I had teared up. She asked if I wanted an evaluation now. I said I did not. We finished the interview, and, in closing, she asked if I was sure I didn't want a PTSD evaluation. I suddenly decided that I did. I had sold my last airplane, so why not. She made an appointment for me with the PTSD Psychologist, which I kept in the fall of 2016.

I had a meltdown during the interview. He got me to talk about a tragedy I had never discussed with anyone before, involving the killing of two young children. I killed their killer, who was really after me. I was his target, and he missed, and the children were killed. The interviewer was a guy my age, a licensed psychologist, and very good at what he did. He quickly suggested that his job was to get me help when needed, and I should quit bluffing and avoiding. My meltdown occurred shortly thereafter. He delved into things I had never discussed or faced.

I was not surprised. I become emotional reading certain books and watching certain movies. Visiting "The Wall" is always a traumatic experience. I am only truly comfortable discussing wartime experiences when with my Academy classmates. Not all such experiences—I suspect we all hold back some. I have, up until recently, been able to lock my worst experiences away. Compartmentalization is the term for it, I think.

Some habits reflect past experiences. I am never comfortable with my back to a crowd, for example. I have a CIA friend and we always want the same seat when we go out to dinner. He is bigger than I am, so I tell him he gets it. He has the watch—he is bigger and tougher. It has become a standing (sitting?) joke. Friends kid us about this. They have never had the experience of being the hunted instead of the hunter. There was that time when I even had a price on my head! There was the time when that habit saved my life.

May has always been a very difficult month. Some of my best friends were killed that month. One was killed May 4, 1969, while flying his last scheduled Vietnam mission. You may recall an earlier discussion of Mike Adams. I have never really gotten over that. He put me on the plane home a few days before and we made plans to reunite back in the states. He was to call when he got settled. The call never came. When I followed up, I learned of his death from his grandmother. I had a meltdown then. On May 31, 1966, nine friends died in a special operations mission. But for my wedding date a few days later, I would have been killed also.

Those dates and Memorial Day have always been tough on me. Everyone has always considered me to be the most unaffected vet they know. Little did they know; but then, little did I really know.

About five years ago we were invited to the Country Club to have drinks and dinner to celebrate Cinco de Mayo. Patti and I love things Mexican and we were having a great time. Something was said that made me think of the anniversary of my friend's death the day before. Because of that fact, his memory was on my mind. I remember responding to a question someone asked. I said,

"Yesterday was the anniversary of when one of my best friends was shot down and killed in Vietnam. He went out and he never came back." I broke into uncontrollable sobs. I just couldn't stop sobbing. I suppose it was only a couple of minutes, but it was an embarrassing eternity to me. I could not will myself to stop.

After that incident I began to think about my reactions to certain things, and how I had down days. They seemed to be increasing in occurrence and severity. Recently I have started to have related dreams again, although they are not particularly scary ones. This summer I had two horrible ones about a month apart and my wife struggled to awaken me. When I awakened, I didn't understand why she had all the lights on and was shaking me and yelling. I have no idea what was going on in my mind. I just knew it was something too horrible, apparently, to remember.

Now I am convinced I do have a problem. I am not the one who escaped completely unscathed. Did anyone? What did I do about it? I asked the VA for help. I was introduced for evaluation by a new doctor. He referred me to Dr. Regina Striegel, PhD, at the VA Hospital in Des Moines. In four months of regular visits she has helped me immensely. Veterans with issues like mine should not hesitate to avail themselves of the expert mental health care available at the VA. I feel much better and am able now to discuss events that have troubled me greatly for years. I still react more than I would like, but so far, so good.

Now there is one less secret to keep!

To be continued—I hope! An epilogue yet to be written.

The End for Now—Finally!

# ABOUT THE AUTHOR

KEITH LUCHTEL grew up in Milford, Iowa, where he graduated from High School and was appointed to the Class of 1964 of the United States Air Force Academy. He graduated with a Bachelor of Science Degree from the United States Air Force Academy in June 1964.

Following graduation, he completed Air Force Jet Pilot Training in the fall of 1965. He then was assigned to Sewart Air Force Base near Nashville, Tennessee where he trained as a pilot of the four-engine C-130 turbo prop airplane and was assigned to the 61st Troop Carrier Squadron based at Sewart. He gained worldwide experience as a pilot and became an Aircraft Commander as a First Lieutenant.

In 1966 he married Patricia Ann Moss. They have two daughters and six grandchildren.

In January of 1968 he began training to become a Forward Air Controller (FAC) at Hurlburt Field, Florida. FACs were used in Vietnam as directors of air strike missions.

In April of 1968 he deployed to South Vietnam where he directed 243 air strike missions and instructed new FACs as they were deployed to Vietnam. He flew 722 combat hours as a FAC. After his FAC tour he was assigned to the 347th Troop Carrier Squadron based at Dyess Air Force Base near Abilene, Texas. He flew the C-130 aircraft on 18 combat missions in Vietnam and several more in other parts of the world before and after his FAC tour, logging approximately another 190 hours of combat flying time in three continents. About 50 of those hours involved covert operations.

He was awarded the Distinguished Flying Cross for Heroism, and eighteen Air Medals.

In August of 1970 he resigned from the Air Force with the rank of Captain and entered Drake University Law School in Des Moines, Iowa. He was Surveys Editor, Volume 22, of the Drake Law Review. He graduated in December 1972 and was inducted into the Order of the Coif academic honor society.

He entered the practice of law with the Nyemaster Goode Law Firm in Des Moines. He became a shareholder and practiced with that firm until 2013. He practiced primarily as a litigator from 1973 through 1983 and tried cases in state and federal courts and the Supreme Court of Iowa. He was retained by the City of Clive as its City Attorney from 1980 to 1987. He began a legislative practice in 1981 which became his primary practice area from 1984 – 2012. He represented business and professional associations and business entities as a registered lobbyist before the Iowa Executive and Legislative Branches of state government.

In 2001 he was designated an Honorary Pioneer Lawmaker by a Joint Resolution of the Iowa General Assembly.

In 2006 he was the recipient of the Iowa Freedom of Information Council's Friend of the First Amendment Award. He was also inducted into the Iowa Broadcasters Association's Hall of Fame. The Iowa Medical Society bestowed its highest non-physician award, the John. F. Sanford Award.

He received the Iowa Newspaper Association's Distinguished Service Award in 2013.

He received the Iowa Center for Public Affairs Journalism Randy Brubaker Free Press Champion Award in 2015.